FIRST PEOPLES OF GREAT SALT LAKE

A CULTURAL LANDSCAPE FROM NEVADA TO WYOMING

Steven R. Simms

Original art by Eric S. Carlson
Cartography by Chelsea McRaven Feeney
Photography by François Gohier

The University of Utah Press
Salt Lake City

The Utah Series on Great Salt Lake and the Great Basin publishes scholarship committed to better understanding this extraordinary place from artistic, cultural, historical, natural, and scientific perspectives. The series brings together studies of the lake and its surrounding geographies from different disciplinary lenses, genres, and personal points of view. Together, the volumes in this series reveal the natural and human processes at work on Great Salt Lake and the urgent need to raise public consciousness to ensure the lake's enduring presence.
Series editor: Jeff Nichols

Copyright © 2023 by The University of Utah Press. All rights reserved.

 The Defiance House Man colophon is a registered trademark of the University of Utah Press. It is based on a four-foot-tall Ancient Puebloan pictograph (late PIII) near Glen Canyon, Utah.

LIBRARY OF CONGRESS CATALOGING-IN-PUBLICATION DATA
Name: Steven R. Simms, author
Title: First Peoples of Great Salt Lake: A Cultural Landscape from Nevada to Wyoming / Steven R. Simms.
Description: Salt Lake City : University of Utah Press, [2023] | Includes bibliographical references and index.
Identifiers: LCCN 2023943907 | ISBN 9781647691370 (paperback) | ISBN 9781647691479 (hardback) | ISBN 9781647691387 (ebook)
LC record available at https://lccn.loc.gov/2023943907

Cover photo courtesy of R. Nial Bradshaw.
Cover illustration, *The Pronghorn Charm*, courtesy of Eric S. Carlson.

Errata and further information on this and other titles available at UofUpress.com

Printed and bound in the United State of America.

FIRST PEOPLES OF GREAT SALT LAKE

For Hadley and Judy

Contents

Preface ix

Acknowledgments xiii

1. Great Salt Lake Genealogy 1
2. From Bonneville to Great Salt Lake 8
3. Explorers in an Ecological Moment 14
4. Pioneers and First Settlers 26
5. Transformations of Place 46
6. A Human Wilderness 58
7. Indigenes, Immigrants, and First Farmers 76
8. The Most Populous Part of Utah 91
9. Upheaval 108
10. Descendants 130
11. Indigenes Meet Travelers 145
12. Denouement 161

Notes 165

References 185

Index 211

About the Author 221

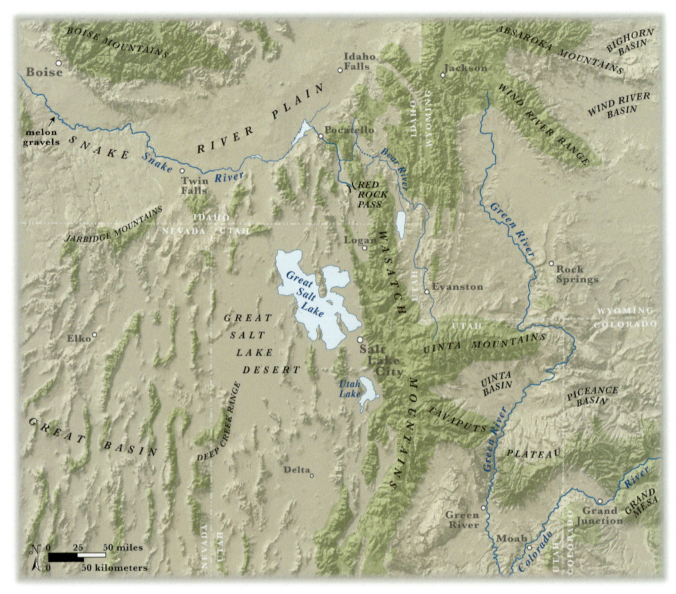

F.1 Great Salt Lake centers on a cultural landscape that renders modern state lines irrelevant. Diverse topographically and biotically, the region of Great Salt Lake represents an ebb and flow of cultural unity over the millennia. Cartography by Chelsea McRaven Feeney.

Preface

This is a story of nearly 700 generations of Native Americans in a cultural landscape centered on but much larger than Great Salt Lake. The story employs the findings of the natural and social sciences, but this is not a science book. This is a story about where people lived and how they lived. It is a story of language histories; the mingling of peoples, Indigenes and immigrants; and the transformations that arise from the processes of interaction, both cooperation and conflict. It is a story of cultural resilience, persistence, and the changing roles of people in landscapes and ecosystems. These things shape sense of place, thus making the concept of place historical.

This story challenges the Pristine Myth, the cultural bias that Indigenous peoples were timeless, changeless children of Nature. The myth that America was sparsely populated—that Native Americans were too primitive and too few to have had a role in shaping the places where they lived. Native Americans arrived in the Great Salt Lake region over 13,500 years ago—675 human generations—and likely much earlier. The first migrants to the Americas encountered landscapes and ecosystems that had never felt the presence of humans. After that it became a Human Wilderness. The Indigenous peoples became active agents in ecosystems—keystone participants. Native America, even the harsh Desert and Mountain West, became fully populated. The people knew everything they needed to manage their environments. They modified the forests and understory vegetation, and encouraged economically important plants such as nuts, seeds, roots, and medicines. They shaped wildlife populations. As with all members of ecosystems, the mere act of living alters the environment. Sustainability means adapting to long-term climate change and to other people and cultures. Adaptation means avoiding extinction, even though every organism that goes extinct is adapting up to the day the last individual dies. The Native Americans of Great Salt Lake were very much part of their world, and the story here is one of long continuity through dramatic culture change.

A landscape approach implies the importance of the concept of place. The power of landscape in Annie Proulx's short stories about Wyoming and, by extension, the Desert and Mountain West is a form of geographic determinism—where you live shapes how you live. Place and history are central, and characterization of the land serves a larger purpose: one of shifting circumstances overlaid upon natural surroundings.[1] Place is important to this story. It helps us envision the story, one of heritage and genealogy. The story moves from the old to the recent, enabling a causal flow of interpretation and offering an atypical genealogy that emphasizes tracing descendants rather than ancestors.

The Great Basin, a desert of warm tones yet studded with hundreds of mountain ranges, is center stage west. The stage extends beyond the eastern rim of the Great Basin to the northern Colorado Plateau of high mesas and rising mountains, all dissected by intricate canyons. It reaches northward across the Wyoming Basin and into the Wind River and Bighorn Basins. It then swings west to the cold mountain ranges of western Wyoming, northern Utah, and eastern Idaho, and across the Snake River Plain. Great Salt Lake is centered in this world. It is a cultural landscape that dissolves state lines. The landscapes across this region we know today transformed over millennia, and so did the people. This story can only be told on scales of time that transcend the lives of individual actors.

The story told here takes a different approach to understanding the ancients than is typical of archaeology. Like all sciences, archaeology requires attention to categories and labels—for artifacts, peoples, and periods of time. Here I use but de-emphasize those things. Science is a product of Western, Occidental culture and the Judeo-Christian cultural tradition. This cultural lens shapes how we see the anthropological Other—the Indigenous, the different, the "primitive." This is not a fault, or wrongheaded, because all peoples understand the Other through the lens of their culture. Yet to tell the story of the ancients in a different way, it is necessary to challenge the notion that the story must be told as a sequence of discrete events among bounded peoples and cultures bumping into each other like billiard balls, yet staying true to their origins as they wander the earth. I call this the Biblical Model.

For this to be a story about the lives of people, it needs to be about more than what they ate, how they built their houses, and the names of their tribes. For the earliest periods of Indigenous history, I trace changing environments, climate, and peoples through the notion of place. I emphasize roles that different peoples played over time and across places. Rather than referring to a sequence of cultural periods, I employ the terms "explorers," "pioneers," and "settlers" to signal contrasting roles and sense of place. These terms are not substitutes for the archaeological cultural terms, nor do they match with the notion of "a people." I explain these terms further as we encounter the story.

For more recent millennia, I bring language history into the story. This is not to say we know the specific languages ancient peoples spoke. Language history is distinct from ethnicity and identity. It is different than a label for a culture, and different from the notion of a singular "people." Anthropological linguistics has a lot to say about the history of the hundreds of Native American languages, and I employ that body of knowledge. Other aspects of culture that enrich the story include ideology, continuity in ritual expression, and regionalization in style. I propose that while some of my interpretations might be speculative, they temper some of archaeology's received wisdoms about ancient Native American history. This story is far deeper in time than any modern genealogy can trace, but genealogy it is, and that is where we begin our journey.

Comments about Dates, Terminology, and Science
I have attempted to streamline the dating by rounding and referring to "thousands of years ago" as often as possible (for example, 13,000 years ago). As we approach the past 2,000 years, I switch to AD/BC because it is familiar to readers of history. The dates I use are based on archaeological methods ranging from radiocarbon dating, tree-ring dating, and optically stimulated luminescence to some novel methods developed for dating rock imagery. All dates are in calendar time. Significant progress has been made to calibrate radiocarbon ages with calendar time, a more approachable form of time for us living souls. This can create confusion because many dates have been reported, especially in the past, as uncalibrated radiocarbon dates. One of the first examples we will encounter is the date of the Lake Bonneville Flood. That has long been cited as an uncalibrated age of 14,500 years ago, but the calibrated calendar age is 17,500 years ago. Similarly, the Clovis culture has long been assigned an uncalibrated age of 11,500 years ago, but the calibrated age is closer to 13,350 years ago.

I generally avoid reciting categories and jargon, but do employ some. The story offered here is historical, but it is by intention a deviation from the familiar culture histories—histories of cultures as units. Not because those are wrong, but because we might gain insight from a different telling.

This story is supported by abundant chapter notes, usually clustered to cover several points at once, to avoid the distraction of in-text citations and numerous notes. I employ the academic rigor of citing page numbers of longer, and especially book-length, treatises to support my arguments. The notes themselves are conversational, intended to identify topics and encourage approachable reading to expand the discussions. Distinctions between quick reads or summaries and the scientific details are also made in some cases. The citations are many, but they are exemplary rather than exhaustive.

Given the vicissitudes of artistic interpretation, I employ the term "rock imagery" rather than the traditional "rock art." I capitalize the words "Indigene" and "Indigenous" because they should be used as proper nouns and adjectives for the peoples who lived in the Americas first. I use the word "Indian" only if I am quoting others who used the term because it was a convention for so long. I do not use the word "prehistory" because there is nothing "pre" about Native American history. Such words pit the written and oral against each other and imply a sequence of progress or betterment. The Indigenous peoples of the Americas lived and recorded history, and we will see how.

I only mention the names of scholars who have studied the past if they are deceased, or if it seems important to identify them. This is not a story about the scientists who investigate the past, but many of them are mentioned in the chapter notes for those who are interested.

I refer frequently to human generations because it is a useful tool to convey deep time in terms recognizable on the short scale of a human lifetime. Many demographers employ the convention that one human generation is 25 to 30 years. I shorten this to 20 years because in ancient times life spans were shorter, and children arrived earlier everywhere in the world.

Science is more about questions than answers, but this story deviates from scientific uncertainty. The fact that scientists change their minds, and frequently remind us of what we don't know, is not a weakness, as some in a politicized public perceive. Rather, it is a strength because it shows that science is not chained to an immutable ideology and agenda. I do privilege the telling of the story by occasionally adding a dose of conclusiveness that tests the limits of the evidence. I avoid the words "perhaps" and "maybe" as much as possible. Thus, my cut-to-the-chase telling may strike some readers, and my colleagues, as speculative. For those who might feel that way, the notes and references will be useful.

Much of the information I offer about lifeways, societies, identities, and interactions of ancient peoples is based on anthropological analogy—letting the present serve the past. The greatest discoveries of anthropology are not the things that are dug out of the ground, but the striking structural parallels in culture processes and organizational forms that occur as conditions vary. Without going into anthropological theory, I employ the use of analogy—something common to all science. I understand that the tone of the story may risk making it sound like I'm referring to consensus beliefs or understandings, but by making the story appear more finished, it can be more human and approachable. Of course, the story will never be finished, and there is much that scientists do not know.

Acknowledgments

Borrowing from L. P. Hartley's novel *The Go-Between*, an introductory world archaeology textbook states, "The past is a foreign country: they do things differently there." Approaching the past as the anthropological Other is at once an opportunity and a responsibility that everyone shares whether we are Native or foreign, Indigene or immigrant, lifelong resident or newcomer. I am not Native American and hence cannot write a history from an Indigenous perspective. I grew up loving the landscapes of the Desert and Mountain West, and since my early teen years I have lived in a figurative time machine. For over 70 years I found a sense of place in California, Nevada, Wyoming, and, for most of those years, Utah. I acknowledge and am grateful for a multivocal society to have the opportunity to write about this expansive landscape, and the eons of human beings who individually and collectively created and lived place.

This book moved from aspiration to action because of a new series about Great Salt Lake being published by the University of Utah Press—its history, hydrology, birds, wetlands, minerals, and politics. I am proud that the too often ignored Indigenous peoples of the Great Salt Lake region and the perspective of deep time are first in the series. I thank series editors Jedediah Rogers and Jeff Nichols as well as my old friend Reba Rauch (formerly at UUP) for encouraging me to attempt this. Thanks to acquisitions editor Justin Bracken for guiding me during the writing stages, and thanks to acquisitions editor Jedediah Rogers for guiding me through the editing, design, and production stages. Thanks also to UUP director Glenda Cotter for your support; Jessica Booth, the designer, for another superb job; and Alexis Mills, whose copy editing significantly improved the manuscript.

Richard Shipley is a Utah State University graduate in history, a successful businessman, a former member of the Utah State University Board of Trustees, and a lover of archaeology. Born in southern Idaho, he seems to know so many others who share his interest in the Native American past. He has supported many projects over the years, and I thank you, Richard, for your support of this project, which allowed us to employ the talents of Chelsea Feeney, Eric Carlson, and François Gohier.

Thank you to the manuscript readers chosen by the University of Utah Press, who both identified themselves. Geoffrey Smith, at the University of Nevada, Reno, made important suggestions and kept me on my toes about Paleoindian archaeology. Thank you also for the reality check, Geoff. Chris Merritt, the Utah State Historic Preservation Officer at the Division of State History, brought the eye of someone who lives and collaborates to make archaeology public. Thank you, Chris, for the observations, suggestions, and encouragement.

I solicited reads of early versions, selected chapters, and, later, more polished versions so I could trace progress and reflect from different angles. Thanks to Jack Oviatt, Kansas State University, for increasing the sophistication of the early chapters on Lake Bonneville geomorphology and paleoclimate as well as other parts of the manuscript. Mark Stuart is an avocational archaeologist and a friend for over 35 years who seems to know everyone and shares his deep knowledge of archaeology around the Utah/Idaho/Wyoming nexus. Thanks again, Mark. Arie Leeflang, Utah Division of Wildlife Resources, is a former USU student who now operates across bodies of knowledge and elements of state government. Thank you, Arie. I have long respected the scholarship of Scott Ortman, University of Colorado, Boulder. His ability to synthesize archaeology, anthropology, and linguistics is inspirational. Thank you, Scott, for the insightful comments, especially on the history of the Fremont peoples. David Hurst Thomas, American Museum of Natural History, New York, produces some of the most synthetic reporting of field archaeology in our business. In his forthcoming volumes on the high-altitude site of Alta Toquima in central Nevada, Dave pushes the envelope into Shoshonean ethnogenesis and history. His recent publication on prayerstones and my good fortune to be a draft reader of the Alta Toquima volumes were inspirational and gave me confidence to foray into an area I have long wanted to explore. Thanks also, Dave, for so many good suggestions. You, and Geoff Smith, are right: it can no longer be "prehistory." There is nothing "pre" about Native American history.

I have known Patty Timbimboo Madsen of the Northwestern Band of the Shoshone Nation for many years. Patty and her sister, Shoshone elder Gwen Timbimboo Davis, read the manuscript and offered valuable insights into, feelings about, and reflections on my telling of ancient history. Thanks to both of you.

The exciting recent work at the Promontory Caves, Utah, by Joel Janetski, Brigham Young University, and Jack Ives, University of Alberta, was also inspirational. Their work on the "Promontory problem," beginning in 2011, opened my eyes to a riddle so persistent that I shied away from it in my 2008 book, *Ancient Peoples of the Great Basin and Colorado Plateau*. Thank you, Joel, for your thoughtful correspondence, and thank you, Jack, for your help in connecting me to people and your compelling writing.

Many others provided photos and artwork, answered odd questions, held conversations, and suggested leads. Thanks to Jim Allison, Pat Barker, Allan Baxter, Bruce Bjornstad, Pete Bostrum, Diana Call, Molly Cannon, Noel Carmack, Mark Connolly, Daron Duke, Judson Finley, Tom Flanagan, Merry Lycett Harrison, Jim Henderson, Bryan Hockett, Randy Langstraat, David Lanner, David Madsen, Martin Magne, Jim O'Connell, Jim O'Conner, Laura Patterson, David Rhode, Katie Snow, and Sean Toomey.

Thank you to Anne Lawlor and Glenna Nielsen-Grimm of the Natural History Museum of Utah for showing me so many potential artifacts suitable for photography. You went beyond duty by enabling the photography to be done in-house by Alyson Wilkins. Thank you, Alyson. Thank you to Kati Corneli, curator at the Prehistoric Museum, Utah State University Eastern, and Bonnie Pitblado, University of Oklahoma, for help and permission to photograph the Pillings figurines. Thanks for tips from Aileen Reilly, University of Alberta, and Ryan Silke, Prince of Wales Northern Heritage Centre, Northwest Territories, Canada. Thanks to Christina Cain, University of Colorado Museum of Natural History, for the Mantle's Cave fishhooks image. Thanks to Martin Magne, Parks Canada; Brian Vivian, Archaeological Society of Alberta; and Karen Giering, Royal Alberta Museum, for the Grotto Canyon images.

A body of knowledge I re-engage here to frame part of the story is anthropological linguistics. My linguistics professors, Wick Miller, University of Utah, and Kay Fowler, University of Nevada, Reno, realized I was at heart an archaeologist, but they instilled an ethic to at least try to "keep up" with the anthropological linguistics of Native American languages in the American West.

It has been rewarding to work with the geologist and cartographer Chelsea McRaven Feeney. Her maps are not only informed and informative, but beautiful art. I have worked with artist Eric S. Carlson before. Eric is an archaeologist who has made a name for himself as an illustrator. His interpretation of ancient scenes conveys a past that is accessible, thought-provoking, yet murky in the depths of time. François Gohier and I wanted to work together again after our book, *Traces of Fremont: Society and Rock Art in Ancient Utah*, was such a success. We anticipated additional fieldwork and more new photography, but the Covid pandemic, as well as the obligations and constraints of being senior citizens, limited our ambition. Nevertheless, photography by François is the best.

My forays toward the end of my career into writing books and articles for a broader audience than my colleagues and students derive from all that those colleagues and students have taught me over the decades. To all of you, a cumulative thank-you.

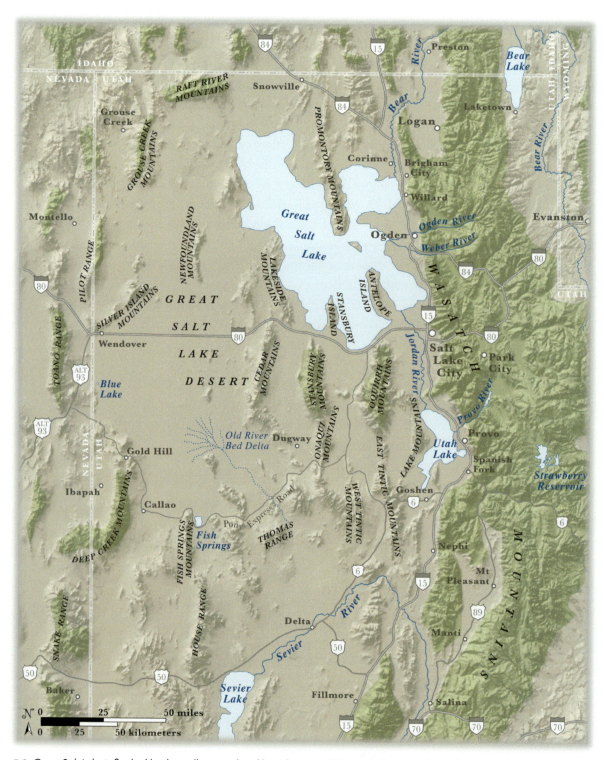

F.2 Great Salt Lake is flanked by the well-watered and heavily snowed Wasatch Mountains footed by rich wetlands to the east, and the arid, mountainous, high desert terrain to the west. Cartography by Chelsea McRaven Feeney.

Great Salt Lake Genealogy

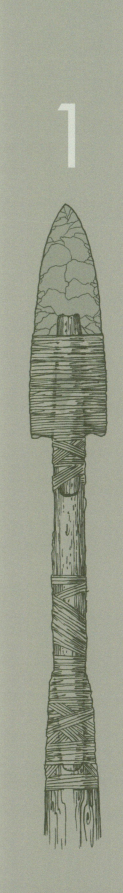

The Bonneville Shoreline Trail is a popular recreational resource on Utah's Wasatch Front stretching from Spanish Fork to the Idaho border. Several sections between Salt Lake City, Ogden, and Logan are completed and offer trails for hikers, cyclists, and, in places, equestrians. The trail follows or is near the ancient ancestors of Great Salt Lake. A genealogy would reveal previous versions of Great Salt Lake, and these would be interspersed over the millennia among versions of a far larger lake called Bonneville, the trail's namesake. The iterations of both lakes combine to create a heritage. The distinctive shorelines known to many Utahns as The Benches are remnants of the last and largest Lake Bonneville. About 30,000 years ago a lake the size of Great Salt Lake began growing. Over the next 10,000 years these ancestral versions of Great Salt Lake and Lake Bonneville alternated as the lake rose and fell repeatedly. A conspiracy of forces we will explore caused Lake Bonneville to reach its last and highest stand 17,500 years ago (calibration to calendar time of a radiocarbon age of 14,500 years ago). Easy numbers to say, but in fact it is a span of time so beyond the moments, hours, weeks, and years of a human lifetime as to be an inconceivable abstraction.

Paleoscientists are accustomed to large chunks of time and arranging them in chronologies. This takes practice and a bit of self-deception. Colleagues in geology scoff at the tiny scales of time that archaeologists work with. Archaeologists smile at the infinitesimal scales of historians. All historical sciences—whether they be geology, anthropology, astronomy, or evolutionary biology—as well as the time-conscious questions in the humanities and the arts dwell in a figurative time machine. We not only want to know what happened, we want to understand it and feel it. We want to be there. Yet time is fluid—a river—not just an accumulation of moments. It can be classified, but never diverted, slowed, or captured. Engaging time, the fourth dimension, is central to my goal here to explore ancient peoples, landscapes, and a changing sense of place.

Pick a section of the Bonneville Trail, such as where it passes Red Butte Garden above the University of Utah Hospital. If we could step into a mental time machine and dial up 17,500 years ago, the resulting view to the west would not only overwhelm our sensibilities of time, but emphatically situate humanity within

1.1 The Bonneville Shoreline Trail looking south in Utah Valley. Maple Mountain. Photo by Wendy LeFevre.

the constraints of nature. The view toward the Oquirrh Mountains and Stansbury Island would be oceanic.[1] Bonneville was a lake so deep and powerful that we would witness wind-driven breakers gnawing at the flanks of the Wasatch Mountains. The open-water fetch of the lake reached to the northwest past Antelope Island and beyond, over 120 miles into the prevailing winds. During storms these winds produced ocean-sized breakers over the area of Holladay and Draper that stripped sediments from the Traverse Mountains and transported them to Point of the Mountain.

Similar situations are found above North Salt Lake, north of Pleasant View/ Ogden, and a striking example occurs at the Stockton Bar along the western slopes of the Oquirrh Mountains. It now looks like a man-made earthen dam, but the Stockton Bar was formed by powerful waves that ripped material from the mountain slopes above Tooele. A railroad cut bisects the bar today. The magnitude represented by these geological features is well known along the coasts—of the world's oceans!

Lake Bonneville and Great Salt Lake had contrasting personalities, but all versions were an inland sea with no outlet to the oceans. Ancestors of Great Salt Lake were shallow and salty, and stood within the historic period range of the lake known since about 1850; during only one or two periods over the past 12,000 years was it slightly deeper. In contrast, the ancestors of Lake Bonneville were far deeper and larger. A taste of desert waters they were not. Bonneville waters were cold, fresh, and deep and harbored Bonneville cutthroat and bull trout, various whitefish, and minnows, suckers, chub, and sculpin. The remains of trout from Lake Bonneville times excavated from Homestead Cave near the Lakeside Mountains show that some trout exceeded six pounds, but surely even larger specimens were possible in such waters.

1.2 *The Great Bar at Stockton, Utah*, by G. K. Gilbert, in *Lake Bonneville* (1890), United States Geological Survey Monograph 1. The view is to the east, with the site of the modern town of Tooele to the left. Courtesy of Utah Geological Survey.

In stark contrast to Lake Bonneville, the Great Salt Lake we are accustomed to is a skillet harboring a veneer of moisture. North of Tooele, Lake Bonneville was 1,000 feet deep, a steep-sided bowl rimmed by mountains along most of its extensive shoreline. In addition to Great Salt Lake, Lake Bonneville included Utah Lake and Sevier Lake, and covered 20,000 square miles of western Utah. It was similar in size to Lake Michigan.

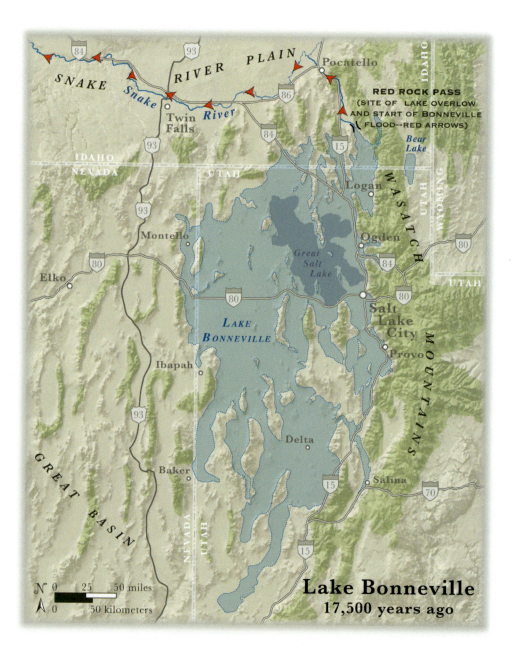

1.3 Map of Lake Bonneville at maximum extent, 17,500 years ago. Cartography by Chelsea McRaven Feeney.

This dramatically different visual experience would have extended to the ecosystems surrounding Lake Bonneville. Limber pine, spruce, and fir, which now live as much as 3,000 feet higher, surrounded the lake. Some of the nearby mountains harbored bristlecone pine, a species that now inhabits terrain between 10,000 and 12,000 feet above sea level. Large shrubs such as hackberry were common, and sagebrush was more plentiful. The pinyon pine and oak brush we are so familiar with had yet to arrive in the region.

The sagebrush and subalpine forest zones above the Lake Bonneville shoreline may have appeared as a narrow band because much of the Wasatch was cloaked in perennial snowpack. Glaciers formed where the Brighton and Alta ski areas are today, and glacial ice rambled down the canyons. Studies at the mouths of Little Cottonwood Canyon and Bells Canyon show there were two pushes of ice near the time of Lake Bonneville's high stand. One glacial event occurred over 19,000 years ago and deposited rock debris, called moraines, that extended from Little Cottonwood Canyon out into the Salt Lake Valley. The ice receded and the moraines were inundated as Lake Bonneville rose for the final time. Another glacial episode about 18,000 years ago pushed ice to the mouth of the canyon and deposited moraines along the edge of the lake.

The glaciers did not cause Lake Bonneville but rather represent the climate of North America during the Pleistocene epoch. This part of the story can be witnessed today at the interpretive display at G. K. Gilbert Geologic View Park's interpretive display near the mouth of Little Cottonwood Canyon.[2] A mental image of glacial ice calving into the frigid waters of Lake Bonneville is irresistible, if for no other reason than it highlights what a different place it was from the Salt Lake Valley of today. Add to this a veritable Scandinavian image of Lake Bonneville fingering into some canyons. This effect was pronounced in the case of Logan Canyon, where a sliver of the lake reached 4 miles up the narrow slot. Other less dramatic drowned valleys existed in the Oneida Narrows northeast of Preston, Idaho, and in Blacksmith Fork, Ogden, Weber, Provo, and Spanish Fork Canyons.

Away from the Wasatch Front, the Bonneville shorelines traversed more-arid terrain. There juniper and sagebrush dominated, with shadscale at the lower elevations. Even the mountains of western Utah, many of them islands in Lake Bonneville, harbored subalpine conifers, but not the depth of snowpack of the Wasatch flanking the eastern shores of Bonneville.

The productive wetland ecosystems that are so much a part of today's Great Salt Lake were present along Lake Bonneville, but in dramatically different locations. Marshes with cattail, bulrush, native reed grass, and sedges were more constrained by the steep shorelines and exposure to wind-driven waves during Bonneville times.

1.4 A finger of Lake Bonneville extended 4 miles up Logan Canyon to the place near the lower center of the photo. Readily visible from the highway are deposits of sands and gravels that were truncated when Lake Bonneville receded. At its high stand the lake inundated all of Cache Valley to the Wellsville Mountains, visible in the distance. Photo by Steve Simms.

Pollen cores from Blue Lake, south of Wendover, Nevada, show that wetlands and marshes existed in places along the western shore of the lake even though Blue Lake was submerged under hundreds of feet of water. The drill cores deep enough to date to Bonneville times show that wetlands along the lake's western shores shed their pollen into the lake waters, where they were transported and buried in lake-bottom sediments.

Lake Bonneville wetlands were able to form where gradients were shallow and along east-facing coves and embayments sheltered from wind and waves. Wetlands could also form in the shallows along meandering streams where they debouched into Lake Bonneville. Some examples might be the flats in Gentile Valley southwest of Soda Springs, Idaho, where the Bear River met the lake. East-facing bays along the western shores of Bonneville southwest of Wendover could also be the source of pollen found in deep sediments under Blue Lake. Just to the south there is an embayment near the mouth of Deep Creek, west of Dutch Mountain. The tip of Lake Bonneville reached into the Sevier Valley, and the broad flats northwest of Salina may have been an extensive wetland.[3]

Eighteen thousand years ago, many animals familiar to us would have been present, including mountain bighorn sheep, mountain goats, elk, mule deer, moose, bears, mountain lions, wolves, and a host of small animals, from jackrabbits, cottontails, and pikas to rodents such as marmots, wood rats, gophers, and voles. Wetlands harbored fish, small mammals, waterfowl, and deer.

The presence of extinct Pleistocene megafauna, however, would present us with a stark contrast to the landscape we know today. Extinct megafauna found along the Wasatch Front and in Cache Valley include American mammoth, horse, Yesterday's camel, ground sloth, musk ox, and giant bison. A saber-toothed cat was found near Park City. The range of now-extinct species was surely greater than this. Across the Great Basin and Intermountain region, a diversity of megafauna species has been documented, including American mastodon, short-faced bear, several species of ground sloth and pronghorn, large-headed llama, American lion, scimitar cat, dire wolf, Harrington's mountain goat, giant bison, and short-faced skunk.[4]

Lake Bonneville and Great Salt Lake repeatedly traded the roles of ancestor and descendant. The Great Salt Lake we know in today's blink of an eye is a complex genealogy. Genealogy implies heritage and humanity. Visualizing the history of Great Salt Lake as genealogy offers an opportunity to know the lake as a collective heritage. This legacy began with Native Americans of the deep past and continued throughout the dynamic history of ancestors and descendants. The legacy has continued over the last two centuries as immigrants with diverse heritages from around the world came to the region. Together Indigenes and immigrants comprise a human legacy 700 generations deep.

I have stood many places on Bonneville shorelines over the past 50 years and mused with students and colleagues, but mostly myself, about whether humans stood in the same places when the lake was here. Did this happen 17,500 years ago? If humans were in the region, that would have been the last time they saw Lake Bonneville before it drained like a colossal bathtub in a matter of months to a level hundreds of feet lower. It remained Lake Bonneville, just smaller, for another several thousand years.

There is no evidence that humans saw Lake Bonneville at its maximum expanse, only tantalizing shreds of inconclusive evidence that any humans at all were in the Western Hemisphere 17,500 years ago. Some seem to believe that humans were here, and someday there may be convincing evidence. But belief is distinct from material reality, no matter how passionately the belief is embraced. Thus, my time machine, conceivably just a vehicle to explore a romanticized past where people hunted mammoths in wetlands within sight of Lake Bonneville, must be set aside for now. It remains possible that humans saw Lake Bonneville, but that is something we do not know.

2

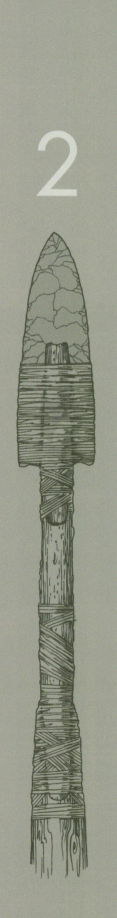

From Bonneville to Great Salt Lake

Lake Bonneville was named by Grove Karl Gilbert, explorer, geographer, geologist, founding member of the National Geographic Society, twice president of the Geological Society of America, and a friend and colleague of John Wesley Powell. In the 1870s, by horse, mule, and foot, he saw much of the expanse once inundated by Lake Bonneville. His 1890 monograph, *Lake Bonneville*, was published by the United States Geological Survey, which had been founded only a decade earlier by way of a last-minute amendment to an unrelated congressional act. It's a fascinating read; Gilbert got a lot right about Lake Bonneville.[1]

Gilbert's work is a model of empirical observation, hypothesis testing, and revision of alternative models. His process of inquiry led beyond a mere description of the ancient lakes to something more sophisticated: an understanding of the *causes* of their history.

Gilbert built upon a written history of observation. The expedition of Captain Benjamin Bonneville in 1833–1835 produced what may have been the first map of Great Salt Lake.[2] When Howard Stansbury made a detailed survey of Great Salt Lake in 1849 and 1850, he noted the "benches," recognized them as shorelines, and was able to estimate the size of the ancient lake. Standing on the salt flats near Lakeside, on the western edge of historic Great Salt Lake, Stansbury commented,

> This extensive flat appears to have formed, at one time, the northern portion of the lake.... Upon the slope of a ridge connected with this plain, thirteen distinct successive benches, or water-marks, were counted, which had evidently, at one time, been washed by the lake, and must have been the result of its action continued for some time at each level. The highest of these is now about two hundred feet above the valley.... If this supposition be correct, and all appearances conspire to support it, there must have been here at

2.1 A survey party camped at Camels Back Cave (*upper right*) in 1901. G. K. Gilbert was known to have returned to the region that year to further support the interpretations in his monograph (Gilbert 1890). This party may or may not have been associated with Gilbert, but Camels Back Cave is prominent in the story to come.

some former period a vast inland sea, extending for hundreds of miles; and the isolated mountains which now tower from the flats, forming its western and southwestern shores, were doubtless huge islands similar to those which now rise from the diminished waters of the lake.[3]

Lake Bonneville, like many other lakes in the Great Basin, was known to be a closed basin with no outlet to the sea. In 1854, E. Griffen Beckwith recognized, as did John Fremont before him, that the Great Basin is a land of internal drainage. Yet regarding Lake Bonneville he remarked that "it would seem impossible for the waters which formed them to have escaped into the sea, either by great convulsions, opening passages for them, or by the gradual breaking of the distant shore (rim of the Basin) and draining them off."[4] Years later, when Gilbert was conducting his fieldwork in the 1870s, he reasoned, "It is quite conceivable that a basin like the Bonneville…should discharge its surplus water at one time over one pass and afterward over another; and this possibility was one of the considerations leading to an examination of *its entire coast line*" (emphasis added). As all good scientists do, Gilbert formed a working model of lake processes based on observable geomorphic processes. He traversed the region over the course of a decade and targeted observations necessary to test and reject, revise, or support his hypotheses. His recognition that he needed to survey the entire rim of the lake turned out to be prescient.[5]

Again, as all good scientists do, Gilbert altered his views over time, but even so, he made mistakes. Prior to his years of direct fieldwork, he assumed, as Beckwith did 15 years earlier, that Lake Bonneville had a long history of stability. But stability in a closed basin lake requires regulation of the lake level; there must be overflow out of the lake somewhere. Gilbert also assumed that considerable time would have been needed to form the prominent Bonneville shoreline bench. His field observations led to changes in these assumptions.

Gilbert recognized that the Bonneville bench is not cut into the rocky slopes and cliffs of the Wasatch. The shoreline was, in fact, constructed; it is depositional and was built by sediments moving down from above. Thus, the shoreline could have formed relatively quickly in geological time. The Bonneville shoreline also marks a contrast. It is the last and highest stand, and all the deposits and features below it resulted from smaller versions of Lake Bonneville earlier and later, and of course from the much lower Great Salt Lake.

Calculations of Lake Bonneville's volume in relation to sources of inflow led Gilbert to realize that the water contained in glaciers and perennial snowpack surrounding the lake would have been insufficient to account for the volume of water it contained. Indeed, recent studies show that glacial ice provided less than 3.5 percent of its maximum volume. As we will see, there was a relationship between glaciers and the lake, but the glaciers were not the singular cause driving the final transgression of Lake Bonneville.[6]

Gilbert's thorough survey of the coastline found the lowest passes along the north rim, where water would have flowed into the Snake River and on to the Columbia River. The survey party went to each pass and determined that only one had evidence of overflow. Gilbert and his team were narrowing the possibilities.

Another clue emerged from geological work near Soda Springs, Idaho. Gilbert observed volcanic deposits, suggesting the course of the Bear River may have changed in recent geological times. In fact, it had since time immemorial flowed north into the Portneuf River and on to the Snake River. At some point, volcanic activity left deposits that blocked the path of the Bear River in Gem Valley, west of Soda Springs, and diverted its flow to the south. By 55,000 years ago, the Oneida Narrows had been carved open, and water was flowing into the Bonneville/Great

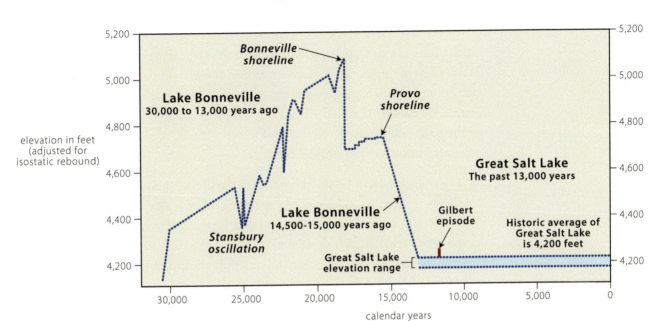

2.2 The history of Lake Bonneville and Great Salt Lake showing relative levels and important events. Chart by Chelsea McRaven Feeney from Oviatt 2015. Courtesy of Jack Oviatt, Kansas State University.

Salt Lake basin. This was the missing supply of water required to create a lake of the size documented by Gilbert and others before him. The actual ages were unknown in Gilbert's time beyond the notion that the lake was geologically young, on a scale of tens of thousands of years. What we now know is the Bear River alone was not enough to cause Bonneville to reach its high stand.

The transgression of Lake Bonneville to its highest level occurred because of climate changes that increased precipitation, decreased evaporation, and caused the last two glacial advances of the Pleistocene epoch: one before 19,000 years ago and another around 17,500 years ago. Pleistocene temperatures were about seven degrees cooler in terms of a yearly average, but there is more to climate than averages. One factor recognizable to contemporary Utahns is the "lake effect." Far larger than Great Salt Lake, Lake Bonneville had a massive thermal capacity to moderate winter temperatures. It also served as a reservoir stimulating higher precipitation. The Pleistocene climate made for cooler and cloudier summers, causing less evaporation and less distinction among the four seasons—a climate that would seem strange to contemporary dwellers of the Wasatch Front.

The Bear River diverted the waters of the western Uinta Mountains for tens of thousands of years, but it was the final climatic spasms of the Pleistocene that led to the climax of Lake Bonneville. As with all climate change, the combination and timing of multiple factors are what trigger novel and unexpected changes—changes, in this case, that caused Lake Bonneville to rise to what would be a catastrophic event: the Bonneville Flood.

In fits and starts, Lake Bonneville oscillated higher and lower by more than 50 feet for 1,300 to 2,000 years, until about 17,500 years ago.[7] Then one day, in the literal sense of the term—perhaps a stormy day with wind whipping the waves and stirring up frothy whitecaps—the rim of the lake failed north of Cache Valley at the Zenda Threshold, near Red Rock Pass.[8] From his vantage atop his horse standing at the pass, Gilbert observed the geological evidence of a flood that had quickly expanded into an unfathomable torrent:

> as soon as a current began to flow across the divide, it must have commenced the excavation of a channel. As the channel increased, the volume of the escaping water became greater, and this increase of volume reacted on the power of erosion. In a short time a mighty river was formed, and the lowering of the lake surface resulted. For a time the out pouring was a veritable debacle.[9]

Gilbert estimated the outflow would have been the size of the Missouri River, but this was one of the things he got wrong. The Bonneville Flood was much bigger than that: for the first few days its volume was larger than 75 percent of the flow

2.3 The Lake Bonneville Flood was so powerful that it trimmed and polished the basalts along the Snake River, visible here as flattened mesas along both sides of the river. Courtesy of Bruce Bjornstad, geologist/author (www.brucebjornstad.com).

of all the rivers in the world. Over the next few weeks the volume diminished to merely the size of the largest flood ever recorded on the Amazon River.[10] Everything in the path of the flood was washed to the Pacific Ocean. Not only every fish, but every moose, deer, elk, bear, rabbit, wolf, and mouse were scoured from the Snake River Gorge along with boulders up to 30 feet in diameter creating a wild torrent that filled the corridors of the Snake and Columbia Rivers and flooded the adjacent plains. In less than a year, the overflow slowed and finally eroded its way to bedrock. Lake Bonneville was now 400 feet lower.

Some overflow continued for another thousand or more years, but the deposition of the Provo shoreline began immediately. The lake was still 600 feet deep and remained stable until about 16,500 years ago. The Provo bench is a prominent feature, and its sinewy length provides the favored eminence for siting several of Utah's institutions of higher education: Utah State University, Weber State University, University of Utah, Utah Valley University, and Brigham Young University. Salt Lake City residents are largely unaware that Foothill Boulevard from the University of Utah to the mouth of Parley's Canyon loosely follows the Provo shoreline.

Climate change was again afoot. The glaciers of North America receded, and temperatures warmed. Once again, Lake Bonneville regressed. There is no direct evidence that humans saw Lake Bonneville while it was at the Provo shoreline, but there is evidence of a human presence in what is now the United States, including our own Great Basin, by about 14,500 years ago. My vision may be just romantic wishful thinking, but I venture the possibility of ancient peoples seeing a version of Lake Bonneville to make a point.

The genealogy of the transition from Lake Bonneville to Great Salt Lake was not a moment in time. Even as the lake receded from the Provo level, it remained a vast freshwater lake for several thousand more years. Although such a span is only an instant in geological time, even a mere thousand years represents 50 human generations. By 14,500 years ago, Lake Bonneville still stood at an elevation around 4,475 feet. The valleys along the Wasatch Front remained largely inundated. The Utah State Capitol would stand less than 50 feet above the shoreline. Even at 13,500 years ago, the lake extended all the way to the Nevada border. But Lake Bonneville was doomed. We would have to change the moniker once again to Great Salt Lake.

There is increasing evidence that humanity had spread widely across the Western Hemisphere, albeit sparsely and in fits and starts, by 14,500 years or more ago. We have firm evidence that by 13,000 years ago people had been living around Great Salt Lake for several centuries. The span between that time of sparse evidence and abundant evidence, about 1,500 years, encompasses 75 human generations that may have lived their lives along Lake Bonneville.

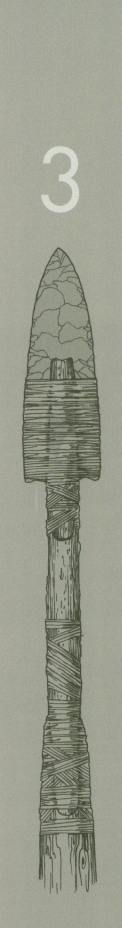

3

Explorers in an Ecological Moment

The immigration of humanity to the Western Hemisphere, the Americas, was a culmination of the prolonged spread of humans to every terrestrial ecosystem on planet Earth. The peopling of the Americas was the last migration of humanity into uninhabited landscapes of continental scale. They are known to archaeologists as Paleoindians to signal they are direct ancestors of living Native Americans. A proposal to refer to the era of the First Americans as the Upper Paleolithic, a term traditionally limited to the Old World, is significant. The Eastern and Western Hemispheres are of the same process. Native Americans are a part of, not apart from, the history of the world.[1]

Those first to come were the true explorers, and they were followed by pioneers who were peoples with distinct cultures, but whose numbers were few. The process of filling the land was consummated by the settlers, diverse peoples during what archaeologists call the Archaic period. The descriptive names I use here—explorers, pioneers, and settlers—are not standard archaeological terminology, but make a point important to a broad understanding of our country's past. My terms direct attention away from the names of "peoples" or, worse, "tribes," or even compartmentalized cultures, and toward the different *roles* people played in their landscapes over the span of many human generations. By emphasizing their roles, we can understand the different ways ancient Indigenous people were active participants in ecosystems. Roles also offer a glimpse of who they were—their perceptions and their sense of place.

These relationships with landscape and place, which in turn shaped life, began with the arrival of the explorers, changed with the pioneers, and changed again as the settlers spread across all the landscapes. The migration of humans to landscapes populated by plants and animals but devoid of humans is an ecological moment, a geologically brief circumstance spanning a few millennia during which ecosystems first become altered by the hand of humanity—an original wilderness that in most cases did not exist again on large scales once humans joined those ecosystems.

There are no contemporary analogies for this ecological moment on the scale of continents and millennia, making it difficult to conceptualize. Sure, frontier peoples in recent and ancient history encountered new landscapes, and some landscapes were at times abandoned. Here we consider the *initial migration* of humans into landscapes never seen before. Such things are utterly unfamiliar to written history, no matter how much anthropologists and historians have studied the cultures of living people. Once humans enter an uninhabited continent, even in fits and starts over centuries or millennia, they become participants in the ecosystem they now call home. If "wilderness" means landscapes untouched by humanity, then wilderness became extinct long ago. Such a notion of wilderness today is an impossible irony.

The ability of humans to spread and to overcome adversity has, in my opinion, been subtly discounted. Culturally deep notions of human societies arranged on a scale of progress from primitive to advanced are amazingly resistant, even among scientists. But evolution and adaptation have a complicated relationship with progress seen as an evaluation of rank. Yet evolution is not foreordained, and adaptation has neither intent nor purpose. It is an outcome, not a road to perfection, or even a pathway to success. Extinction is always one potential consequence of adaptation. Evolution and adaptation are scientific concepts that help us understand how and why nature is as it is. In contrast, progress is a cultural value judgment that positions ancient humans in stages from rudimentary and primitive "upward" to an illusion of the present as civilized and accomplished.[2] Popular archaeology is often written to thrill the reader by sensationalizing the accomplishments of ancient peoples, as if we should be surprised that they were so capable despite their so-called primitiveness. Well-meaning perhaps, but such views are as subtly ethnocentric as the ethnocentrism it hopes to rectify. This pervasive cultural undertow obscures so much human potential and capability.

One of the major scientific discoveries of anthropology is that humans were physically, intellectually, and culturally modern no later than 40,000 years ago, and probably much earlier. These are times long before the Americas were peopled, yet we still allow notions of the primitive to constrain expectations of the human capacity to migrate and innovate. For decades, scholars were resistant or just dismissive of the idea that the Americas were initially colonized along the west coasts of North and South America. Now there is substantial evidence of that very thing happening 15,000 years ago, and perhaps earlier. Notions of ancient Indigenous peoples as incapable primitives are not limited to the Americas. Archaeologists were long resistant to the possibility of humans living at altitude in the Himalayas before the last few thousand years because the environment was seen as too harsh. Now there is evidence the Tibetan Plateau was colonized as early as 30,000 years ago.

Such resistance extends to many more cases, and even one close to home: the alpine environments of the Rocky Mountains and Great Basin. Decades ago, the mountains were given short shrift because of the perception that the Indigenes did not spend much time in alpine environments, let alone live there. Too few opportunities, too many alternatives. Or just too harsh. This perception was only enhanced by the mistaken notion that Native Americans were few and inconsequential. No reason to bother with the high mountains. This view has changed because the evidence was expected, searched for, and found.[3]

Our interest here is the peopling of the Bonneville/Great Salt Lake region from Nevada to Wyoming. I have argued for years that one fault of archaeology is that we tend to assume the answers lie within a defined study area. On the contrary, many of the causes of human history operate on larger scales.[4] Let's situate our quest to know the Bonneville region by looking outward. We emulate the scientific path of G. K. Gilbert and use an understanding of current processes to develop expectations of what we might find. Often in science, with no expectations, finds are not made.

First, let's place the timing of initial human exploration of the Lake Bonneville region in hemispheric context. Then we can shrink the scale to our regional cultural landscape. An opening premise is the explorers faced dramatically different circumstances than all those who followed because they occupied an ecological moment. This enables us to develop some expectations about behavior, the nature of their lives, and the nature of the remains they might leave behind.

The evidence has continued to build over the last few decades for the initial peopling of the Western Hemisphere by 14,500–15,000 or more years ago. Debate over individual sites continues, but the pattern gains strength from the geographic extent of the evidence. The earliest sites are not limited to the Arctic but are found throughout the Americas. No matter where the earliest confidently dated sites are found, they fall in a remarkably tight window of age: a few thousand years or so. There is no apparent progression of ages from north to south, but there is no reason to expect that. Given the time involved, it is not that far. In 2018, Holly "Cargo" Harrison walked 14,181 miles from Ushuaia, Argentina, to Prudhoe Bay, Alaska, in 530 days. Others made similar walks before him, including George Meegan in 1981. He took a leisurely 2,425 days. Generations of ancient migrants living their lives would have migrated through the hemisphere much slower, and in stops and starts over many human generations. Rates of ancient human migration are known in some cases, but on subcontinental scales. Nevertheless, the first exploration of the Americas seems fast given the tight window of dates. If people advanced only seven miles per year, they would have been able to explore the entire hemisphere in about 2,000 years, or about 100 human generations. Such a migration seems fast on the one hand, but is in fact a longer span of genealogy than any living person can trace.[5]

A sample of sites occupied 14,500 or more years ago includes some that have stood critical analysis for decades, such as Meadowcroft Rockshelter in western Pennsylvania and Monte Verde in coastal Chile. Archaeologists have also found new sites and reinvestigated old ones using new methods. Examples of sites studied more recently include Schaefer and Hebior, Wisconsin, where mammoths were butchered with stone tools after being hunted or scavenged between 14,000 and 15,000 years ago. The Debra L. Friedkin site in Texas yielded stone tool debris in sands 15,000 years old. The Page-Ladson site in Florida contains the remains of a

3.1 Map of the Americas showing the first explorers' migration routes and sample sites referred to in the text dating between 14,000 and 15,000 years ago. Cartography by Chelsea McRaven Feeney.

3.2 Examples of Western Stemmed Tradition point types: (*top, from left*) some of the earliest: Haskett, Cougar Mountain, and Windust from Cougar Mountain Cave, Oregon; Lind Coulee from Cooper's Ferry, Idaho; and Parman from Cougar Mountain Cave, Oregon; (*bottom, from left*) later but still early Western Stemmed Tradition points: Lake Mohave, Bonneville, Silver Lake, and Stubby from the Old River Bed Delta, Dugway, Utah. From Smith and others 2020. Courtesy of Geoffrey Smith, University of Nevada, Reno.

spectacular mastodon hunt, with tools dating to 14,500 years ago. Sites in South America and Mesoamerica complement the strong evidence from Monte Verde for occupation by this time. A host of other sites have produced evidence for even earlier human presence, but have complicating factors that urge restraint and additional study. The human footprints at White Sands, New Mexico, reported in 2021 and claimed to be 23,000 years old, are one example. The critiques of this age are strong and indeed urge restraint despite the media furor over the find.[6] Nevertheless, the case for widespread human occupation of the Americas as early as 15,000 years ago signals a sea change unimaginable to scientists only two decades ago.[7]

Perhaps the most exciting advances in the study of the First Americans are in human genetics research using DNA from ancient and living descendent populations. Genetic evidence also makes a strong case for colonization of the Americas by 15,000 years ago or earlier. It suggests the possibility of failed migrations, and perhaps multiple migration events. It is clear that the source populations were in Eurasia and migrated across the enormous continent of Beringia, connecting what is now Siberia and Alaska. About 20,000 years ago the Native American founder groups genetically diverged from the Eurasian groups.[8] The genetics are complemented by archaeological evidence of similarity among some stone artifacts between Kamchatka, Siberia, and North America, particularly what are called stemmed points—something we will find relevant to the Lake Bonneville/Great Salt Lake region.

How the explorers made their way to what is now the United States, and beyond, is still debated, but there is increasing evidence that the earliest migrations were along British Columbia coastal environments by a combination of land and boat. An inland route along the eastern front of the Alberta/Montana Rockies was also available, but recent dating suggests it was not passable until 13,800 years ago. The coastal environments that were submerged under the Pacific Ocean during the Pleistocene epoch became rich ecosystems dubbed the Kelp Highway. Coastal terrestrial ecosystems became free of ice between 18,000 and 14,000 years ago, and were recolonized by a wide variety of animals, from caribou to foxes and bears. We should expect, rather than express doubt or surprise, that human opportunists participated in that recolonization.[9]

Closer to home, the Paisley Caves in southeastern Oregon have a long history of occupation: human fecal material has yielded DNA dating to as early as 14,500 years ago, and blood evidence for processing Pleistocene horses and mammoths. At Cooper's Ferry, in western Idaho near the confluence of the Salmon and Snake Rivers, another long record of human occupation that began over 15,000 years ago also includes stemmed points, a type of tool widespread in early sites in North America and eastern Siberia.[10]

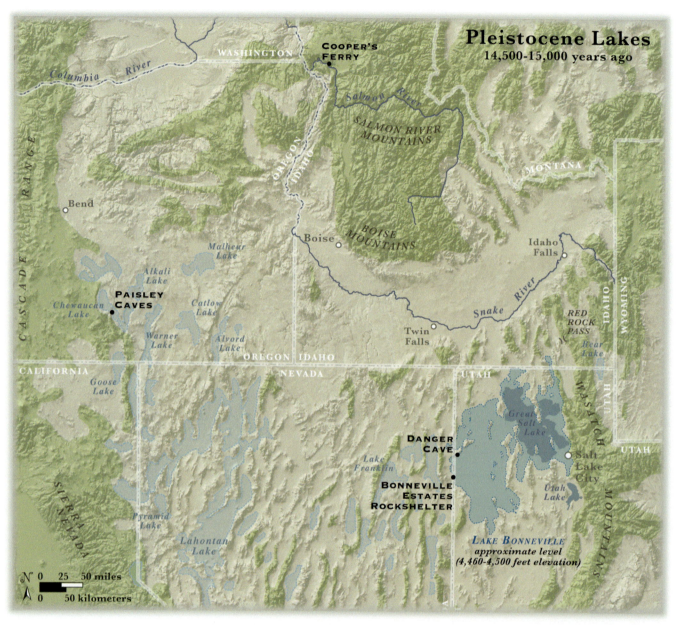

3.3 Map of Lake Bonneville 14,500–15,000 years ago. There is evidence of occupation during this period at the Paisley Caves, Oregon, and Cooper's Ferry, Idaho, as well as other sites across what is now the United States. Danger Cave and Bonneville Estates Rockshelter are important to the story, but they were occupied after Lake Bonneville transitioned to Great Salt Lake. The extent of the other lakes shown on the map are approximate because precise levels between 14,500 and 15,000 years ago are poorly understood. Cartography by Chelsea McRaven Feeney.

Evidence from across the Americas and the Desert and Mountain West suggests that humans may indeed have seen a version of Lake Bonneville. Between 14,500 and 15,000 years ago they would have gazed upon a huge, deep, and fresh lake that submerged most of the Wasatch Front where today's cities are. The shorelines remained steep, and the places where shallow water and wetlands formed were in dramatically different places than where they would be only a thousand years later. As documented by archaeologists, explorers lived very different lives compared to the later peoples who lived around the earliest Great Salt Lake of 13,000 years ago. The landscape and the peoples' sense of place would have been different from everyone who followed. Who were they?

The explorers' presence was sparse, and they entered ecosystems that for the first time became hunted and gathered. It is easy to say their lifeway was nomadic. This is consistent with their spread on a time scale of millennia, but remember, each millennium spans 50 human generations. To simply say they were mobile glosses over too much. There are cases of historic period hunter-gatherers who move every day or every few days. Mobility is not one-dimensional but takes two forms that I like to call tempo and mode.[11]

The mode of mobility of these hypothetical Bonneville explorers was shaped by opportunities to skim the cream off the top of the uninhabited landscape. It would veer dramatically between settlement driven by local activities versus wide-ranging reconnaissance and tracking of herds of mobile animals. Thus, the mode of settlement for the explorers was neither nomadic nor sedentary, but an oscillation between the two in varying tempos. Activities might have included hunting a mammoth or a herd of bighorn sheep or elk. Or culling a stream so full of trout they could be taken by hand. Or driving and clubbing enormous flocks of flightless geese during the summer molt. It was a hunting society, and of course among hunters, this is not something one simply does, but something one is and lives. The processing of a hunt—preparing the meat, but also the hide, the blood and sinew, and bone for tools and clothing—shifted the mode of mobility toward the women's economy. Also, hunters often fail, whereas plant foods offer stability, again shaping the mode of mobility. The harvesting of dozens of acres of yampa, bitterroot, or biscuitroot for drying and transport involved everyone. But again, the processing of plants and animals, toolmaking, and weaving of textiles for everything from string to bags to clothing symbolize the women's economy that underwrote what is naively stereotyped as a male-centered hunting society. The activities of the women's economy tethered the people for a while, thus dampening the tempo of mobility. Yet the tempo inevitably quickened with the promise of abundance in the uninhabited wilderness that lay ahead.

3.4 *The Atlatl and Dart Hunter*, by Eric S. Carlson. The atlatl is a tool that increases the velocity of a dart spear. Darts in the Great Salt Lake region were made of native cane with a hardwood (often greasewood or mountain mahogany) or antler foreshaft tipped with a stone projectile point. The atlatl can be used in positions other than kneeling or sitting. The learning curve is steep, but with training, modern atlatl/dart athletes are effective up to 30 meters, although the dart can be thrown farther.

The tempo and mode of mobility over the scale of human generations and the need for extensive social networks in a land of human isolation fostered broad similarities in their technological kit. It is likely that the stemmed points used in Siberia, across the Beringian continent, and in places along the migration paths across the Americas were the foundation of the Bonneville explorers' tool kit. Stemmed points often served as darts affixed to shafts and propelled by a throwing stick called an atlatl. Most stemmed points are generic and multipurpose, serving as knives and other tools used for cutting, scraping, and piercing a variety of materials.

Stemmed points are easy to fabricate from common toolstones such as basalt, chert, quartzite, and obsidian. The explorers would not know all the sources of exotic high-quality stones, hence they did not invest in a technology that required it. That would come later. The tool kit was complemented by scrapers, gravers, drills, and often just expedient flakes of stone that could be put into service. Such a stone tool kit is not necessarily an end but the means to manufacture the most common tools, ones made of wood and bone. These materials were constantly available and light to transport, but unfortunately, such tools are perishable and survive the millennia only under limited circumstances.

Explorer campsites could be anywhere, and likely fleeting, even if the group size was, upon occasion, large. They did not use caves and rockshelters—not because they were unaware of such places, but because occupation of caves and rockshelters requires planning depth and an expectation to return to them as, for example, landmarks and locations of caches. But although planning depth directed toward caching was not a useful trait for the explorers, planning was necessary for monitoring the whereabouts of large game. Thus, redundancy in occupation was not a strong feature of the explorer lifeway.

Perhaps most important, both the tempo and mode of mobility responded to the importance of nurturing social networks, which were an invaluable source of information about a landscape where distances between groups of people could be enormous. Daily life was spent in families and camp groups that could fluctuate in size and membership, and included kin in the broadest sense of the term. Anthropological discoveries about the social organization of hunter-gatherer societies suggest that among small groups of explorers, the reckoning of descent was likely flexible and included male and female lines, thus gathering lineages together—a system known as bilateral descent. Over a lifetime, there may have been a bias toward one lineage or another. Kinship in Indigenous forager societies can be based on more than blood and marriage, capable of extension to include associates, friends, neighbors, captives, and foundlings via rituals of adoption. Kinship systems are not fixed but are adaptations that respond to the tyranny of circumstance. The explorers had

3.5 *An Explorer Encampment,* by Eric S. Carlson. The explorers of 13,500 to perhaps more than 15,000 years ago did not wander aimlessly in search of big game. The degree of organization employed by historic Native Americans living in subarctic conditions can help us envision this ancient past when the explorers entered the Americas. Settlements such as this served as base camps, and the explorers would have had a diverse diet of waterfowl, roots for drying and transport, and the occasional large mammal such as mammoth. Variations of the kind of housing depicted here exist in subarctic landscapes around the world.

a social network appropriate to an expansive wilderness under conditions of low population density.

School for the explorers was daily life, and knowledge was passed on through the generations. From the time children could walk, they learned about the plants and animals, including what each is good for and which are poisonous. Children in foraging societies use sharp tools early on, and along with adults and the elderly, they manufactured everything from housing, clothing, containers, and trays to string, snares, and all manner of stone, bone, and wooden tools. They learned about the healing arts and medicine from the elders.

Young explorers grew up in habitats lived by their parents and grandparents, even if they might have never seen the places of their grandparents' birth. They would know many homes, and the notion of "home" might have been a sequence of places unique to the life history of individuals, not a concept of homeland shared by a group tethered to a particular place. Family was thus fluid, not a fixed unit with clear boundaries of membership standing in isolation from others. A lifetime of movement would have been familiar and expected, and sense of place would have been extensive, plastic, and inclusive.

Movement across the North American continent would have been imperceptible to the explorers but codified in the stories passed down for generations about where they came from. The size of hunter-gatherer populations under such conditions can experience dramatic swings of boom and bust. Some lineages went extinct. Genetic bottlenecks and dead ends were perhaps common.[12] Archaeologists do not agree on the relationships between these explorers and those who came later, although the evidence indicates they were indeed Native Americans. The explorers would be absorbed by later peoples, yet we are learning that the Americas were widely explored very early. Humans may indeed have seen Lake Bonneville. However, despite their successes, like many explorers in history, they left few traces.

Currently there is no solid evidence of explorers in the Bonneville Basin. Their record would be scant, as it is everywhere in the Americas. Much of northern Utah would not be expected to reveal the explorers because Lake Bonneville remained large prior to 14,000 years ago. Some of the sites with early remains—such as Danger Cave, just outside of Wendover, Utah—were submerged 14,500 years ago. Nearby Bonneville Estates Rockshelter, south of Blue Lake, Nevada, was not submerged and has yielded evidence of human occupation over 13,000 years ago, but not earlier. It is important to note that the earliest dates for the cave sites do not necessarily mean these are the earliest dates for human presence in the region. In the Great Salt Lake region, some caves within sight of each other remained unused until thousands of years after the first humans entered the region. In archaeology, we always know that the earliest dates are for specific places, and they will remain the earliest dates until an earlier place is found.

If humans were present around a late version of Lake Bonneville 14,500 or more years ago, they lived in a different landscape than later peoples. The mountains continued to harbor perennial snowpack at high altitudes, with limber pine, spruce, subalpine fir, and bristlecone forests lower than they occur today but compressed between lake and snow. Places where we might expect to find sites older than those we already know would be near the wetlands associated with the lake at that time. These would be very different places than the locations currently yielding evidence of the earliest occupations. The excursion here is speculative, but that will diminish as the evidence is found. For now, we turn our attention to the period of the pioneers and settlers, Native American ancestors with a widespread presence in the Great Salt Lake region from Nevada to Wyoming.

4

Pioneers and First Settlers

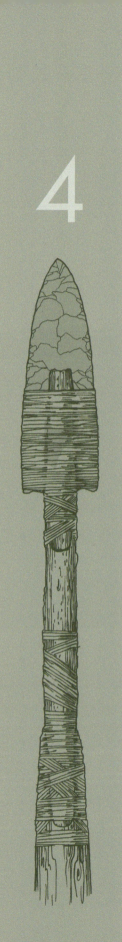

The obscurity of the explorers contrasts with the stronger archaeological signature of the pioneers of the Paleoindian period and the subsequent settlers of the Archaic—those who filled in the spaces behind. Some of the North American pioneers were of the well-known Clovis culture, but others continued to use versions of stemmed points that became known as the Western Stemmed Tradition. The preceding explorers remain anonymous out of skepticism or incomprehension, labeled only by reference to their successors as "Pre-Clovis." Yet differences in their circumstances are sufficiently dramatic to deserve description and comparison to the later peoples.

The explorers during the earliest fits and starts of human entry into the Americas were few, but they did manage to spread throughout the hemisphere. That itself is a sign of success. By the time of the pioneers the ecological moment was ending. The presence of the pioneers is easily recognizable across the North American continent. As the Pleistocene ice sheets receded, humans became endemic members of North American ecosystems over 13,000 years ago.

The recession of Lake Bonneville from the Provo shoreline after 16,500 years ago was complete before 13,000 years ago. Lake Bonneville transitioned into Great Salt Lake, which persisted as a narrowly fluctuating skillet of a lake until the present. The landscape the pioneers knew contrasted with the one known by the explorers who came before them. Neither was it like later times. Remnant Pleistocene aquifers in the mountains and foothills supplied water for thousands of years, making wetlands more abundant 13,000 years ago than they would be only a few thousand years later. The Pleistocene megafauna were largely gone, but the animals familiar to us, including the mule deer, pronghorn, and elk, persisted. Some plants that characterize the region today, such as the pinyon pine, had yet to reach the Great Salt Lake region from their ice-age home in the Southwest and southern Great Basin.

The Clovis culture is clearly recognizable in the Great Basin and Intermountain West. It features a distinctive stone projectile with consistent characteristics such as channel fluting and an associated set of stone debris and tools.

Many Clovis points are found in Utah, where they are most common in valley settings, but they also occur in the foothills and even at higher altitudes in the moderately tall mountain ranges scattered across the Bonneville Basin. I have seen them in private collections from the northern tip of Lake Bonneville near Preston, Idaho, surprising numbers of them from the Sevier Desert near Delta and the Beaver Bottoms areas harboring vast wetlands. Clovis points in the Great Basin and Intermountain West are overwhelmingly surface finds, and all Clovis points in private collections are out of context. Archaeologists can only tentatively infer that Clovis in Utah is similar in age to the well-dated Clovis chronologies developed for the American Plains and the Southwest, where they fall within a relatively tight window of time between 13,000 and 12,700 years ago.

The Clovis lifeway is much written about. The people remained mobile, but in a different way than the explorers. People continued to make light use of caves, and Danger Cave on the outskirts of Wendover yielded a fluted point that was not mentioned in the final report.[1] The nature of Clovis mobility was shaped by higher population densities and the existence of widespread and redundant networks. This is seen in their stone points. Although many Clovis points were made of local stones of varying quality, what really stands out is the toolstone transported long distances and used to fashion spectacular specimens of Clovis craftsmanship that convey abundant social signaling and ideological significance. A Clovis point found at the famous site of Blackwater Draw, New Mexico, near the Texas Panhandle border was made of obsidian from near Milford, Utah, a walk of over 1,000 miles. Similar distances are known for exotic stone fashioned into Clovis points across the breadth of North America.[2]

The spectacular Clovis caches found across the West are a symbol of these long-distance networks, the artistry, and the fusion of the utilitarian, the social, and the sacred. The Fenn Cache is such a trove from our own Great Salt Lake region. It consists of 56 large Clovis era points, knives, and bifaces and weighs 18 pounds. The cache was found by a rancher around 1902 east of Bear Lake and passed down by the family until it was brought to light in 1988 by a New Mexico collector and art dealer. The circumstances of the Fenn Cache discovery are vague.

> One report says that the collection was plowed up in a field, another says it was recovered in a skin bag in a dry cave. Because there are none of the distinctive metal scratches or breaks that occur when stone artifacts are hit

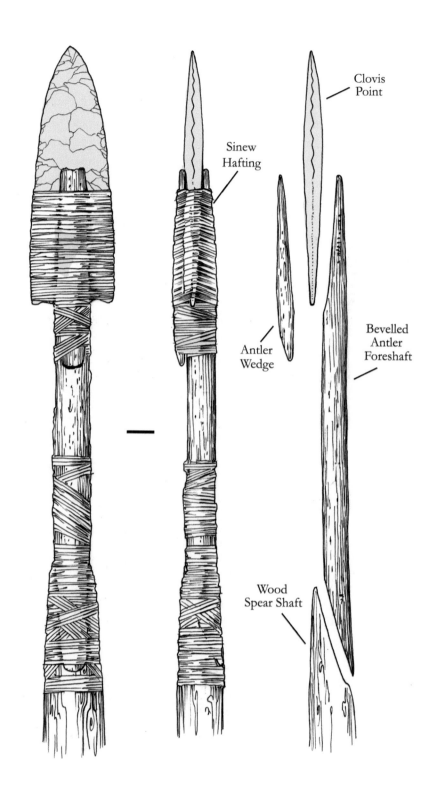

4.1 A Clovis point found in the northern Rocky Mountains is shown as it would appear when mounted on a dart. Artwork by Eric S. Carlson.

with a plow, we think that the second story is most likely. Originally, the discoverer placed enough value on the items to preserve them together in a frame, but later they were stored in his son's basement and forgotten. The collection came to light when it was given to a daughter-in-law as a wedding present. It was she who subsequently sold it in Santa Fe. From the family's scant recollections, we believe the cache was discovered somewhere in the three corners area where Utah, Wyoming, and Idaho meet.[3]

A long-time avocational archaeologist in Utah whom I have worked with for over 35 years talked with local ranchers in the 1970s about Clovis finds in the Bear Lake area. He suspects that the Fenn Cache came from Six Mile Creek, east of Bear Lake, which drains east into the Bear River in Wyoming. A rancher from Sage Creek, a few miles south of Six Mile Creek, found some large bifaces that he said came from a "cache" in a rockshelter up Six Mile Creek. Another local rancher had a big collection of Clovis era artifacts, including Cody knives, that came from the same area.

Perhaps important are the natural routes offered by the landscape. Six Mile Creek is along the best natural access route connecting the extensive Bear River wetlands along the Wyoming and Utah border with the Bear Lake Valley. One would expect caches along natural travel routes. Hikers of the region know that after traveling up Six Mile Creek and reaching the south end of Bear Lake, the natural trail heads south from Laketown up Strawberry Valley, granting access to the Cache Valley via Blacksmith Fork (Hardware Ranch). Or the traveler can continue southwest up Ant Valley and gain access to the rich Ogden Valley, known to the fur trappers of the early nineteenth century. From there the Wasatch Front is a half-day walk.

The Fenn Cache is likely the work of one artisan. Many of the bifaces were unfinished, and those that were remained unused, yet most showed polish and scratches from being carried in a bundle or a bag. Their significance was sanctified by a coating of red ochre, an iron oxide pigment used in ritual contexts across the Americas and in Eurasia since Neanderthal times. In Indigenous societies, there is no binary distinction between the utilitarian and the sacred. Debates over whether something is one or the other say more about us than it does about them. Nature, culture, time, landscape, and place are of a single cloth.

Geographically expansive social networks are exemplified by the sources of stone in the Fenn Cache: chert from the Green River Formation in southwestern Wyoming, agate from east-central Utah, obsidian from southeastern Idaho, and red jasper from the western slopes of the Bighorn Mountains in north-central Wyoming. Stones from these sources are also part of other Clovis caches found in

4.2 Photo of the complete Fenn Cache. Courtesy of Pete Bostrum, Lithic Casting Lab, Troy, Illinois.

the West. Like the Fenn Cache, some of the other Clovis caches were found by locals and some remain in private collections. Other caches include the Simon Cache in south-central Idaho, the Richey Cache in central Washington, the Drake Cache in north-central Colorado, and the Anzick Cache in central Montana. The latter three caches also contain ivory fragments and rods.

The Anzick Cache is special and speaks to a far larger issue—deep connections of heritage past and present. The Clovis cache at the Anzick site was interred with

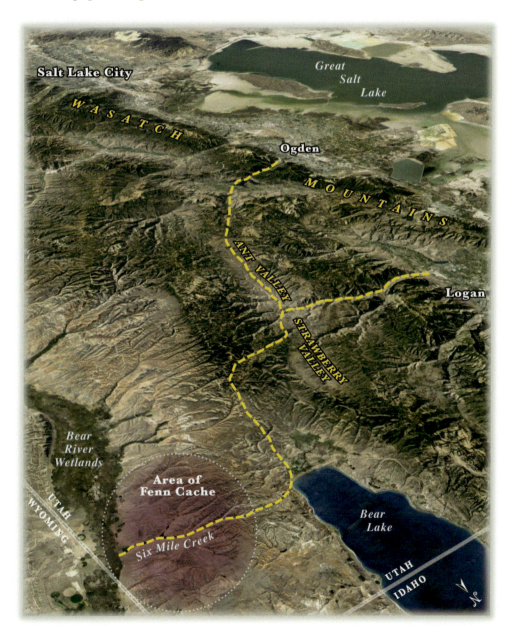

4.3 Aerial view of the Six Mile Creek area and the approximate location of where the Fenn Cache is suspected to be from. There are natural travel routes from the Bear River wetlands, along the border of Utah and Wyoming, to fertile areas such as Cache Valley, Ogden Valley, and the Wasatch Front in Utah. Pedestrian routes can be very different from those of historic roads. They feature a dribble of debris left from millennia of stopovers, camping, and retooling of stone implements that is not found in nearby areas that were not as frequently traveled. Natural routes should harbor caches of equipment, of which the Fenn Cache is exemplary. Cartography by Chelsea McRaven Feeney.

the burial of a child 12,900 years ago. Through collaboration of the landowner, Native American tribes, and scientists, it was learned that ancient DNA from the child shows deep roots with peoples of Siberia and a close affiliation with living Native Americans.[4]

Clovis epitomizes a broad presence of humanity across North America, but in the Great Salt Lake region, it is only part of the story. Here and across the Great Basin and Intermountain West, the points of the Western Stemmed Tradition take center stage.[5] The tradition is far more common there than Clovis. The earliest stemmed point types, such as Haskett, are as early as Clovis, and there is increasing evidence that some are older than Clovis and thus associated with the preceding explorers.

Again, my monikers of "explorers," "pioneers," and "settlers" are not intended to just be different names for the "cultures" identified by archaeologists—especially when whole peoples are parted out by the kind of projectile points they made. The Western Stemmed Tradition preceded but continued through Clovis times. The stemmed points of the pioneers eventually changed as life changed, and new forms of stemmed points persisted among the settlers of the Archaic until about 8,000 years ago, long after Clovis disappeared. A variety of stemmed points continued to evolve over the millennia, creating a link with the living Native Americans of the region. It is more probable to suspect that many "peoples" used these technologies.

The Western Stemmed Tradition also connects the earliest Americans with their roots because stemmed points are found in very early contexts in eastern Siberia and Kamchatka. Stemmed points are most common in western North America, suggesting they may be a tangible remnant of explorer migration along the Pacific coast. In contrast, explorer migration south through the inland corridor along the Rocky Mountain Front populated the interior of the continent. Clovis arose subsequent to those migrations and developed in the Plains and eastern United States, eventually returning north to Alaska. The Western Stemmed and Clovis traditions symbolize the diversity among even the earliest Americans, and a long path of connection with living Native Americans. What were the lifestyles among these early peoples of the Great Salt Lake region? What were the landscapes like?

The famous Clovis sites of the Plains and the Southwest that gave the culture its name are mostly places where large animals were killed, especially mammoths. It is likely, but to a lesser extent known, that Clovis people also hunted Pleistocene horses, camel, bison, and musk ox. This leads to a stereotype of Clovis people as specialized big-game hunters. The location and movement of these animals would strongly influence Clovis decision-making and suggest a distinctive form of mobility. But archaeologists have long realized there was more to Clovis-period life than big-game hunting. Over the seasons, and through the lives of individual hunters, people subsisted on a variety of plant and animal foods. Not only did the availability of large game vary, but the ability of individuals over the course of their lives changed. Young boys hunted more approachable game, such as rabbits and waterfowl, and likely participated in root and berry collection, as did girls, young women, and the elderly, both women and men. Women in many hunter-gather societies hunt using snares, clubs, rocks, and their hands, and diverting streams to flood the burrows of small mammals. The sacred ritual of big-game hunting begins for men in their teens, but once a hunter approaches his thirties, his abilities diminish, just as they do for pro athletes today. In Indigenous societies, they would then transition into the role of spiritual leaders, advisors to the hunt, and their knowledge of the sacred and proper execution of the rituals became a power greater than physical prowess. When the life history of individuals is taken into consideration, we glimpse cultural texture rather than cultural stereotypes.

The tilt of the food system toward a broad range of plants and animals is especially true in the Great Salt Lake region. Bonneville Estates Rockshelter, south of Wendover, Nevada, yielded deposits dated as early as 13,000 years old that include the early Haskett type of the Western Stemmed Tradition. The excavation also yielded a variety of stone, bone, and wood tools and scraps of plant fiber ranging from knotting to nets. The primary foods at Bonneville Estates were sage grouse and rabbits, with lesser amounts of pronghorn, mule deer, mountain sheep, and bison. The seeds of grasses, shrubs, and marsh plants indicate a broad and opportunistic diet. The rockshelter is situated on the Bonneville shoreline in a sagebrush and shadscale desert, but the wetlands around spring-fed Blue Lake are nearby. The same can be said of Danger Cave, just outside of Wendover, Utah, where occupation over 12,000 years ago centered on a spring-fed marsh. Upland environments were also used at this early time, including Smith Creek Cave, Nevada, 30 miles north of the town of Baker. The cave is situated 1,500 feet above the Bonneville shoreline. There, a variety of upland plant and animal resources were harvested as early as 13,000 years ago, and use of the cave continued for thousands of years.[6]

Archaeologists talk a lot about stone points and other tools because they preserve well, so we have a lot of them. The understanding of perishable artifacts is limited by fragmentary finds in small samples, but such finds do reveal a sophisticated material culture. A variety of distinctive plain weave mats and bags of fine execution were made by the earliest peoples in the Americas. Some are decorated with leather and contrasting colors of fibers. Some appear to be made on looms. Sandals and moccasins were made to exacting techniques and styles, and those traditions lasted for thousands of years, testifying to intergenerational persistence across large geographic areas. There are bone needles and awls for sewing, and all manner of cordage of

4.4 These exquisite fishhooks from Mantle's Cave in Dinosaur National Monument, Colorado, urge us to think broadly about foods. These hooks were stored in a basket along with a bundle of small mammal snares and other objects. Each hook is about 5 centimeters long and made of bone and wood bound together by string and cemented with pine pitch. One hook was attached to a cord 3 meters long. The other two were on opposite ends of a cord 3.5 meters long. Photo by François Gohier. Copyright University of Colorado Museum of Natural History, Boulder.

soft dogbane with excellent pliancy, milkweed for strength, and sagebrush bark for durability. There are nets for carrying and as parts of snares to capture small rodents. Long rabbit nets were used for rabbit drives, harvesting hundreds for meat and precious skins. The skin is easily pulled from the rabbit with a single movement. Then it is cut into strips and wrapped around a central fiber cord to make a thick yarn. These are sewn together to form a cape. Rabbit-fur robes took hundreds of hours to manufacture and were repaired and passed down for generations. Such

Great Basin Sandal Types

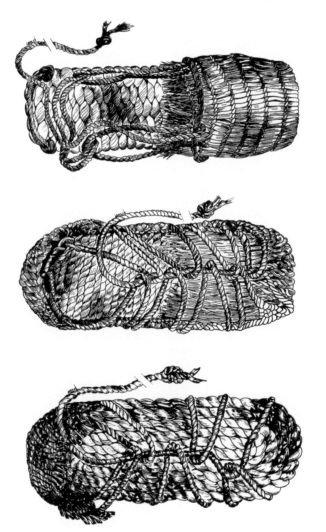

4.5 These sandal types are characteristic of the northern Great Basin of Nevada and Oregon during the time of the pioneers and early settlers. From Connolly and Barker 2004. Courtesy of Tom Connolly, University of Oregon Museum of Natural and Cultural History.

robes are known from lab tests to have heat retention superior to a down coat and comparable to a modern sleeping bag.[7]

Mobility that was variable in tempo and mode remained the pattern during the early phases of the Clovis and Western Stemmed Traditions although the larger continental scales of population compared to the explorers was a significant difference. The twin management problems—keeping track of large game and keeping track of other people—were not as difficult. The pioneers gained a deeper attachment to places compared to the explorers, who held an attachment to the new and unfamiliar. Larger and more extensive populations and a tilt toward the notion

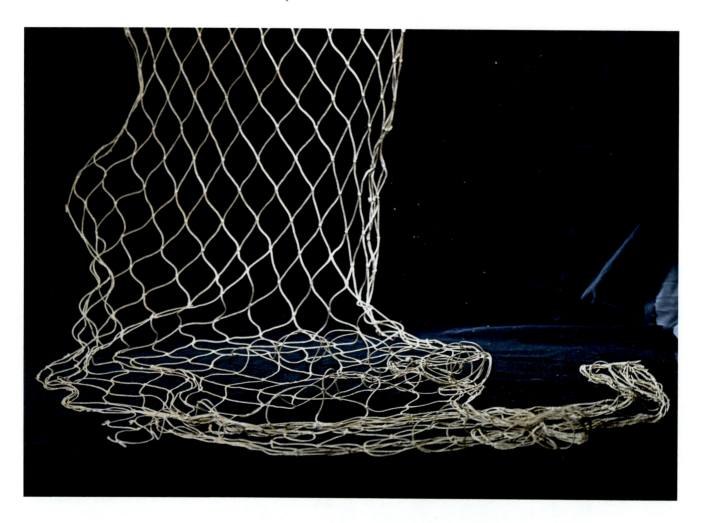

4.6 A Southern Paiute rabbit-hunting net from the ethnographic period. Photo by Alyson Wilkins. Courtesy of Natural History Museum of Utah.

of place as places made the long-distance social networks of information more redundant. The Clovis caches are only one facet of this, but they do symbolize a connection to place that was different from that of the explorers.

One difference between the Clovis and Western Stemmed Tradition lifeways might be described as the provisioning of individuals versus the provisioning of places. Clovis people transported everything each time they moved. Their tools needed to be durable, they maintained large networks, and they traversed the landscape extensively. Western Stemmed Tradition people did not cache spectacular tools and blanks of exotic toolstone to the degree known for Clovis. However, there are assortments of Western Stemmed points and blanks in private collections that may be caches.[8]

There seems to be greater redundancy in the use of landscapes by Western Stemmed Tradition peoples, implying notions of place that are more tethered. We will find this in the association of very early rock imagery in landscapes yielding a strong signature of the Western Stemmed Tradition. However, both Clovis and Western Stemmed pioneer lifeways exhibit a form of planning depth, and none of these early peoples wandered aimlessly. Far from it. They were intimate with the landscape, even though there were cultural differences in how people conceptualized landscape and place. These things only hint at the transition from pioneers to settlers in the roles they played in the landscapes of the time.

The difference between conceptualizing place in terms of transience and newness and in terms of homeland is evident in the Great Salt Lake wetlands. Nothing speaks to this like the Old River Bed Delta, a fascinating remnant of Lake Bonneville located within Dugway Proving Ground and the United States Air Force Utah Testing and Training Range. Both are closed to public access. Travelers on the Old Pony Express Route can see the upper channel of the Old River Bed about 7 miles west of the Simpson Springs Pony Express Station. The channel is readily apparent, but today it is a stark, sunbaked desert wasteland. G. K. Gilbert visited the Old River Bed and his description conveys a sense of wonder:

> the chance traveller finds nothing to quench his thirst from Simpson spring to Fish Spring, a distance of 40 miles. One who stands here in the midst of a desert, where the only vegetation is a scattering growth of low bushes, and looks on an ancient river course 2,000 feet broad and more than 100 feet deep, cannot fail to be deeply impressed.... the Bonneville shore-line, which is visible upon the adjacent mountains and buttes, is 700 feet higher than the highest part of the old channel; and our exploration demonstrated that the entire site of the channel was submerged during both Bonneville and Provo epochs.... In a word, the channel was opened at a time, during the final desiccation of the lake, when the level of the water in the main body fell below the bottom of the strait.... Neither end of the channel is visible from the crossing of the stage road, but both are commanded by neighboring peaks. It is about 45 miles in length, and holds a direct course from the heart of the Sevier Desert to the edge of the Great Salt Lake Desert.[9]

Gilbert recognized the Old River Bed as a stark reminder of what the Bonneville Flood created when the Gunnison arm of Lake Bonneville, occupying the Sevier Desert of west-central Utah, drained north into the Great Salt Lake arm. He also recognized that the flow of water continued as the lake retreated below the Provo level. We now know that water continued to flow either on the surface or as groundwater from the Sevier Desert across the Old River Bed for thousands of years because freshwater clam shells yield a strontium signal of a Sevier water source. Miles north of the upper channel, the water disperses onto a vast mosaic of channels and ponds known as the Old River Bed Delta. It lasted from over 13,000 years ago to 9,000 years ago. A great deal of recent archaeology describes hundreds of ancient camps, activity areas, and thousands of Western Stemmed Tradition artifacts, mostly points of different types spanning the 4,000-year history of these vast wetlands.[10]

As the landscape filled with people, the social organization shifted in response to changes in lifeway. The redundancy in mobility and the less widely traveled, more tethered movements would have partitioned groups into structured lineages and bands. Rules of exogamy would dictate that one must marry across lineage lines, and even slightly higher population densities and changes in long-distance mobility made that feasible. Such connections create relatives, alliances, obligations, and conflicts of interest. These same networks structure the notion of place. Sense of place would become more tied to places of use, to birthplace, and to homeland.

Decisions about hunting and gathering shaped group membership and size, and these decisions were likely gendered. A wide range of activities is apparent in the archaeology. Hunting remained important, as attested by the large Western Stemmed point types. One such point found on the Old River Bed Delta is a Haskett, an early Western Stemmed Tradition style. The point was associated with deposits between 12,000 and 13,000 years old. It must have been buried quickly and remained buried for a long time because it showed very little erosion. An astute researcher realized the potential and submitted the point for protein residue analysis. A long shot paid off. Blood protein residue was found on the Haskett point. The blood was tested against two dozen animal taxa as well as the sediment surrounding the point. All were negative except for a positive match to elephant antiserum. The Haskett point from the Old River Bed Delta was evidently used on a mammoth.[11]

The images of hunting or scavenging a mammoth contrast with the relatively mundane vegetable and animal resources found in the wetlands. Akin to the aisles of a modern supermarket, the wetlands yielded harvestable birds, all manner of small mammals, and large game such as deer and pronghorn. Wetlands also harbor important root crops such as cattail and bulrush. Roots, collectively known to botanists as geophytes, can be eaten fresh or cooked, or pounded and dried for storage and transport. Bulrush and cattail roots are about 75 percent water. They can be strung together by the hundreds and thrown over the shoulder like a bandolier to provide sips of water on journeys across the desert. These tiny canteens were discarded by the hundreds in the dry caves of the region, where they survived for thousands of years as chewed up fiber "quids."

Some of the stone tools found in the wetland sites are for root preparation. Just as the modern potato is important to us, the ancient roots were important to the

Western Stemmed Tradition pioneers and settlers. One can envision groups of men, women, and children spending weeks harvesting cattail and bulrush in the marshes of the Old River Bed Delta. Such mundane activities would have been part of everyday life, but an opportunity to harvest a mammoth would not have been passed up.

The fullness of life at this time of transition from pioneers to settlers is evident in the same part of the Old River Bed Delta where the evidence for mammoth processing was found. The Wishbone site yielded a fire hearth 12,300 years old containing the wishbone of a duck. The hearth also yielded four seeds of wild desert tobacco. This is the oldest find of tobacco known in North America by a long shot. About a half mile away, tracks of human footprints were found in summer 2022. The barefoot prints were left by adults and several children between 5 and 12 years old. The geological context suggests the footprints and the hearth with the duck and tobacco seeds are about the same age—between 12,000 and 13,000 years old. These finds offer a glimpse of a social life that was much more than a struggle for existence in the wilderness.[12]

The Old River Bed Delta was likely the largest, but it was not the only wetland fringing Great Salt Lake. Other early wetlands are found at nearby Fish Springs, Blue Lake, Danger Cave, Public Shooting Grounds, the lower Jordan River, the Weber River, and the Bear River.

The archaeology is clear that the wetlands tethered the people of the Western Stemmed Tradition for thousands of years, thus ushering in the transition from pioneers to settlers. One way to see that is in the acquisition of stone for tools. Because the wetlands do not produce toolstone, it had to be brought in. Most tools found on the Old River Bed Delta were made from fine-grained basalts, typically from a half dozen sources 35 to 50 miles away. Obsidian was also used, much of it from sources near Topaz Mountain, about 50 miles to the south. At times the distances were much greater; obsidian was also transported from a dozen sources in Nevada, Utah, and Idaho up to 100 and even 200 miles from the Old River Bed Delta.

Sense of place, and its role, changed everywhere during the transition to the time of the settlers. Sacred landscapes provide a dramatic illustration of place. We will encounter these across the Great Salt Lake region, but we begin with the rock imagery along the Snake River Canyon south of Boise and east toward Twin Falls. Dozens of rock imagery sites are scattered along the route of the Lake Bonneville Flood. Over 90 percent of the rock imagery is placed on what is known as the Melon Gravel, basaltic boulders ripped from the canyon walls by the Bonneville Flood and rolled into spheres ranging from the size of a watermelon to several times larger than the size of an SUV. The gravel bars and stringers of these rounded boulders create a striking landscape along the sections of the Snake River Canyon where they

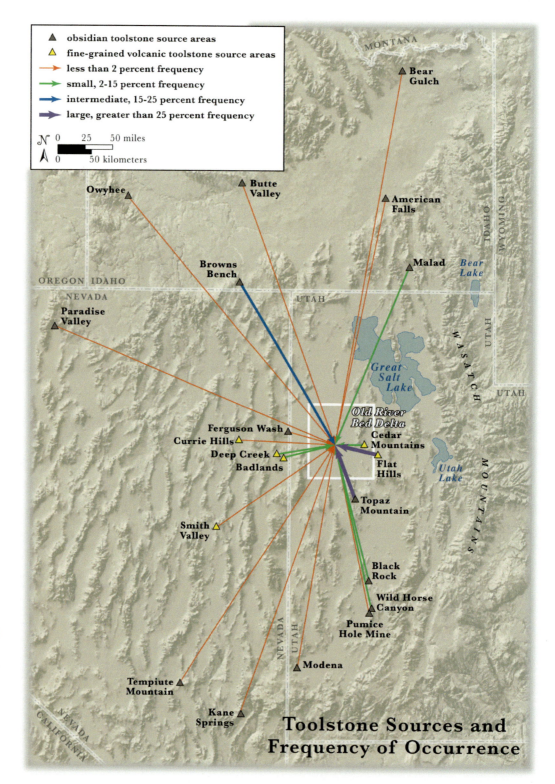

4.7 Toolstone sources and frequency of occurrence at the Old River Bed Delta. Redrawn by Chelsea McRaven Feeney from a map in Page and Duke 2015. Courtesy of Daron Duke, Far Western Anthropological Research Group.

4.8 Melon Gravel rolled, rounded, and left behind by the Lake Bonneville Flood, including an exceptionally large boulder that dwarfs the SUV. Courtesy of Bruce Bjornstad, geologist/author (www.brucebjornstad.com).

accumulated as they came to rest. The Melon Gravel is the most obvious evidence of the power of the Bonneville Flood, and its association with water would be evident to people who knew the land. The association of rock imagery with the Melon Gravel is compelling given the rarity of imagery on literally tens of thousands of easily accessible angular basaltic faces on talus and the walls along the canyon. But those were mostly untouched, and it was the Bonneville Flood debris that became a sacred landscape.

Some of the early rock imagery on the Melon Gravel continued to be produced by the Shoshone of the historic period. The earliest imagery is of the Great Basin Carved Abstract Style, typically associated with Western Stemmed points in the northern Great Basin. A relatively new and tentative method for dating rock imagery has produced dates within the broad span of time indicated by the different styles, but also indicates that some rock imagery on the Melon Gravel may be 10,000 to 13,000 years old.[13]

The connection of Melon Gravel with water is not incidental. In Indigenous societies, water holds mythic power that is manifested in stories from purification rites, legends of floods, and origin stories. In desert societies the affinity of water to life itself takes on special meaning. The creation of rock imagery does not occur in a vacuum. It is not the imagery that gives the landscape its meaning; rather, it is

4.9 Panorama of the sacred Melon Gravel landscape at Celebration Park, Idaho. Courtesy of Allen Baxter Photography, Boise.

the sacred landscape that motivates the creation of rock imagery. The makers did not witness the Lake Bonneville Flood, but the landscape it created exemplifies the construction of place as descendants formed a lasting relationship with deep time.

The image of wetland superabundance is seductive, but it was not static. Climate change is inevitable, and the millennia from 13,000 to 9,000 years ago were a time of significant climate change. About 12,900 years ago, and after several thousand years of a warming and drying trend, the climate of the Northern Hemisphere swung back toward glacial conditions during a period called the Younger Dryas. The transition was unusually rapid as climate swung toward cooler conditions on the scale of a geological moment—a few human generations. Thus, the cause of this change may be novel. The Younger Dryas lasted until 11,700 years ago.

About a century later, climate again swung, and Great Salt Lake reached levels never to be seen again. Called the Gilbert Episode, it began 11,600 years ago, and the lake inundated the Bonneville Salt Flats all the way to Wendover and east to the edge of downtown Salt Lake City, near the Gateway center. Another, smaller expansion of the lake occurred around 11,000 years ago, flooding the site of the Salt Lake City airport and again across the salt flats toward Wendover. Such fluctuations can be short-lived and evoke the personality of this erratic inland sea.[14]

4.10 The rock imagery on Melon Gravel at Celebration Park and Wees Bar, Idaho, evokes a mix of styles and ages. This example is at Celebration Park. Courtesy of Allen Baxter Photography, Boise.

These were dramatic changes on time scales that could be incorporated into oral histories and passed down over generations. Events such as the Younger Dryas and the Gilbert Episode symbolize the degree of climate change that can occur even as life goes on. Some wetlands that were vital to the people of the Western Stemmed Tradition were flooded during transgressions of the lake, yet even the Gilbert Episode did not inundate the wetlands at the Old River Bed Delta or at Fish Springs. In some areas, such as the lower Bear River, the larger lake simply changed the location of wetlands, and they likely reached upstream north of Brigham City past Honeyville during Gilbert times.

After the Younger Dryas and Gilbert Episode the climate returned to the pattern of warmer temperatures and increasing desiccation. Sagebrush retreated from the valley floors and gave way to shadscale and other desert shrubs. Drought-tolerant grasses increased their range. The vast expanse around Great Salt Lake became more similar to what we see today. Evidence of human life in these early times is most apparent in the lowlands, but the uplands and mountains were not ignored.

The earliest types of Western Stemmed Tradition points are scattered lightly across the higher country. An early Haskett point is known from near Pineview Reservoir in Ogden Valley, and other stemmed points have been found in Wasatch Back valleys. As time went by, use of the uplands increased. Despite the imagery of lowlands found in names such as Bonneville Basin and Great Basin, it is the mountains that dominate this region. Nevada is the most mountainous state in the country, with over 300 ranges. As writer John McPhee observed, "Each range here is like a warship standing on its own, and the Great Basin is an ocean of loose sediment with these mountain ranges standing in it as if they were members of a fleet without precedent."[15] A flotilla of mountain ranges rises across the Great Salt Lake region. The Oquirrh Mountains, the Cedar Mountains, the Stansbury Mountains, the Fish Springs Range, the Deep Creek Range, the Raft River Mountains, the Grouse Creek Mountains, the House Range, the Snake Range, and the Mineral Mountains are only the big ships in this vast convoy.

As climate continued to dry the valleys, limber pine retreated to cool canyons along with spruce and subalpine fir. The bristlecone died out in some ranges but survived in the high altitudes of the Snake Range along the Utah–Nevada border. The mountains increasingly featured sagebrush parks with aspen forest, montane brush, and juniper. The pinyon pine so familiar to us who know the region today was not present or was rare in these early millennia, as was the oak brush so familiar now along the Wasatch Front.

The mountains would have offered attractive resources to the early settlers, and we know from the movement of toolstone that people did travel. Rock imagery again offers a portal into the life of the times. Most apparent in the northwestern Great Basin, the Western Stemmed Tradition is significantly associated with areas of the earliest rock imagery, the Great Basin Carved Abstract Style. The dating is typically sparse, but there are hints that this style of rock imagery could date to the time of the pioneers and early settlers. At Long Lake, Oregon, rock imagery is partially buried under Mazama Ash from the volcanic explosion that created Crater Lake, hence it is no less than 7,700 years old. At Winnemucca Lake, Nevada, rock imagery buried in calcium carbonate tufa deposits dates within one of two windows: 10,500–11,300 years ago or 13,700–14,800 years ago. The strong representation of the Western Stemmed Tradition in upland settings in association with rock imagery shows redundancy in the use of this higher country, which was attractive for big-game hunting and the all-important collection of roots. The same areas with rock imagery and Western Stemmed points have also yielded stone tools used to pound roots. Camp groups of multiple families would have been present in such places when conditions were right.[16]

Around Great Salt Lake the upland signal is weaker, and it may be that the tethering to place was more episodic and opportunistic—like the place where the mammoth was taken in the Old River Bed Delta between 12,000 and 13,000 years ago. As elsewhere though, use of the mountains would eventually change.

Sometime between 9,500 and 8,300 years ago, the Old River Bed Delta diminished or dried up. Great Salt Lake was also declining and would never reach the level of the Gilbert Episode again. For the next 9,000 years Great Salt Lake would be confined to a relatively small range identical to the direct measurements of Great Salt Lake levels from the 1850s to the present.

5

Transformations of Place

Maude Moon, an elderly Shoshone woman, told the story of the Pickleweed Winter to linguist Wick Miller in 1971. Mrs. Moon was born in 1888 and lived most of her life at Goshute, at the foot of the Deep Creek Range near the Utah–Nevada border. Pickleweed grows on the salt flats where the water table is near the surface. In the fall it bears an abundance of tiny seeds, smaller than poppy seeds. Pickleweed chaff is a major component of archaeological deposits found in the caves of the Great Salt Lake region.

> The pickleweed grows there at the edge of the salt flats. The earth is salt. Only there it grows well.… In the winter time they [the ancient Shoshone] used to live on it. There were just seeds. One winter when the snow melted, it did like this (made waves with the hand). The water did thus (to the seeds), and (seeds) came over there to rest. Just its seeds (the waves) would deposit the seeds at the edge of the salt flats. The people then gathered it, pushing it into their burden baskets with their basketry scoopers. In this fashion they dried it. Just the seeds. It was like that, and they gathered just the seeds. The pickleweed had very tiny seeds.… During the winter, one ate all he wanted.… They ate it with pine nuts, they say. They ate it with jack rabbits. Times were good they say. They didn't go hungry.… They lived on the pickleweed in the wintertime, made sacks, put it inside, and dug a hole in the ground. That was their storehouse. It would not get wet. They did like this (covered it) here with any kinds of seeds. All seeds. That's it, the rat's tail (came off).[1]

The story of the Pickleweed Winter is a symbol of a settling process that is one of several transformations that occurred between 9,000 and 2,000 years ago. Central to this process were changes in the economy and the consequences of those changes for life and society. All Indigenous peoples ate a variety of foods, even the explorers and pioneers who followed large game, and they sometimes hunted Pleistocene megafauna such as mammoth. Seeds were consumed from the beginning, especially larger seeds such as pigweed, which is in the amaranth family, and likely some of the large-seeded grasses such as Great Basin wild rye. Roots, too, were consumed from the beginning. More important than a laundry list of foods eaten is the structure of the diet, including the frequency and quantity of different kinds of food, the extent of processing, and the decision to prepare foods for storage or transport. Decisions about the economy shaped the rest of the culture, just as they do today. The settlers of Great Salt Lake occupied a different landscape and lived different lives than the pioneers before them.

The early settlers were more numerous than the explorers and pioneers of the preceding millennia, although well below the populations that foragers would eventually attain. In fact, the archaeological signature of the explorers is so faint that their very existence remains a point of contention. The archaeological signature of the pioneers is so much stronger than that of the explorers, it is taken for granted, even though we know very little about them. Their signal remains weak. In comparison, the archaeological signature of the settlers is an order of magnitude greater. Their record and impact during what scholars call the Archaic period are everywhere. The settlers played a different role in the environment after 9,000 years ago; their use of the landscape changed, and sense of place became variations on a theme for the next 7,000 years. The first transition was multidimensional and entailed small seeds, technology, a built environment, food processing and storage, mobility, territory, kinship, and ideology.

Small seeds from dozens of plants native to the Great Basin became more important in the economy, not just a supplement. The chaff from processing pickleweed is readily apparent in the layers of fill in the caves around Great Salt Lake, including Danger, Hogup, Bonneville Estates, and Camels Back Caves. The story of the Pickleweed Winter illustrates the irony of small seeds. Pickleweed seeds are so small that when scattered across your hand, it is incomprehensible that these could be collected in sufficient quantity to make even a snack. Mrs. Moon knew that large quantities can be collected by waiting for rain on the salt flats and skimming the seeds from shallow pans of water where the wind and wavelets push them into windrows. Huge quantities of pickleweed chaff and plant parts are found in excavations of the caves. Whole pickleweed plants were cached in the caves so the long hours of separating and processing the tiny seeds could await winter, when people had time on their hands. But even with the expertise that Mrs. Moon had that comes from living on the land, small seeds remain an irony. They are abundant, yet they are expensive food relative to hunting a rabbit or a mule deer or digging biscuitroot. On the other hand, processing seeds into a flour makes them more nutritious and, importantly, more storable. Food storage reduces the risk of shortage and starvation, especially during the harsh winters of the Great Salt Lake region.

Elevating a reliance on seeds required an investment in technology. Grinding stones can require hours—even dozens of hours—to shape and to create a surface by pecking a slab with a harder stone tool. Seeds eaten in quantity must be ground into meal or too many will pass through the gut as undigested empty calories. Grinding stones are not routinely transportable and become part of a built environment that tethers people to places.

5.1 This coiled basket was lined with pine pitch to serve as a water bottle. Coiled basketry represents an investment in costly technology to deal with changes brought by the settling process. Such baskets could be curated, repaired, and handed down over generations of users. Photo by Alyson Wilkins. Courtesy of Natural History Museum of Utah.

Processing and storage required tighter baskets made by the painstaking coiling process, in which split fibers such as willow form a rod or bundle that is wrapped and coiled upward or outward to form a variety of vessel sizes and shapes. Varying the species of fibers enables the introduction of color and designs. Basketmaking is an art learned at an early age and a skill honed over a lifetime. Most baskets represent hundreds of hours of work. Dating of baskets suggests they were passed down over generations. In one case, two baskets dated nearly 300 years earlier than the foods they contained! Twined basketry trays are used to parch the seeds with hot coals to prevent them from germinating and dries them to prevent spoilage. Coiled basketry vessels can be watertight and are used to cook the seed flour into a gruel using water heated with hot rocks. The gruel may contain a variety of seed flours and serves as the base of a stew laced with everything from roots, berries, nuts, and greens to bits of rabbit, duck, muskrat, sage grouse, venison, pronghorn, and so on.[2]

Then there is the construction of a place to store the parched seeds. Maude Moon declared they "dug a hole in the ground." She was referring to a variety of ways that stored food can be protected if someone knows what they are doing. Her reference to storage may be the most significant thing about seeds. When something is stored, it presumes the necessity to return. Stored food is an insurance policy, but also a ball and chain.

The transition to an economy with a big role for seeds is not the only symbol of the settling process. The storage of all manner of food increased. Although roots

5.2 A pine nut storage facility at the Bustos site in the White Pine Range south of Ely, Nevada. It was constructed on bedrock to improve rodent resistance. The scatter of rocks outside the circle are rocks that were removed to open the cache, which was covered by layers of cedar bark, limbs, and earth over the pinecones and bags of nuts below. Photo by Steve Simms (Simms 1989).

5.3 *The Root Collectors*, by Eric S. Carlson. Roots, known to botanists as geophytes, were important in Native American diets from the earliest times. They are nutritious, starchy, and store well. When dried, they can be transported. Here a camp group is using digging sticks to harvest what could be yampa (*Perideridia* spp.), biscuitroot (*Lomatium* spp.), or bitterroot (*Lewisia* spp.). Crescent-shaped stone tools are sometimes found in root-collecting areas that have persisted for centuries and even millennia. Crescents are multipurpose tools and are also found in wetlands. Courtesy of Eric S. Carlson.

were eaten by the earliest peoples, their role may have broadened. Starch grains from dryland roots such as yampa, bitterroot, and biscuitroot were found on grinding stones, milling stones, and basket fragments from Hogup Cave, located west of the northern arm of Great Salt Lake.

Evidence for a trend toward the mass collection of jackrabbits at Camels Back Cave suggests group hunting using nets and clubs to take large numbers of jacks in the early winter when they form large groups. This kind of hunting produces so much meat that at least some was surely jerked and stored.

Storage benefits from increased processing and the tether of settling would favor investment in all kinds of processed foods, whether seeds, dried roots, game and fish jerky, nuts, berries, or dried grasshoppers. Lakeside Cave, west of Great Salt Lake, was a grasshopper collecting and processing station. People from far and wide knew that when water spread across the salt flats west of the cave, and the winds were right, millions of hoppers would drown and blow onto the shore in windrows several inches high and miles long. They were scooped up with flat basket trays along with incidental amounts of the oolitic sand that lines some shorelines of the lake. Oolitic sand grains are concretions of lime formed around a brine shrimp fecal pellet or other tiny debris, creating tiny pearl-like spheres. It occurs only on the shorelines. The practice of bringing the hoppers to the cave introduced significant amounts of oolitic sand into Lakeside Cave, where it would not naturally occur. The grasshoppers were then pounded into a paste that could be mixed with seeds, root paste, animal fat, and such to form desert fruitcake, an early version of a power bar: nutritious, storable, and transportable. Lakeside Cave was used to collect grasshoppers as early as 5,000 years ago, and the activity occurred whenever the opportunity arose until about 1,000 years ago. I can attest that grasshopper meat is edible. Indeed, the tiny strip of white meat is like crab or lobster. Lakeside Cave symbolizes not just the tethering process, but the erratic tempo of opportunism.[3]

The underpinning of the settlement process is something that modern people take for granted—infrastructure. The explorers and pioneers had little infrastructure, nor did they process and store much food given their life on the move. There are hints of redundant, and even local, use of places among the pioneers, but a recognizable change brought by the settlers began 9,000 years ago, and the settling process would unfold over the next seven millennia. The ups and downs of this process, often shaped by climate change creating wet periods and long droughts, anchored the tyranny of circumstance that underlies all human life in all times and places.

If seeds, roots, and the storage of a wider variety of foods as an investment in place have so many advantages, why did it take so long to make this transition? Surely it could not be that the explorers and pioneers were too primitive—too ignorant. Was it just because they could not progress? Or the genius or prophet who would lead the people into the future had yet to be born? But wait—people had been living in the Great Salt Lake region for 5,000 years, or 250 human generations, before the seed transition even began. It seems improbable that such explanations can account for such a long wait for the magic of genius and progress. The answer is not found in the motives or aptitudes of individuals, nor in a random sequence of historical events. It is not found in events at all, but in the processes that shape the culture that people are born into, learn, and live. The answer is found in the consequences of humans living their lives as shaped by culture. In the case of the ancient Indigenous inhabitants of the Great Salt Lake region, the transformation was a consequence of the process of settling. Humans became endemic participants in ecosystems. Indeed, they became the keystone participants. The settlers of the Archaic period began to change the nature of wilderness by a process that over the centuries and millennia created a Human Wilderness.

The archaeology and paleoecology of the Great Salt Lake region offer dramatic evidence of the transformation process and a degree of explanation as to how and why it occurred when it did the way it did. The cave sites around the lake provide powerful evidence because they contain layer after layer of deposits, often with excellent preservation of perishables, and opportunities for modern dating. They contain a record of human life over hundreds of generations and thousands of years. They enable us to understand cultural change that is difficult to comprehend from the vantage of our relatively brief lives, especially lives ensconced in post-industrial society.

Caves also contain a record of changing climate and its consequences for the ecosystems humans depended on and, in turn, shaped. Climate can be gleaned from the plants and animals found in the caves, and from the wood rat middens that preserved evidence of changes in vegetation and, by extension, climate. The locations and changes in wetlands are documented in geological trenches in places like the Old River Bed Delta. A comparison of regional versus local vegetation is documented by the study of pollen from trenches and from cores drilled into the lakebed. Temperature and moisture records have also been preserved in tree rings, such as those of bristlecone pine in the Snake Range of eastern Nevada. Some caves contain animal bones deposited not by people, but by other predators. A spectacular example was found in Homestead Cave on the Utah Test and Training Range operated by Hill Air Force Base. For more than 13,000 years, owls deposited pellets of digested food in layers that record changes in habitats and climate. It is estimated that Homestead Cave contains over a million bones of rodents, fish, lizards, and birds. The transition from freshwater Lake Bonneville to a saline Great Salt Lake is seen in Homestead Cave in the decline of freshwater fish bones. The transition to desert by 10,000 years ago is evident as a nosedive in the abundance and diversity of rodents. This change in climate marked the transition from the Pleistocene to the Holocene geological epochs.

By 9,000 years ago the enormous wetlands so important to the Western Stemmed Tradition pioneers had disappeared or had become a scatter of small wetlands. The amount of time spent in wetlands decreased, and stays were shorter. There was greater use of upland habitats. The first use of limber pine nuts by 9,000 years ago was followed by the harvesting of pinyon pine nuts by 8,000 years ago. The adoption of these key nut species is a strong signal that uplands were much more of an attraction than before.

The record at Bonneville Estates Rockshelter shows that small mammals, especially rabbits, were the most common prey, but the meat diet also included mule deer, pronghorn, bison, and sage grouse, and montane prey such as bighorn sheep and marmot. The technology of hunting changed, with smaller versions of Western Stemmed Tradition points becoming favored, and new styles of smaller, triangular points being produced. Camels Back Cave had an abundance of cottontail rabbits harvested 9,500 to 8,000 years ago. Cottontails require dense cover to avoid predators, so this indicates that substantial shrublands persisted even as the wetlands shrank. However, after 8,000 years ago jackrabbits increased at the expense of

5.4 *The Pine Nut Harvest*, by Eric S. Carlson. The pinyon pine became an economic staple as it spread across the Great Basin beginning over 8,000 years ago in the northeastern Great Basin and 6,000 years ago or later in the central and western Great Basin. Groves of pinyon can produce nuts every year, but they cycle individually. Nut production can be predicted a year, and sometimes two years, ahead, enabling planning. The fall harvest required equipment that was cached in pine nut groves, such as the pinyon hooks seen here. Grinding stones to hull the nuts were stored by leaning them against tree trunks or lodging them in a tree crotch. Pole and log wickiups used for housing in previous years were refurbished. Courtesy of Eric S. Carlson.

cottontails, showing that desertification was creating a more open habitat. Jackrabbits run from predators and thrive in open shrubland.[4]

As people invested in place, the move toward processing and storage constrained how far they could travel, even as those changes were beneficial. We explore the process of settling by beginning with hunting because that is the underlying catalyst of the transition to a broader food economy, the storage of food, the first steps toward a built environment, and settlement itself.

One thing that did not change from the time of the pioneers in the Great Salt Lake region is that large game—mule deer, bighorn sheep, pronghorn, and occasionally elk, moose, and bison—were always hunted when possible. Recall that the twin management problems for the explorers and the pioneers were keeping track of large game and keeping track of other people. The location and abundance of large game drove the decision-making. Along the way, all the other resources were taken to sustain the hunt. Local abundance of resources such as roots provided the opportunity to obtain transportable supplies to sustain the next round of travel, as well as to pause to retool and associate with other people. That mode of mobility promoted long-distance social networks of information and long-distance moves, albeit moves that occurred in spurts. Humans living in an ecosystem with few neighbors, or after an absence, will reduce large game numbers by hunting. They also displace large game as the animals learn to move away from the humans who are hunting them. This co-evolution is as old as humanity, and humans are the keystone predator. Humans can hunt a broader array of age groups, and they target what they need, such as males for meat and females for quality hides. Humans prey upon and readily displace competing predators, including wolves, cats, and even bears. The use of the teeth and claws of these animals for ornamentation and tools was widespread and simultaneously symbolizes the sacred nature of such animals and the capability of human hunters.

When the human presence is sustained as it was for the settlers, populations of large game are liable to be cropped to levels well below carrying capacity. In other words, the abundance of large game is driven from the top down by predation, not from the bottom up by limited food. None of this mattered much for the explorers and the pioneers because their populations were low, but, more significantly, their mobility kept them moving to maximize game encounters from small-bodied to mega-bodied. The long-distance movement during the early millennia enabled game populations to rebound, and large game can rebound rapidly in the absence of human predation.[5]

One consequence of the settling process and the cycling among smaller territories, whether they were small wetlands or upland patches, is that resources were more rapidly used up. As people exploited more locally, game populations were kept at low levels. The cave sites in the Great Salt Lake region show clearly that small game dominated the meat diet. In fact, the representation of large game decreased as the people were increasingly tethered to places. The shrinking of wetlands, which are magnets for large game, exacerbated the trend. The desertification of the uplands compressed the ranges of animals that favor uplands, making them even more susceptible to human predation. The goals of hunting did not change much, but the declining numbers had the twin effects of making more expensive foods such as seeds a bigger part of the diet, and making it worth the extra effort to process and store a wider range of foods. The insurance policy of storage to hedge risk came with the ball and chain of smaller territories, which ensured that large-game populations would be shaped by a human presence anchored to places.[6]

At first glance it may seem that people remained as mobile as those of the preceding millennia and, in a sense, became even more mobile. The tempo of mobility may indeed have quickened, but the mode of mobility became tethered and redundant. Moves were shorter and cycled through contrasting ecosystems within smaller

5.5 *Caching Pine Nuts for Winter*, by Eric S. Carlson. Large groups could assemble for the pinyon harvest to lay in winter supplies. The storage facilities were often constructed on bedrock to hinder rodents, and the caches of nuts in hulls and cones were covered with layers of juniper bark to provide further resistance to insects and rodents. Layers of rocks and earth also protected the nuts, although the loss rates could have been significant. People moved among the storage locations over the course of the winter. The pinyon zone is a good place to be in winter. It provides firewood and is in a warmer thermal zone than the valley bottoms and the higher elevations. Courtesy of Eric S. Carlson.

territories. In such circumstances, food storage to manage risk is advantageous but consequently tethers people to place in a vicious cycle. More local and sometimes lower-quality tool stone was used. The local distinctiveness and regional variation in projectile point and knife styles indicate a degree of compartmentalization compared to earlier times.

Changes in basketry and textiles such as sandals show diversification even as there was continuity with earlier times. The movement of exotic trade goods such as Pacific shell show that broader connections existed and implies that large camp groups from far-flung locations gathered for opportunities such as rabbit drives, the pinyon harvest, and root collecting. Such events fostered trade, marriage, alliance building, and the all-important flow of information. The ethnographies describing

5.6 Mobility can be contingent and vary on the small scales of days, months, or an annual round. Individuals and groups can conceptualize a territory on these small scales. The larger temporal scale of the life history of individuals helps us see mobility and concepts of territory as evolving processes rather than as immutable attributes of cultural groups. Ethnography among Indigenous foraging peoples shows that lifetime ranges can exceed 8,000 square miles. The hypothetical range shown here is borrowed from the Nunamiut Eskimo in northern Alaska to imagine the scale of lifetime mobility in a portion of the Great Salt Lake cultural landscape. Individuals' sense of place derives from personal experiences, hence territory is not just a fixed parcel of land. Cartography by Chelsea McRaven Feeney from a sketch map by Lewis Binford (1983:115).

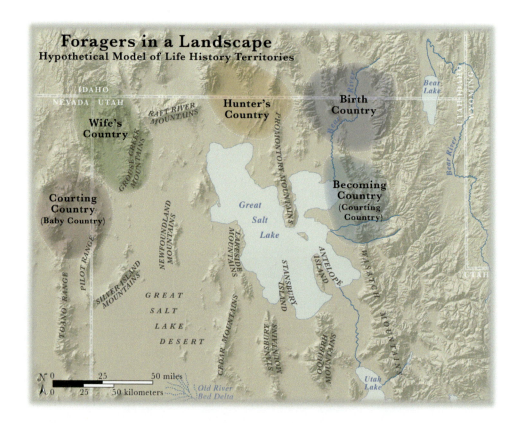

Indigenous life and perspectives in the Great Basin convey the feeling that one of the first things people discussed when they met up, along with matters of kinship, was the location and status of food sources.[7] The availability of nuts could be predicted over a year out, sometimes two, and everyone knew that when the rabbitbrush turns yellow, the pine nuts are ready to pick. When it was time to pick yampa roots, or the wind and water were perfect for brine fly larvae or grasshoppers, news could travel widely, and people would walk for a week to participate.

The settling process does not mean everyone just stayed home, in contrast to the wanderlust of the explorers and even the pioneers. It is tempting to atomize ancient foragers as living their entire lives in one place—one valley, one mountain range. Mobility is not a state of being, even though anthropologists of the twentieth century employed the device of the seasonal or annual round to describe the lives of foragers. A consideration of temporal scale adds dynamism to such descriptions. The territorial range of a family or camp group of foragers during an annual round may bear little resemblance to the territorial range traversed over a lifetime. Large territories would be favored during times of drought, which peppered the millennia during the settling process.

Territory on the scale of a human lifetime can be astonishingly large. An analogy from the Nunamiut Eskimo helps envision this.[8] Over the course of their lives, Nunamiut adjust their foraging range depending on the productivity of animals and plants, marriage, childbirth, and deaths of family members. All the places that an individual encounters over their life are remembered and named according to where that place fits into their life history. For some Nunamiut these stages and places translate as Birth Country, Courting Country, Baby Country, Wife's Country, and Hunter's Country. Each place is a reference point, and collectively the places where an individual's unique experiences occurred overlap to create a life history territory that may be geographically expansive. Nunamiut lifetime territories can be 8,500 square miles.

The lifetime accumulation of cultural knowledge about landscapes is conveyed and perpetuated in stories and rituals. These in turn serve as a map of the land that is also a map of social networks. The stories are passed down from the ancestors and may be commemorative in character by reference to historical events. As such, territory can be scaled according to season, annual round, and life phases, and all are linked to the ancestors. Territory is more of a concept, and a way of living, than it is a parcel of land. As Nick Thompson, a Western Apache elder, told the ethnographer Keith Basso about the stories of landscape and place that he was recording at Cibeque, Arizona, "White men need paper maps. We have maps in our minds."[9]

Landscape, lifeway, and sense of place are foundational to the genealogy of the living Native Americans of the Great Salt Lake region. From the time of the first settlers up to around 3,000 years ago, the ancient Indigenous people were of nature, and the wilderness was theirs. It was a Human Wilderness.

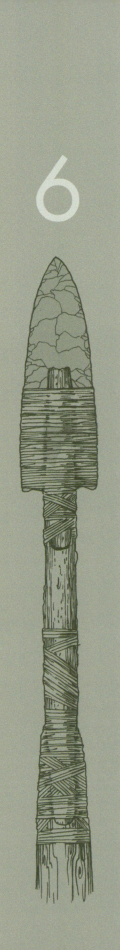

6

A Human Wilderness

The Pristine Myth—as envisioned by early American writers from James Fenimore Cooper to Henry David Thoreau, and articulated in the eighteenth century by the heirs to Jean Jacques Rousseau's notion of the Noble Savage—is enshrined in American heritage. The Pristine Myth justifies the belief that America was a wilderness ripe for the taking and necessarily relies on the belief that Native Americans were few, primitive, and benign.[1] As Luther Standing Bear (1868–1939), chief of the Oglala Sioux, expressed the manifestation of the myth, "Only to the white man was nature a 'wilderness' and only to him was the land 'infested' with 'wild' animals and 'savage' people."[2]

If wilderness is a place untouched by humanity, then its demise began during the ecological moment when the explorers arrived and the pioneers spread throughout the continent. As America became a Human Wilderness, landscapes became increasingly managed as the settlers transformed places over the ensuing millennia. Even in the desert expanse of the Great Salt Lake region, and all the mountain ranges east and west, the footprint of Indigenous peoples changed as the settling process played out over the millennia.

Indigenous peoples everywhere employ a range of practices that amount to environmental management and conservation. In some places and times, portions of the landscape became anthropogenic, taking their characteristics from the hand of humanity. The people also experienced the outcomes of their decisions. The mere act of living life produces a tyranny of circumstance that lead to consequences for the environment and for the future life of the people. By the end of what archaeologists call the Archaic period, about 2,000 years ago, a cultural sea change had occurred in the lifeways of people and how their societies were organized. We explore this by beginning with changes in climate and landscape, and then trace the changes in daily life and society.

Climate and landscapes in the Great Salt Lake region changed. Ancient vegetation records show wetter periods, including one around 6,500 years ago, that caused the return of wetlands and grass meadows. There were cool intervals between 4,400 and 3,400 years ago and 2,700 and 1,500 years ago, spans of time equal to many human generations.

During the Archaic period, Great Salt Lake fluctuated between 4,170 and 4,215 feet. At the lower elevation, Great Salt Lake would have been a mere puddle. At its upper elevation, it would have flooded all of the area around what is now Interstate 80; a few miles west of the where the Salt Lake City airport is and west past Tooele, there would also have been flooding in the area of what is now Interstate 15, the Legacy Parkway, and Centerville. The Bear River Bird Refuge marshes would have been inundated. Within this narrow range of elevation, this skillet of a lake fluctuated rapidly and frequently rather than gradually, with fluctuations on the scale of centuries or millennia.[3] The ancient settlers experienced a Great Salt Lake much like the one measured since 1850. Changes in ecosystems around the lake were primarily spatial adjustments and variations on recognizable themes—without, of course, the effects of over a century of cattle and sheep grazing, roads, dams, water diversion, alfalfa production, invasive species, mining, fire suppression, and urbanization.

We met the concept of a built environment previously, and it offers a portal into the changes that occurred during this long process of settlement. The attribution of a built environment to ancient Indigenous peoples may seem like a stretch for modern people with our homes, factories, roads and rail, electrical grids, waterways and dams, schools, churches, sports stadiums, sewers, fiber optic systems, and such. But the built environment of the ancients was just as important. It was intelligent and tuned to the needs at hand, even though the inventory of tools and facilities was small, and the technology relatively simple. The investment in a built environment and a redundant use of ecosystems increased specialization and reduced the need to transport gear. Caches could be placed to serve specific needs, and activities were increasingly redundant.

When Northern Paiute women in southeastern Oregon showed anthropologists and botanists in the 1980s the techniques for collecting biscuitroot and yampa, they would pick up stone scraping tools that had been left on the ground in the root stand from the previous trip—and the previous trips of their ancestors. Botanists know that some of these stands have life spans measured in millennia. Root fields were managed using fire, and experiments show that regular fire increases yields. But those yields were sustained by routine collecting of biscuitroot and yampa because digging the roots acts as tillage, thus stimulating further root production and complementing the benefits of fire.[4]

6.1 A patch of yampa in northwestern Nevada near Surprise Valley in 2019. Its white flowers are prominent in the background, where a controlled burn years before reduced the sagebrush, making it more favorable for yampa. The area of sage and less yampa in the foreground was not burned. The root patches do not have to be burned every year, but over the span of decades, repetition improves the yield, as does harvesting the roots by digging, which serves as tillage. Photo by Steve Simms. Courtesy of James O'Connell, University of Utah.

Caching of equipment, along with residential and storage facilities, would have been essential to the pinyon pine nut harvest. Bundles of snares and spare bows and arrows could be tucked into a rocky ledge. Specialized equipment such as fishing line, bone hooks, duck decoys, nets, and sinkers could be cached near wetlands and picked up on the way in. Some items were specialized. The hollow leg bones of duck might be included in such a cache because they were used as snorkels by submerged hunters to capture ducks by pulling them underwater by their legs.

One dramatic example of built environments that emerged during the process of settling is found in mountains at altitudes so high that archaeologists did not recognize them until recent decades. In these cases, the mountain environments were engineered, reflecting both material and social investments. People hunted in rugged alpine landscapes for thousands of years, but a little after 3,000 years ago, the human presence surged with the construction and habitation of substantial alpine villages. The surrounding alpine landscapes changed from logistical use to residential, with entire family groups moving to altitudes of 10,000 to nearly 12,000 feet for the summer. Circular houses with stone foundations were built, and significant refuse middens accumulated. The three best-known examples are numerous villages at each Alta Toquima on the Mount Jefferson Tablelands in central Nevada, the White Mountains in eastern California, and the Wind River Range in Wyoming.

Together they symbolize the extensive, and intensive, nature of the settling process. High-altitude villages were built or reoccupied again and again, in some cases right up to recent centuries. Considered together, the occupations were not synchronized and cannot be explained by a broad historical event, or by continental climate events. They are individual opportunistic responses to local situations by diverse peoples. The Native American settlers were using more and more of the landscape.[5]

People did not traverse the landscape randomly, but used known routes made permanent in the stories—the mental map. Archaeologists know of many routes identifiable by a sinewy dribble of stone tool debris that goes for miles—much like the continuous stream of trash thrown from car windows along modern highways. I have hiked ridges to access high country that had almost no evidence of human presence at all, while an adjacent ridge on a natural route is packed with campsites and debris along its entire length. These were not ancient highways that people could easily follow, but routes of access learned from the elders. Most of the time, they were not used enough to leave the defined trails that we moderns are accustomed to, but in some geologically stable environments, such as desert pavements, ancient trails are graphic and have persisted for millennia. These routes are the natural passages that a good outdoor navigator would find because the ancient people knew intimately how to best traverse the land. As noted earlier, the Clovis era Fenn Cache was placed along a natural route between the Bear River in Wyoming and the Wasatch Front of Utah. The alpine villages do not occur on every mountain range in the West because they are attuned to specific landscapes. Contrary to popular belief, Indigenous peoples did not—as I have read and heard countless times—"wander aimlessly in search of food"!

Tools and structures for obtaining food were just part of the built environment. Medicines were cached in bundles such as the Patterson Bundle found near Thompson, Utah—a skin bag containing pouches of individual doses of curing herbs.[6] Another skin bag was found in central Utah near the Great Gallery rock imagery site. It contained several smaller pouches and included local chert flakes, an antler flintknapping tool, and a softball-sized mass of edible marsh elder seeds.[7] The Shaman Bundle from Lovelock Cave, Nevada, contained pouches of vegetal cakes, pitch, ocher, other small objects, and a stuffed weasel pelt with feathers in its mouth. A shaman's sucking tube, used on a patient to extract disease, was found in the wetlands west of Ogden. It was made of steatite from eastern Washington. Tool stone continued to be cached, but most caches were not as dramatic as the Clovis caches of the pioneers.

The routes of the settlers traverse sacred landscapes that empower and animate the land. By collaborating with Native American elders and experts, archaeologists

6.2 The Patterson Bundle of herbs organized into pouches of doses. The bundle was found near Thompson, Utah, and dates between AD 1438 and 1522. From Harrison 2003. Courtesy of Merry Lycett Harrison.

6.3 This sucking tube, used to extract illness from a patient, was found west of Ogden, Utah. It is made of steatite sourced to the Spokane area of eastern Washington. As with other powerful objects, long-distance movement is common. Photo by François Gohier.

6.4 *Retrieving the Cache*, by Noel Carmack. A small pit that was dug in the wetlands of Great Salt Lake west of Ogden contained 88 obsidian tool blanks. They were awaiting retrieval, and those who left them there would have made them into knives, scrapers, arrowheads, drills, and gravers. The obsidian is from a source near Malad, Idaho, over 60 miles away. Such caches are emblematic of the built environment, and this cache was commemorated by the placing of a rounded quartzite pebble with the obsidian tool blanks. The cache was never retrieved, but this reenactment reminds us that it was part of someone's life. Courtesy of Noel Carmack.

are becoming more adept at identifying sacred landscapes, where every place is named, sometimes marked, and associated with stories that trace the ancestors and history—a sort of social geography.[8] Rock imagery can be one element of the social geography, representing places of power and significance. The rock imagery on private property at Connor Springs north of Great Salt Lake and along the west side of Utah Lake were created over millennia and form dense clusters. Smaller displays of rock imagery are scattered widely across the Great Salt Lake region. Rock imagery is not created and situated randomly. Nor is it graffiti or doodling. I am often asked, "Why did they put it here when there are so many smooth rock faces that contain no rock imagery?" The answer resides in the significance that places embody, which in turn inspires the rock imagery. Not the other way around. One cannot know the rock imagery unless one knows the meaning of places and something about the lives of the people who created it.

> Rock imagery is one element of a "social geography." It offers a glimpse of the agency of individuals who did not act alone, but who were part of a social fabric that included a worldview that extended beyond the household and the family. Nor is rock imagery just about the makers and the meaning it held for them. This is because rock imagery remains meaningful on time scales that transcend the lives of individuals. Indeed, the initial intent fades and the importance of the maker diminishes as future users and caretakers construct the meaning of rock imagery for their own times. Rock imagery does not passively reflect a meaning, but is a vehicle used to construct meaning as history proceeds.[9]

As the millennia of the settlers proceeded, the people became more and more a part of the landscape. Even though populations grew slowly, and with booms and busts, by 3,000 years ago the Human Wilderness had become more managed, the environment more domesticated. The process of settling is symbolized by the single greatest environmental management tool employed by Indigenous forager societies across much of the world: fire. No other topic seems to reflect the error of the Pristine Myth—the notion that Native Americans were few, benign, and children of nature—than does the use of fire.[10] According to the fire ecologist Stephen Pyne,

> Because the concept of wilderness has been linked to the discovery and settlement of America by Europe, any enterprise that predates the reclamation, no matter how extensive, is considered wild. Thus, Indian fire practices, which were enormously powerful as landscape modifiers, have been dismissed. The return of natural fire to wildlands is less likely to "restore" an ancient landscape than it is to fashion a landscape that never before existed.[11]

The reasons Indigenous peoples employed fire are diverse. One of the most common reasons, and the best-documented in eyewitness accounts from across North America, including the Great Basin, is the use of fire to drive and concentrate game to improve hunting success. Fire was employed in early winter to facilitate rabbit drives. In the summer small fires of less than an acre drove grasshoppers into piles of brush to seek cover, and then the brush was ignited to kill and roast the hoppers, which could be gathered by the thousands. Fire was used across North America to drive large game, and in the eastern United States such hunts occurred on grand scales, covering many square miles and involving multiple tribes.[12] In the 1930s the ethnographer Isabel Kelly described a communal deer hunt by the Northern Paiute in Surprise Valley northeastern California, a landscape as stark as the Great Salt Lake region:

> The only means of taking deer wholesale was by firing.... When deer were sighted on a hill, a group of hunters hastened there.... They started fires, working them around until the band was completely encircled. This accomplished, the fires were brought closer, constricting the circle until the animals were bunched on the crest of the hill where they could be shot conveniently.[13]

6.5 *Hunting Deer with Fire*, by Eric S. Carlson. This scene is based on stories of the old days shared with the ethnographer Isabel Kelly by Northern Paiutes in Surprise Valley, northeastern California, during her fieldwork there in the 1930s. Hunting by fire was well documented in the eastern United States in the eyewitness accounts of seventeenth- and eighteenth-century European settlers. Courtesy of Eric S. Carlson.

Members of John Wesley Powell's expeditions observed fires for driving game adjacent to Desolation Canyon on the Green River: "For two or three days the air was hazed with the acrid smoke of a distant forest fire. Great fires, which often were set by Indians driving game, ravaged thousands upon thousands of acres of timber."[14]

To members of government survey parties like Powell's, the ubiquitous nature of fire was seen as wasteful behavior, "this great destroyer," because the survey parties were there to help Euro-Americans appropriate the land and make "proper" use of it. Every one of the government surveys witnessed huge forest fires in Colorado and Utah that "destroyed more timber than had been taken by the people (Euro-Americans) since the occupation of the territory."[15] In California, cultural burning by Indigenous peoples was seen as so illogical that it was criminalized.

Hunting was not the only reason for setting fires. In the Great Basin, favored plants—such as the grass seeds that were as foundational to the food economy as wheat is to modern people—can benefit from firing sagebrush where it has grown too thick. Clearing areas around stands of medicinal plants with fire protects them. Setting fire to forests to open the understory favored game of all kinds and encouraged seed-bearing forbs such as Blazing Star. Firing improves aging pinyon-juniper woodlands that have become so overgrown and dense that virtually no understory exists at all—only barren gravels. Not only does nut production improve, but rabbits, squirrels, birds, and deer increase in number. Firing dense quaking aspen forest has the same effect.

Firing the wetlands reduces insect populations and clears areas for habitation. It also thins some plants, such as the phragmites that can choke the flow of water and reduce the productivity of other plants and animals.

Firing massive stands of roots reduces competition from unwanted plants and favors the economically important roots. In this way, root stands can be sustained for centuries if there is a rotation of fire and regular harvesting by digging. This is long-term land management.

Fire in the Great Basin and Intermountain regions was principally employed in the spring and fall, when burning can best be controlled. Ground moisture and wind were considered, and areas were targeted for specific reasons. Runners dragging pine pitch torches sometimes traversed miles. Fire management of this type, all done on foot, creates a mosaic of habitat types and ages. It breaks up the monotony that we see today of unending expanses of sagebrush and shadscale. The modern-day pinyon and juniper forests, and those represented in photography over the past century, are expanding because of fire suppression. It is typical around the Great Salt Lake region to see younger juniper trees out ahead of the main body of forest as they colonize new terrain. Both pinyon and juniper are intolerant of fire, and they expanded dramatically after fire suppression became widespread in the late nineteenth and early twentieth centuries.

When the Indigenous peoples populated and managed the land, the pinyon and juniper forests were a mosaic of trees and shrubs of differing ages. The understory of forbs and grasses was more diverse. The ancient fire regime of the Indigenous peoples along with natural lightning-struck fires created healthy ecosystems. As Stephen Pyne (1982) has noted,

> It is often assumed that the American Indian was incapable of greatly modifying his environment and that he would not have been much interested in doing so if he did have the capabilities. In fact, he possessed both the tool and the will to use it. That tool was fire…without which most Indian economies would have collapsed.[16]

Fire was used across North America, but even the deserts of the Great Basin and the Southwest were subject to Indigenous burning. Individually, Indigenous fires are small in scale, and the low population density of the ancient settlers often left tracts of territory uninhabited at times. Anthropogenic fire was less of a factor early in the settling process, but as the millennia passed, the presence of humans fostered consequences. Populations grew larger, territories became more circumscribed, and economic competition grew apace. Fire became a force with which competing populations could gain an advantage because fire was shaping the land and the ecosystems that drove their economies. Thus, the importance of land management was meager at first but, over time, led to consequences that everyone had to live with.

How much did Indigenous fire shape the landscape? On short time scales of years or a few decades, the human effects were surely circumscribed, creating a mosaic of habitats in different stages of succession. In some locales the ecosystem became anthropogenic, while the hand of humanity in other locales was faint or absent. However, when we expand the temporal scale beyond short-term thinking and consider impacts over human generations, we are jolted by the vantage of deep time. Fires were set across the region as a routine management tool, perhaps a few dozen fires a year for a particular camp group of a few dozen souls, which add up over the lifetimes of individuals. We found that lifetime territories of foragers can be on the scale of thousands of square miles. Add a measure of time spanning dozens of human generations and the landscape becomes an artifact of human agency. It is important, however, to consider that Native American fire regimes were characterized by abundant small fires that created a patchwork of burned and unburned landscapes that burned often, but that only rarely led to the massive fires we are experiencing in twenty-first-century America.[17]

Shaping the landscape extends to activities beyond large-game populations and land management using intentional fire. The mere act of living shapes ecosystems, even among small populations of foragers. Consider fuel for cooking and heating, especially given the winters in the Great Salt Lake region. The only source of fuel was wood. If one camps in the Great Basin in winter, the source of firewood becomes highly significant. In the 1990s we had a tradition with friends from Salt Lake City of camping out to harvest small pinyon pines for Christmas trees from a young forest northwest of Montello, Nevada. This was actual camping, not using an RV with a heater. The weather was always cold in December, but one year the thermometer dipped to −5 degrees Fahrenheit. We began to wonder how much wood a camp of ancient foragers might consume over the course of a winter.

That real-life experience led me to encourage and fund students to experiment with this topic. The experiments were done during campouts in the desert and simulated the consumption of firewood, controlling for group size, numbers and sizes of campfires, and duration of heating. The rate of wood consumption could be measured, as could the amount of wood available in various pinyon and juniper forests, as well as the amount of dead wood available for fuel. Ancient foragers used their fires most of the day and night. This was especially true during winter, with single-digit and subzero temperatures, even though the people had shelters, textile clothing, and rabbit-fur robes. Less fuel was used in the warmer months, but campfires were still made every day of the year, and every year of people's lives. We found that a hypothetical group of 30 foragers could clear the dead firewood from 10 to 30 square miles of pinyon-juniper forest in 10 years.[18]

That might seem like a lot of wood collection, but there is a lot of land in the Great Salt Lake region that contains pinyon-juniper forest. Further, the forests replenish the supply of dead wood over time. How might the human consumption of firewood for fuel by small populations play out over time in Great Salt Lake pinyon–juniper forests?

Let's consider two places. Pinyon-juniper forests extend from the Grouse Creek Mountains in northwestern Utah west to the area north of Montello, Nevada—an area of over 350 square miles. A similar-sized area of pinyon–juniper forest runs along the western slopes of the Deep Creek Mountains, Dutch Mountain, Pinyon Flat, and nearby lower ranges north and south of Ibapah and Goshute, Utah. Indigenous population densities recorded by early anthropologists in the driest areas of the Great Basin are measured in square miles per person, not in persons per square mile, a measurement familiar to the industrialized world. Each 350 square mile tract of pinyon–juniper forest might harbor about 60 people, which would be about eight square miles per person.

Even a conservative use of the experiments and simulations indicates that 60 people living in each of those areas would clear the dead wood from about 100 to 300 square miles over 50 years. Even accounting for the natural replenishment of dead wood, the pinyon–juniper forests of both the Grouse Creek and Deep Creek areas, together covering nearly 700 square miles, would become anthropogenic in only three human generations. Yet the scale we are dealing with in the story of First Peoples deals with dozens and even hundreds of human generations! People matter, especially when the focus expands beyond immediate self-interest and considers the power of deep time.

The small everyday things also matter. The mundane acts of staying warm in the winter and cooking meals produce consequences, and this is true of all people—indeed, all organisms. For us in the modern world, it is the consequences of countless small acts of using dirty fossil fuels to live. For the settlers it was more earthy things, such as deer, rabbits, roots, pine nuts, grass seeds, stone, bone, fibers, medicines—and fuel wood.

The earliest settlers saw landscapes, places, foods, and material as public things. Everyone could use anything, and the rules of society promoted public values. The right to use a place was gained by occupation for a few weeks or months until the group moved to another place. Kinship and marriage practices fostered broad connections that likely spanned languages. When populations were extremely small, this system worked better than a territorial, bounded society, but as the millennia wore on, things changed. By 4,000 years ago, and later in some places, sense of place had shifted from a way of life toward a built environment specific to resource extraction and activities.

The increased importance of places magnified notions of private property, but also fostered cooperation, leadership, and new conventions of kinship that emphasized the maintenance of group identity. There was a decrease in the use of cave caches. Some storage was moved inside the home, where it could be controlled. The use of local, often low-quality toolstone continued, but even the higher-quality obsidian tended to come from sources closer to the village than in earlier times.

The archaeology of the Great Salt Lake region only hints at these shifts, a pattern that is clearer when the whole of the Great Basin and Intermountain region is considered. The human presence around Great Salt Lake extended to new sites after 4,000 years ago. Several caves at Fish Springs were used for the first time even though the wetlands there had been used since the time of the pioneers and first settlers as part of the network that included the Old River Bed Delta a bit to the east. As pinyon forests spread after 5,000 years ago, occupation intensified in the Grouse Creek and Deep Creek Mountains, and the number of known archaeological sites increased overall. The Prison site in Draper shows that people were investing in more substantial housing between 3,000 and 2,000 years ago, a clear mark of settling. At the Dimple Dell site in Sandy, substantial housing spanned a period between 1,800 to 1,400 years ago. The same occurred at the Hot Springs and Airport sites north of Salt Lake City. American Fork Cave, a bighorn sheep hunting camp located a few miles above Timpanogos Cave, began to be used 3,500 years ago. The high country—from the Bear River Range above Cache Valley, along the Wasatch Back, and south to the Wasatch Plateau—was used more intensively after 3,000 years ago. The concept of territory gained ground.[19]

The landscape effects of the human hand are symbolized by measures of fire. At Blue Lake, on the western edge of the Bonneville Salt Flats, pollen cores show an increase in burning in the vicinity after 2,000 years ago, a pattern that persisted for centuries. A regional study of fire in a zone straddling the central Utah–Nevada border found that early- and late-season forest fires, the times when fires are more likely to be human caused, were common until about 1850, when Native land management was disrupted. A study of sagebrush fires in Newark Valley, central Nevada, spanning nearly 10,000 years has shown that fire had always been present but increased after 2,000 years ago.[20]

The attention to place, part-time village life, cooperative relationships, and private rather than public goods are evident in the willingness of people to invest in the long term. The built environment traces this transition, and perhaps nothing shows this better than increased investment in hunting facilities. I refer to the phenomenon of building stone and wooden walls and enclosures to divert and trap pronghorn (often referred to as "antelope," but pronghorn [*Antilocapra americana*] are technically not antelope), mule deer, and bighorn sheep, which are known across the Great Basin and Intermountain regions. Some drive facilities are nearly 5,000 years old, but construction increased over the last few thousand years. A sense of the enormous investment in such a facility is conveyed by the Fort Sage Drift Fence north of Reno, Nevada. Built of rock, it is almost three feet high and extends for over a mile. Pronghorn would drift along the obstacle and could be ambushed. It may also have been used for bighorn sheep. The bone associated with the facility shows that animals were butchered there for transport, probably to a central village. Construction of the Fort Sage Drift Fence began about 3,700 years ago, and it continued in use for over 2,500 years. The enormous investment of labor shows a commitment to place for over 125 human generations.

The D.C. Corral, at 7,600 feet on the north slopes of the Jarbidge Mountains in northeastern Nevada, is a spectacular drive facility situated on a steep talus slope. Bighorn sheep will initially run downhill when alarmed, then inevitably turn uphill

6.6 A section of the Fort Sage Drift Fence north of Reno, Nevada, indicates the degree of investment possible in hunting infrastructure; it consists of more than a mile of rock fence. The facility was built nearly 5,000 years ago and was used increasingly in subsequent millennia, evoking the power of landscape and place. Courtesy of Bryan Hockett, United States Bureau of Land Management.

and easily outdistance humans on steep talus. Bighorn sheep or deer were driven downslope along a natural path onto the talus. The animals were diverted by a stone wall in the early days when darts were propelled by the atlatl. Later, after the adoption of the bow and arrow, a wooden fence was built a little higher on the slope. A slightly downward shot is best for atlatl hunting, whereas a level shot is better for bow and arrow hunting. The D.C. Corral fence blocked escape. Blind pits dug into the talus enabled hunters to hide until the game passed below while hunters at the crest of the talus slope awaited. In the corner of the L-shaped fence, the talus was arranged in a circular flattened area to provide a place to butcher the animals. Obsidian tools were found within the talus, and nearby there are campsites where the hunters processed the take. This facility was used for at least several thousand years. When one considers the built environment of the Fort Sage Drift Fence and the D.C. Corral, and dozens of other such sites, how could anyone see the people who lived this way as primitive and benign?

Dozens of pronghorn traps exist in the Great Salt Lake region. Most are made of juniper wood, so they tend to date to the last few centuries. Some are substantial, consisting of large timbers, but others are lightly constructed and discontinuous. There is one in Five Mile Draw north of Montello, Nevada, that is circular with an opening. From the air it looks like a keyhole. It is 600 feet long and 400 feet wide. The placement takes advantage of the terrain and the natural behavior of pronghorn to run from swell to swell and then meander slowly down in the swales. The people knew animal behavior and placed the trap along a subtle swale at the end of two shallow descending valleys, enabling the trap to be used when potential prey were

6.7 The D.C. Corral, Jarbidge Mountains, Nevada. This trap for bighorn sheep and possibly deer contained the animals on a talus slope. Below the more recent wooden fence (used with bow and arrow) is a faint rock wall in the gully bottom, probably from the atlatl and dart period. Blind pits are on the slope of the small ridge in the upper center of the photo, and the flattened talus butchering area is at the lower left, within the corner of the wooden fence line. Photo by David Lanner.

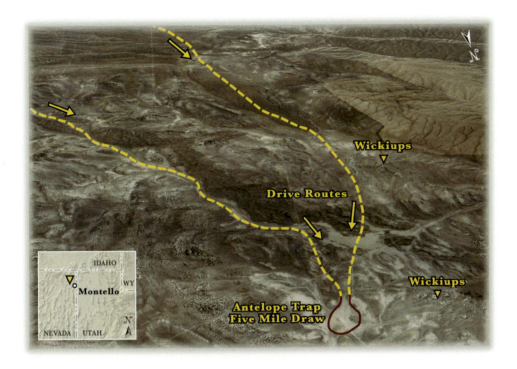

6.8 Map of routes used to drive pronghorn down shallow swales into the Five Mile Draw trap northwest of Montello, Nevada. Archaeological sites with remnants of juniper wood wickiup structures and fire hearths may be camps used in the hunts. Cartography by Chelsea McRaven Feeney.

in either drainage. A shaman adept at hunting pronghorn and spiritually powerful managed the hunt, and his sacred power enabled the attraction of curious animals. The shaman might use a disguise of a pronghorn headdress and an apprentice following behind, holding on to his hips to mimic a pronghorn. The animals are curious and tend to stare at times, hence with special power they can be "charmed." Pronghorns are extremely wary and difficult to hunt alone without firearms, but their tendency to herd makes them susceptible to group hunting.

A hunt in Five Mile Draw likely began miles away the day before. Sometimes only a few hunters would patiently nudge the animals down the valley. In other hunts, men, women, and older children participated. Rock cairns or piles of brush placed along the route to mimic humans multiplied the number of hunters. Once near the trap, the pronghorn would be set into a run, and even a fence only three feet high would have diverted the animals. Pronghorn can easily jump fences, and I have seen hundreds of them leap over multiple four-foot-high barb wire fences, but when they run, they prefer to bend with obstacles so as to maintain speed. Once inside the enclosure, the pronghorn would mill around and herd up. Sometimes they might be killed all at once, but other times they were guarded, with the hunters taking a few a day to allow time to process the meat, hides, bones, and other products. Sometimes broken arrow tips are found inside the enclosures. In one case, the broken stone tip of an arrow point found inside a pronghorn corral matched the broken base of

6.9 *The Pronghorn Charm,* by Eric S. Carlson, showing the culmination of a pronghorn hunt that may have begun days earlier. The lead animal remains curious even at a tilted run. Courtesy of Eric S. Carlson.

the same arrow discarded a quarter mile away at a residential structure where the arrow was repaired. The trap in Five Mile Draw we see today is perhaps 300 years old, but earlier versions may have been in that location for much longer. Dozens of these wooden traps are known in northern Nevada, northern Utah, and eastward into western Wyoming.

In 1917 Howard Egan provided an eyewitness account of a Shoshone pronghorn hunt in Antelope Valley, Nevada, about 20 miles northwest of Ibapah, Utah. The hunt took place over several days and yielded two dozen pronghorn. It had been 12 years since the trap was last used. This indicates the planning depth of the people: they invested for the long term. The elderly men said that they harvested so many animals, they did not expect to use that trap again in their lifetimes because it would take years for the herd to rebound. That probably varied and would depend on how frequently other traps in the area were used. Pronghorn can repopulate rapidly even under conditions of predation.

There are two pronghorn enclosures south of Park Valley, Utah, in Box Elder County. One opens to the south, and another one nearby opens to the north. This would have enabled the hunters to plan drives during either the fall migration, when the animals seek lower ground, or in the spring as they migrate upward. It all depended on when it would be worth it, and who was living in the area.

Pronghorn drive facilities are known across the Great Basin and Intermountain region, and their use increased over time. They symbolize people's tie to the land, an interest in the long-term investment of labor, and the culmination of the settling process.[21]

All these changes convey a sense that people were investing more in the land. They worked harder. This promotes both cooperation and competition. The abundance of deer bones found in some sites in the Great Salt Lake region seems to increase after 3,000 years ago.[22] Part of this is due to a climate favorable for deer, but evidence from around the Great Basin suggests that humans were by that time willing to travel farther and spend an unusual amount of effort to obtain meat from large game for the purpose of prestige—perhaps better termed "social signaling." In the context of a more settled life, bounded social groups, and territories, social signaling becomes a useful ambition.[23]

The final millennium of settlers in the Great Salt Lake region followed a pattern that was widespread across the American Desert West: growing populations, redundancy in settlement, and some measure of leadership promoting cooperation. The people were still few because the deserts and mountains of the vast Great Salt Lake region are harsh, but steadily humans, like all organisms, filled the spaces. The stage was set for even more change.

7

Indigenes, Immigrants, and First Farmers

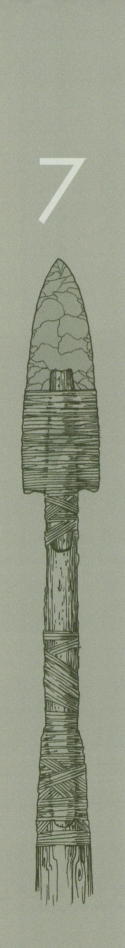

Take a drive west on the Pony Express National Historic Trail—past Simpson Springs, over Dugway Pass, and on to Fish Springs National Wildlife Refuge. Continue west through Callao, north through Gold Hill, and over the north end of the Deep Creeks near Dutch Mountain. Desolate, eerie, beautiful, and remote from the world. Camp at the pass, where there is an ancient stone hunting blind that used to have stone debris from toolmaking before it was all collected by visitors. Look west across range after range of mountains receding into the sunset. The experience is a landscape study in warm pastels. Surely this must be the way it was for Native Americans 2,000 years ago, AD 1, the time of Christ, the time of the Romans.

We get back in our car and head home via ignoble Wendover to our city along the Wasatch Front and rejoin the larger world. The gulf between our times and those of the Native Americans is unfathomable. They were lightly scattered, yet managed and shaped the land through the simple acts of living. They surely were isolated from the rest of the North American continent. Or were they? The seduction of the Pristine Myth withers under a reality that the settlers were caught up in continental forces and a changing America over 2,000 years ago.

Native American populations grew dramatically over the last few thousand years. By 3,000 years ago, consolidated villages of hunter-gatherer peoples in Louisiana constructed the Poverty Point ceremonial site consisting of hundreds of earthworks sprawling across 500 acres. These hunter-gatherers had the time to amass enough labor to construct the earthworks over the course of six centuries, with individual mounds and linear earthworks built in spasms of corporate labor over mere weeks or months. To the north along the Tennessee and Ohio Rivers, village populations practiced selective breeding to enlarge the seeds of native plants such as sunflower and goosefoot, fueling the Eastern Agricultural Complex long before maize arrived.

7.1 *Fish Springs, Great Salt Lake Desert, Utah*, watercolor by Sean Toomey.

By 2,000 years ago California had the highest population densities of nonagricultural Indigenous peoples of any similar-sized place in the world. In the Southwest, maize agriculture spread from central Mexico to southern Arizona by 3,500 years ago, and by 2,000 years ago it was making its way north across the Colorado River.

The Great Salt Lake settlers of the Late Archaic period may have inhabited a desert backwater, but the continental waves of change came to them too. For them, it is a story of farmers emigrating from the Southwest. What happened to the Indigenous peoples? What changes did the immigrants bring to the land and the lives of the people who already lived in Colorado, Utah, and along the Wasatch Front? Typically both Indigenes and immigrants change, and a new culture is created out of that interaction and the upending of lives.

By the time the Three Sisters—maize, beans, and squash—came deep into Utah, between 100 BC and AD 100, agriculture had been practiced in the American Southwest for several thousand years.[1] A multifaceted trail of evidence points to migrations of Southwestern peoples of at least two language histories, differences in material culture, and a shared experience as early farmers.

Immigrants came to eastern Utah across the Colorado Plateau in Utah and Colorado. They followed the natural routes over the Tavaputs Plateau in Utah. In Colorado they ascended the Roan Cliffs to Douglas Creek and the Piceance Basin, a route offering easy access to the Uinta Basin. Natural routes continued west via

7.2 Receding ranges of the Great Basin. The view is to the west, into Nevada, from Dutch Mountain, Utah. Photo by Steve Simms.

the Duchesne and Strawberry Rivers to Utah Lake and Great Salt Lake. This natural passage was evident in the historical period, used by Timpanogots Utes from Utah Lake to make seasonal trips to visit with relatives and other Ute bands living in the Uinta Basin and western Colorado. The walk from Provo, up past Heber and on past Duchesne to Roosevelt, is not that bad. It is shorter than a walk I once did from Glen Canyon Dam to Richfield, Utah, in about two weeks as part of an archaeology crew following a transmission line. Most of these trails display a ribbon of chipped stone debris accumulated over the eons by repeated travel and toolmaking.

These immigrants, the Eastern Basketmakers, spoke an ancient language of the Kiowa-Tanoan language family. Kiowa-Tanoan speakers include Puebloan groups in the upper Rio Grande Valley in northern New Mexico—including Tewa, Towa, and Tiwa—as well as the Plains Kiowa of historic times. The ancestors of the historic Hopi may also have used the same routes to migrate north across the San Juan River and north past Moab, Utah, and on. Like so much migration in history, it

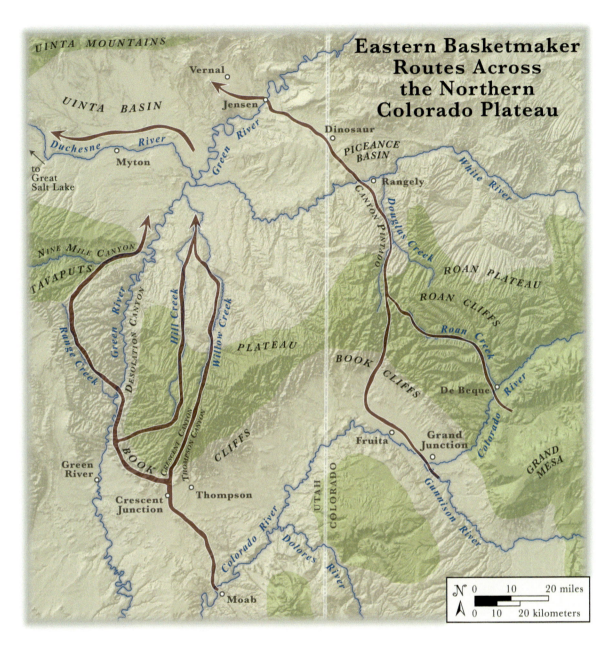

7.3 Natural routes for the migration of Eastern Basketmaker peoples into Utah, where they and the Indigenous peoples of Utah together formed the Fremont peoples. The passageways through the canyonlands, though limited, include Range Creek to Nine Mile Canyon, Hill Creek, and Willow Creek. The Green River corridor is not continuous and requires a swing to the west to circumnavigate Desolation Canyon. A ford of the Colorado River at Moab leads through Valley City, north of Arches National Park, where the trail is littered with chipped stone debris and rock imagery all the way to Crescent Junction. From there, migrants would have been able to reach the routes mentioned above or continue up Crescent Creek past a concentration of rock imagery to merge with Thompson Canyon and reach the top of the Tavaputs Plateau. Routes through Colorado avoid the impassable sections of the Dolores River Canyon, cross the Colorado River near Grand Junction or De Beque, and head north toward Douglas Creek and the Piceance Basin. Cartography by Chelsea McRaven Feeney.

is not neatly bounded by peoples. Upheaval throws different peoples and speech communities together.

The Western Basketmakers, who are archaeologically distinct from the Eastern Basketmakers, crossed the Colorado River in Glen Canyon, a stretch of river that could be forded in various places, but with access constrained by limited routes into the canyon from the south and out of the canyon to the north.

Western Basketmakers would have been able to ford the San Juan River in southeastern Utah, travel west to ford the Colorado River at Bullfrog, and then head north along the Waterpocket Fold, Capitol Reef, and the Fremont River. The Colorado could also be forded farther west and up to a natural crevice that later became the Hole-in-the-Rock Trail used by nineteenth-century Mormons. From there migrants could head north along Fiftymile Bench to Escalante and the upper reaches of the Sevier River. The area around Escalante became one of the hearts of both Fremont and Ancestral Puebloan occupation. The Colorado can also be forded even farther west, such as at Wahweap, bringing migrants along the Vermilion Cliffs, where they could access the upper Virgin River or the Paria River. All these routes emerge into the Great Basin, the ancient homeland of Uto-Aztecan languages dating back at least 6,000 years. From there they spread north along the rim of the Great Basin, and some may have reached the Wasatch Front.

The Western Basketmakers are members of an ancient speech community in the Uto-Aztecan language family. This is a diverse family of dozens of languages sprawling from the Great Basin to southern Mexico. Uto-Aztecan languages include Hopi in northern Arizona and in Utah the Ute, Shoshone, and Southern Paiute languages of historic times. These western Fremont groups, sometimes called the Sevier culture, have long been seen by archaeologists as distinct from eastern, Colorado Plateau Fremont groups.[2]

Basketmaker peoples are collectively the ancestors of a culture often referred to as the Anasazi, but more appropriately called Ancestral Puebloan. They, in turn, are the ancestors of all the living tribes of the Four Corners region, thus they embody a diversity of languages and cultures, and associated ethnicities.[3] The Basketmakers lived in farmsteads and moved among small agricultural plots. Their approach worked, and their bone chemistry shows that most of the calories they consumed during their lives came from maize, centuries before they migrated into Utah.[4] Farming is hard work, but it produces more food, including storable food to weather the lean times. More food, especially a consistent supply of nutrition for weaning infants, leads to reduced infant mortality and population growth. Everywhere in the world, anthropology finds that early farming societies grew faster than forager societies and became demographic centrifuges, flinging immigrant populations into new lands.

Utah north of the Colorado River was a frontier to the Basketmakers. Unlike the landscape encountered by the first explorers, who entered a hemisphere with no human beings, the Utah frontier of 2,000 years ago was already occupied by settlers with a foraging heritage measured in thousands of years—hundreds of human generations. Most immigrant frontiers in history begin with men. They enter the frontier and marry Indigenous women. In subsequent decades whole families follow and transform the landscape, the nature of place, and turn foraging societies into farmers. Even though Basketmaker farmers would have also harvested wild plants and hunted game, the nature of place became agricultural rather than one of hunting and gathering. The Basketmaker immigrants did not overrun Utah in a wave of advance, and they were not all one people, but different peoples with diverse languages and ethnicities. The centrifuge of farming in the Southwest motivated small groups to explore new lands north of the Colorado River, stopping at places favorable to a pursuit of their farming way of life. It was opportunistic and incremental.

Maize is detectable in the archaeology of the Sevier Valley and the Glen Canyon and Escalante River regions, dating between 100 BC and AD 200. Early sites of Basketmaker farmers are found in the San Rafael Swell along the Muddy and San Rafael Rivers, in Nine Mile Canyon, and in the more remote canyons of the Tavaputs Plateau. The best documented example of an immigrant Eastern Basketmaker colony in the wilds of Utah is the Steinaker Gap site, now inundated by Steinaker Reservoir north of Vernal. By AD 250, immigrant farmers had made it to the Uinta Basin. They built a hamlet of residential structures, characteristic Basketmaker storage structures, and irrigation ditches. A substantial proportion of their calories came from maize agriculture, and they occupied the area for 150 years. Similarly early dates for maize farming were found recently in nearby Cub Creek in Dinosaur National Monument.[5]

The Wasatch Front would have been an Eden in the frontier for immigrating Basketmakers because some of the longest growing seasons and the most abundant water in Utah lie along the Front. Old-timers remember the vegetable farms and fruit orchards that stretched along U.S. Highway 89 from Santaquin to Brigham City. Perched above the briny barrens and wetlands at the edges of Great Salt Lake and Utah Lake are fertile alluvial plains fed by springs emanating from the base of the Wasatch. Great Salt Lake and Utah Lake are thermal sinks that moderate extremes of temperature. Thus, the growing season along the Front is weeks longer than in the high desert valleys to the west, or Cache Valley and the valleys of the Wasatch Back.

Most of the excellent Wasatch Front farmland is now urbanized. While we know of hundreds of archaeological sites that date to the farming period, urban sprawl prevents us from learning much about them except in a few places. Nevertheless, there is evidence that farming came to the Wasatch Front early. At the Prison site in Draper, two residential structures were found with numerous samples of organic residues and plant phytoliths (durable microscopic structures of silica specific to different plants) from maize, and nine radiocarbon dates indicate an age of 2,400 years—about 400 BC. Unfortunately, further work at this important site was prohibited.[6]

The Grantsville site at the foot of the Stansbury Mountains is one among a string of small villages along Willow Creek where people were farming maize by AD 500. The recently discovered Dimple Dell site in Sandy has residential structures and evidence of maize farming as early as AD 250, and more confidently between AD 400 and 600. Evidence from several archaeological sites in the Willard Bay and Plain City area shows that people were consuming a mixed diet of maize and wild plants by AD 500. In the wetlands along the eastern shores of Great Salt Lake, maize was added as one more staple among the abundant seeds, roots, and greens common to those wetlands. Stored maize would have been an insurance policy against the lean times.[7]

The Basketmaker presence in Utah in the early centuries AD consisted of a sprinkling of immigrant settlements in a landscape of dispersed foragers. Migration inevitably brings upheaval and tension. The social landscape was transformed by the Other—people whose values, beliefs, languages, adornment, and physical appearance were different and subject to suspicion. Where Basketmaker farmsteads were established, local hunting suffered, and favored places to collect seeds, roots, and nuts were appropriated by immigrant farmers. The farmers felled trees for construction and fuel. Away from villages, fire became a routine management tool to clear the land, restrict unwanted plants, foster economic plants, and reduce insect populations. Indigenous foragers lost access to some lands. Historically, foragers vote with their feet and move to more remote and less desirable places. Over time, however, people socialize, game and gamble, trade, marry, and create kinship ties. Inevitably there is gene flow. Identities may harden into resistance for some, but for others identity incorporates new realities and opportunities.

Analogous cases in history suggest that the more routine the interaction between different ethnic and linguistic groups, the more individuals manage that interaction through maintenance of identity and language. A striking example among many around the world is one from Native California that features a high degree of ethnic and linguistic compartmentalization known as tribelets. Their identities remained strong, but there was a tremendous amount of interaction among California tribelets. The famous case of Ishi, a Yana living on the western slopes of Mount Lassen, northeast of Sacramento, helps us understand that such seeming territoriality and strong identity can reflect interaction rather than isolation. Ishi's tribelet was called

Yahi, and it was one of three Yana triblets each occupying a stream drainage bound by ridges on both sides. There were subtle variations in language and identity among the three Yana groups. Another group, the Wintu, lived to the south and spoke a very different language. Sometimes relationships between the Yahi and Wintu were violent, but other times the two groups were on good terms. Ishi was a master flintknapper, but he did not make his arrowheads the Yahi way. His arrowheads were Wintu. Ishi was either a Wintu who moved and became Yahi while young, or his father was Wintu and taught him to make arrowheads. He saw himself as Yahi, and he spoke Yahi, but his behavior grew out of interaction in a polyethnic world.[8]

The maintenance of identity is fueled by economic ties. Foragers may exchange large-game meat for maize and beans—or stone, special woods, and medicines from far-flung locations. Historical accounts and observations by anthropologists of foragers interacting with small-scale farmers reveal a pattern. Over their life history, an individual might switch between living among farmers and living among foragers, alternating between settled life and wide-ranging travels. There may be periods of resistance to the farmers and times when foragers are recruited and join farmers—leading to marriage, children, and inevitable shifts in identity. As the years pass, the populations of farmers tend to grow until there is a natural catastrophe such as a drought. The ensuing shortfall and suffering may cause migration, even local abandonment, but when the drought is over, farming populations rebound and resume growth. This is the way Fremont life went for centuries. Through it all, the surrounding forager populations remained dispersed.

One relationship between the settled and the nomadic does not change. The foraging life is one of feast or famine subject to the vagaries of natural food production. When times are hard, foragers, especially women and children, will attach themselves to farming villages by building huts on the outskirts and offering labor or nonfood resources in exchange for food. In cases throughout history and around the world, as farmers encroach upon traditional foraging grounds, foragers are marginalized and reduced to associating with the settled farmers under conditions of reduced status. A modern example is the encroachment on Indigenous foragers in the Amazon Basin of South America during the twentieth and twenty-first centuries by loggers, miners, and farmers. Africa has a similar history of farmer-forager relations going back several thousand years. This process creates a landscape where clusters of farming villages become central places against a background of dispersed foragers.

Archaeologists are becoming more adept at recognizing this phenomenon among the Ancestral Puebloans of the Southwest around central places such as Chaco Canyon, Zuni, Hopi, Mesa Verde, and the large pueblos of the Great Sage

7.4 A cutaway sketch of a typical Fremont pithouse. Most have a central clay-rimmed fire hearth, a ventilator shaft for fresh air, and a roof opening for access by ladder that doubles as a chimney. The roof of the structure often served as a workspace. Also known as earth lodges, pithouses occur around the world. They are warm in the winter, cool in the summer, and are often remodeled to extend their use life. Artwork by Eric S. Carlson.

7.5 This spectacular wall mural was found in a Fremont pithouse on private land near Monroe, Utah. It reminds us that a thousand-year-old home that fell into disrepair and became buried was once a nice place to be, and was also a place to care for and live in. From Stuart 2015:79. Courtesy of Mark Stuart.

Plain in southwestern Colorado and southeastern Utah. The Indigenous peoples of the hinterlands were the "fierce, barbarous, and untamed"—the non-Puebloan peoples who may have long histories in the Southwest.[9] The foragers did not die out or disappear. Like the more archaeologically recognizable Ancestral Puebloan farmers, their descendants are among Native Americans alive today. It would have been this way during the Basketmaker immigration to Utah from AD 1 to 500, but in Utah the interaction with Indigenous foragers produced a new culture called the Fremont. In some ways Fremont looks like immigrants, but in other ways Fremont looks like Indigenes.

The name "Fremont" was assigned in the 1920s by Noel Morss, who was part of a multiyear project of the Peabody Museum of Harvard University. The project began near Torrey, Utah, and the Fremont label was taken from the river of the same name before the expedition moved on to Nine Mile Canyon and the Tavaputs Plateau in subsequent years. Morss and other archaeologists recognized the Southwestern roots of the Fremont but referred to the region as a "northern periphery" of the Southwest because the Fremont did not seem like the farmers and builders of masonry structures that the Ancestral Puebloan were known to be.[10]

We can see the Southwestern heritage in several ways. Many of the excavated Fremont houses in the Great Salt Lake region are a type known as pithouses. That term is a bit of a misnomer for what were semi-subterranean structures 10 to 20 feet in diameter with an aboveground timber and adobe superstructure. The Southwestern roots are especially apparent in pithouses with four central posts to support the roof, a clay-rimmed fire hearth in the center, and a ventilation shaft coming in underground from the side. Access was by a ladder through the roof, which also served as a chimney. Variations on pithouse architecture occur on every temperate continent, where they are often called earth lodges. They are cool in the summer, warm in the winter, with storage space for a lot of gear.

The use of pottery tells a mixed story. By AD 500, Fremont peoples had become sufficiently settled and populous that pottery became common—another sign of Southwestern heritage and continued interaction. However, Fremont pottery is overwhelmingly plain ware. Corrugated Fremont pottery certainly harkens to the Southwest but occurs in limited quantities and only late in Fremont history. The relatively small amount of Fremont pottery that has painted designs shows Southwestern roots but is their own style. Small amounts of painted Ancestral Puebloan pottery were directly imported to both Great Basin and Colorado Plateau Fremont sites, but in extremely small quantities relative to the abundance of pottery at Fremont village sites.

Fremont rock imagery traces a mixed heritage with hints of the preceding foraging settlers, such as elements of the Great Basin curvilinear style and elements of the Barrier Canyon style. A Basketmaker heritage is strongly apparent in the trapezoidal body shapes and headdress motifs that persisted in Basketmaker rock imagery from Late Archaic forager times in the Four Corners area. Other Basketmaker motifs—such as horns, bear paws, talons, and wings—are also found in Fremont rock imagery in eastern Utah. Fremont rock imagery shows some affinity with later Ancestral Puebloan styles, but the Fremont tradition is distinctive in retaining its Basketmaker and forager roots.

The Basketmakers' inspired use of trapezoidal anthropomorphs is widespread across Fremont country and taken to high art in the Classic Vernal Style of the Uinta Basin. There it suggests heroic narratives, vison questing, and shamanism. Some Fremont rock imagery may be associated with the oral history of landscapes and ancestors. The anthropomorphs in Fremont rock imagery also appear as decorated clay figurines, such as the Pillings figurines found in Range Creek Canyon, Utah.[11]

Fremont rock imagery varies geographically with strong ties to the Eastern Basketmaker heritage of the Colorado Plateau of eastern Utah. It also shows affinities to the heritage of the Snake River Plain and western Wyoming in the shield imagery found in the Uinta Basin, the Tavaputs Plateau/Book Cliffs area, and the Great Salt Lake region. A Great Basin heritage is evident in Fremont rock imagery of western Utah. The diversity in Fremont rock imagery is consistent with origins among the foraging settlers, likely of several language histories, as well as farming immigrants from the Southwest, also of several language histories.[12]

Biology, too, provides a window into heritage. A large sample of Fremont human burials was saved from destruction by rising Great Salt Lake waters and from vandalism of the exposed bones in the late 1980s and early 1990s. Investigations of sensitive matters such as the deceased cannot occur without the consent and the collaboration of the Indigenous descendants. With permission from the Northwestern Band of the Shoshone Nation in Fort Hall, Idaho, small bits of bone were sampled for ancient mitochondrial DNA. The Fremont living along the Wasatch Front from AD 900 to 1200 show a distant maternal affinity to modern populations at Jemez Pueblo in the upper Rio Grande drainage, the same homeland as the Eastern Basketmakers and the heartland of the Kiowa-Tanoan language family.[13] Unpublished studies of Fremont crania show a Colorado Plateau–Great Basin dichotomy in head shape and facial form, something the Domínguez-Escalante Expedition of AD 1776 encountered. DNA also revealed that the immigrants tended to more often be male than female, consistent with the initial stages of human migration in other historical cases.[14]

Optimistically, more ancient DNA work will eventually help work out the history of the immigrant and Indigenous Fremont, and where the Great Salt Lake

Fremont fit in. To this day we know little about the genetics of the foragers of the eastern Great Basin and northern Colorado Plateau, and their living Ute, Shoshone, Goshute, and Southern Paiute descendants. That part of the Fremont origin story remains to be fully told. In addition, it is likely a gross error to assume that the DNA from the Great Salt Lake Fremont represents all Fremont. We should expect to find genetic diversity given the multiple origins of what became known as Fremont.

We know an Indigenous heritage is part of the Fremont story because it is most apparent in Fremont basketry, a technology that hints at ethnicity in ancient societies

7.6 The complete set of Pillings figurines, including the specimen that went missing in the 1960s and was anonymously returned in 2011. Analysis determined that the lost figurine was indeed part of the original collection through several means: analysis of the textile imprints left when the figurines were laid upon a mat while still wet, analysis of the clays, and the presence of the same chemical coating applied when the figurines were stored at Harvard University in the 1950s. Photo by François Gohier; inset photo by Bonnie Pitblado (see note 7.11). Courtesy of Prehistoric Museum, Utah State University Eastern, Price.

7.7 The distinctive three-piece Fremont moccasin. Photo by François Gohier. Courtesy of Natural History Museum of Utah.

more than any other material culture. Fremont coiled basketry is constructed most often with a one rod and bundle foundation with interlocking stitches. It is a tradition of Indigenous settlers going back over 6,000 years. Another method—a half rod and bundle foundation with non-interlocking stitches—was also used, and this is found in Eastern Basketmaker baskets. In contrast, basketry of the Western Basketmakers is distinct in using a two rod and bundle foundation with interlocking stiches, a technique known among the Ancestral Puebloans.

The influence of Western Basketmaker immigrants is less apparent than that of the Eastern Basketmakers. Migration routes in the Colorado River canyon country along the Utah–Arizona border are far more constrained and rugged than the eastern routes along the Utah–Colorado border. It is as if Indigenous foragers in western Utah adopted more of a Basketmaker way of life, and there was less of an immigrant presence compared to eastern Utah and western Colorado. Despite the diverse language history of Fremont origins and the likelihood that Fremont peoples were polyethnic, the ancient forager roots of the Fremont persisted in a far stronger way than in the Ancestral Puebloans of the Four Corners region. Indigenous women maintained their distinctive basketry traditions regardless of what immigrants and farming brought. Basketry around the world is mostly a women's technology, a skill learned over a lifetime and passed down through generations. The roots of the settlers found in Fremont basketry show the connection of the immigrants with Indigenous women. They nurtured the ancestry.[15]

7.8 A Fremont hock moccasin, in this case a bison hock. Photo by Alyson Wilkins. Courtesy of Natural History Museum of Utah.

As any modern person knows, cultural signaling is found in footwear. The Fremont made two types of moccasins. One was made of three pieces of untanned deer or bison hide curved around the ankle and sewn on top of the foot. Another type was made from the hock of a deer, bison, or elk, creating a single piece sewn together. The Fremont moccasins have Indigenous roots and are distinct from Southwestern styles.

Interaction between Indigenous and immigrant people is occasionally detectable archaeologically. A burial of an adult male found in 1931 in Nine Mile Canyon looks Basketmaker except for the moccasins and leggings, which look Indigenous. Baskets occasionally exhibit mixed traits. A coiled basket's foundation may be an immigrant style, while the body construction is Indigenous, and the finish on the rim blends both. It seems women from different traditions contributed to teaching young girls how to make baskets. Mothers, aunts, and sisters exhibited genealogies that span ethnic and language histories—a female version of the analogy with Ishi, the Yahi from northern California who made Wintu-style arrowheads.

That male traditions of Indigenous foragers also survived is apparent in the projectile points used to tip atlatl darts and in the arrow points used after the arrival of the bow. Although the bow and arrow arrived in Utah about the same time as the Basketmakers brought maize north, it did not come from the Basketmakers; they still used the atlatl and dart. The bow and arrow arrived from the Northwest, where it was present in southeastern Oregon and southern Idaho over 3,000 years ago. Soon after, the bow and arrow reached Hogup Cave west of the Great Salt Lake, but halted. It did not spread east into southwest Wyoming or south to the Escalante canyon country until after AD 1, when the Basketmakers were migrating north. The bow and arrow did not immediately replace the atlatl and dart; both continued to be used for centuries. By AD 500 the bow and arrow had become the most common hunting tool. It also shaped interactions among people because it can be a tool of repression.[16]

The stone projectile points used by the Fremont peoples are broadly distinct from those of the Ancestral Puebloans and tend to reflect Fremont ties with the Great Basin and Intermountain regions. Even when points from the two cultures are identical, they are called different names as if to reinforce the archaeological categories. In central Utah, near Hanksville and south, there is a long, narrow arrow point called Bull Creek. Across the Colorado River in Arizona, the same point is called Kayenta. It is as if the pottery, women's technology among Ancestral Puebloan and Fremont peoples, marks a clear boundary, but the points, men's technology, does not. Does this speak to contrasts in lifetime mobility between men and women?

It must have been a complicated time as the bow and arrow arrived from the Northwest, and immigrant maize farmers arrived from the south—symbols of continental change. The Fremont peoples of the Great Salt Lake region were born of Indigenes and immigrants. What archaeologists lump together as an "archaeological" culture was in actual life multilinguistic and polyethnic. They were the first Utah farmers.

The Most Populous Part of Utah

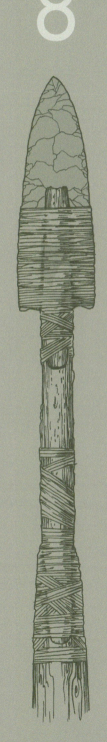

The Great Salt Lake wetlands, sandwiched between lake and mountains, is a continuous archaeological site. Since the days of the Utah pioneers in the nineteenth century, arrowheads were collected by the thousands—to the point where they are now few. Old-timers tell stories of titanic battles between tribes of "Indians," sometimes comparing them to the ancient Greeks and Persians. A farmer in Willard found a cache of 600 arrowheads nestled in a small hole. At the bottom of the hole were maize cobs. The arrowheads were once in a bag with the maize, and the bag did not survive the thousand years it was buried. Was the maize offered as a blessing?

On the opposite side of the Great Basin, 500 miles to the west, the Stillwater Marsh near Fallon, Nevada, has yielded the same staggering abundance of arrowheads and other artifacts. The *Reno Gazette* ran an article in 1976 about an elderly man from Fallon who collected arrowheads all his life. "The points were plentiful if one knew how to spot them," he declared. He felt he was "saving" them for the future. He collected thousands of points, and through illegal digging in caves, he found many perishable items and even human mummies. But sites and artifacts are a *nonrenewable* cultural resource, valuable only when in context. More fragile than an endangered species of animal, artifacts and the history they tell do not reproduce. The old man from Fallon also knew that the arrowhead hunting in Nevada wasn't as good as it used to be, and he complained about people coming from all over the country to hunt for them. In one sense he seems to realize the destruction, but in another he is utterly unaware that merely collecting things does not save them.[1]

The similarity of the Stillwater marshes to the Great Salt Lake wetlands makes one wonder if there was a grand civilization out there in the shadow of the Sierra Nevada, like what was claimed here in Utah. Fortunately, a lot has been learned in both places, not just from the arrowheads, but from the study of the full range of material culture—houses, storage spaces, cooking hearths, refuse dumps, rock imagery, incised stones, the invaluable perishables, and the *context* of it all, which breathes human life into the story. Knowledge of age, health, medical and dental maladies, diets, and genetics can be gleaned by substance analysis of small samples of bone. These biopsies of human bone come from skeletons carefully and respectfully excavated with permission from the Indigenous descendants. The remains are sometimes disturbed by construction, the fluctuations of water and wind, and, unfortunately, vandals searching for trophies.

What we know is that the wetlands of the Great Basin drew people who lived on the natural levees that border every channel and body of water in the marshes. In contrast to the peak populations of farmers along the Wasatch Front between AD 800 to 1300, the people at Stillwater were foragers.

What about all those arrowheads? Were there grand battles between armies of warriors? Romantic, but no. The battle of Marathon between the Greeks and the Persians in 490 BC occurred on an uninhabited plain. The arrowheads in the Great Salt Lake wetlands are scattered among the places where people lived and hunted. The answer is prosaic. When hunting in the marshes among the cattails and the bulrush tules, the loss rate of arrows would have been astronomical. That is why the Fremont farmer cached 600 spare arrowheads.

A colleague recounted a public lecture he gave years ago about the Fremont peoples along the Wasatch Front, which he suggested was the most populous part of Utah in ancient times. Someone in the audience was surprised that "Indians" lived near Salt Lake City because they thought "all the Indians lived in southern Utah." Of course, the archaeological sites in southeastern Utah, with its cliff dwellings and such, are readily apparent to even the disinterested visitor. But ancient Indigenous peoples lived *everywhere* in Utah. The Wasatch Front was rich agricultural land and very well could have been the most populous part of Utah during Fremont times—as it is today.

Fremont archaeological landscapes are also found in Utah Valley, especially near the Provo River delta and around the southern edge of Utah Lake. These places, too, are becoming urbanized, and increasingly along the Wasatch Front, ancient living sites tend to be encountered by bulldozers. This is how the substantial Fremont village and human burials were exposed along City Creek in downtown Salt Lake City near the intersection of South Temple and 300 West. During Fremont times villages existed along most of the creeks flowing from the Wasatch Mountains, and sites are known on the Jordan River, Kay's Creek, the lower Weber River, the Ogden River, and south to the Provo, American Fork, and Spanish Fork Rivers.

Urbanization is only the tail end of the story. The farming conditions favorable

8.1 *The Fremont Hamlet*, by Eric S. Carlson. Hamlets, or rancherías, were the most common settlement. They were hubs for dispersed populations, cycling workers among local landscapes for specific tasks. Agricultural fields were diverse and dispersed, a sort of investment portfolio of varying risk and potential for returns. While a particular individual might live in a hamlet all year, some did not. In addition to the pithouses, notice the ramadas and platforms that served as workshops. Courtesy of Eric S. Carlson.

to the Fremont peoples were also favorable to the Utah pioneers. In the 1870s, the Wheeler Expedition encountered prehistoric "mounds" in the prime farming area of the Provo River delta:

> West of the town [Provo], on its outskirts and within three or four miles of the lake, are many mounds, of various constructions and in different states of preservation.... Those examined were on low grounds, almost on a level with the lake and with Provo River...a number of mounds more or less perfectly preserved; some are entirely untouched, except on the outer edges, where the Mormon's grains [*sic*] patches encroach upon them; others have been almost completely leveled with the surrounding fields.[2]

Fremont mounds dotted the best agricultural land. The mounds offered the diversion of recreational artifact hunting, but in a more serious vein, they were a nuisance; the mounds are the decomposed remains of pithouses and surface structures that were built of or weatherproofed with adobe. After the structures were abandoned, centuries of rain and snow "melted" and spread the adobe, leaving a lump of ground so hard that nothing will grow. By the late nineteenth and early twentieth centuries a growing population made Utah farmland increasingly valuable, and the Utah pioneers realized that removing the mounds made economic sense. Over 400 Fremont mounds dotted the Parowan Valley north of Cedar City in the late nineteenth century, but only half remained by 1915. There were over 200 mounds along the Willow Creeks near Grantsville in the 1930s. They are difficult to find today. Lore has it that one farmer in Utah Valley had a business removing

8.2 After Great Salt Lake receded in 1988, hundreds of archaeological sites were exposed northwest of Ogden as the denuded ground eroded and deflated. This is an exposed pithouse with a backpack near the rear wall and a 25-centimeter scale inside the antechamber. The adobe used to build the pithouse resisted erosion, leaving the feature in bas-relief. Photo by Steve Simms.

unwanted "Indian" mounds. He hired out his services using a horse-drawn scraper to level the mounds and scatter the adobe.

The Big Village at Willard is a dramatic example of the treasures and knowledge harbored in these nonrenewable cultural resources. It became a favored place among locals to collect arrowheads and, occasionally, clay figurines, bone awls, slate knives, pendants, beads, and human skulls. Don McGuire of Ogden—a former mining engineer who had worked with John Wesley Powell and, like Powell, was interested in Native Americans—took a special interest in the Big Village beginning in 1873. Over a span of 15 years, he and his associates excavated a wide range of artifacts, 15 human skeletons, residential and storage structures, and quantities of charred maize, beans, corn cobs, ornaments, and textiles. They also found huge amounts of broken pottery, a few of which were fragments of Ancestral Puebloan black-on-red wares traded all the way from the Southwest. McGuire estimated the settlement covered 25 acres, and he noted an earthen wall around the town.

Four mounds were excavated at Willard in 1932, and a burial was documented. The deceased was flexed in a sitting position and accompanied by slate knives, a bone awl, a projectile point, two manos, small grinding stones, and a lump of red pigment. A large grinding stone was turned upside down and placed across the drawn-up legs.[3]

Some mounds contained pithouses, both round and square. This is significant because over time there was a transition from round to square houses, an indication in architecture across much of the world of increased settling and investment in housing. Occurring here in the eleventh to twelfth centuries, this transition is apparent at other Fremont sites.[4]

The Big Village at Willard was never subject to modern excavation, but three human burials removed from the site in the early twentieth century were recently studied for stable carbon isotopes to evaluate diet. The two who died between AD 600 and 900 ate a lot of maize; the diet of the third, who lived in the AD 1200s, tilted toward more wild foods.[5]

Fremont villages like Willard, which were common, had histories measured in centuries, albeit in stops and starts rather than continuous occupation. Even though it is considered one culture, a lot of change can happen in a century, and individuals experienced change during their lives.

Sense of place became centralized. Villages like Willard were not just somewhere to farm but places of power. Shoshones in the late nineteenth century referred to the Big Village with awe. Even though Willard had long been abandoned, the place remained powerful. Over decades accumulating into centuries, it attracted people, causing the Big Village to grow into a mound readily apparent from a distance.

An illustrative comparison is the Evans Mound in the Parowan Valley near Summit, Utah. Excavation there in the early 1970s exposed a vertical section of pithouses

8.3 This photo of the Big Village at Willard was taken by Andrew Kerr sometime between 1920 and 1930. Most of the hilltop in the photo is composed of the remains of Fremont pithouses that formed an accretional mound during a century or more of occupation. Courtesy of Utah State Historical Society and Mark Stuart.

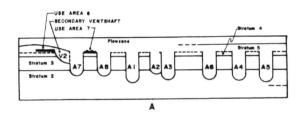
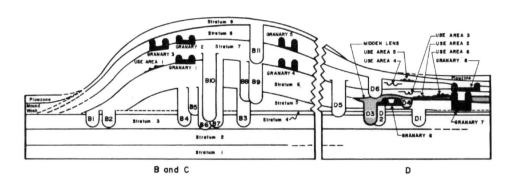

8.4 A schematic drawing of the stratigraphy at Evans Mound near Summit, Utah, showing how structures accumulated over more than 150 years of occupation. Walter Dodd (1982).

and adobe granaries stacked upon one another accruing to a height of seven feet above the surrounding plain over the course of occupation from AD 1050 to 1175.

The secrets still hidden in the Big Village at Willard met an unfortunate end. The dikes creating Willard Bay were constructed in the 1950s and completed in 1964. Despite the existence of preservation laws and the salvage archaeology being done in Glen Canyon on the Colorado River and other places across the United States, the archaeological remains at Willard were given secondary status. Indeed, the area of the Big Village was a source of borrow fill, and giant drag-line shovels were used to excavate material. Construction workers estimated over 20 human burials were encountered, along with masses of corn cobs and many additional housing structures and storage pits. Avocational archaeologists led by Fran Hassell of Ogden became site stewards, salvaging artifacts ahead of the destruction, and wrote newsletter reports on several burials.[6] They could only do so much.

It is likely that many burials became entombed in the Willard Bay dikes, making them an ignoble Native American mausoleum and a sad testimony to the ethic of progress. The place where the Big Village of Willard once thrived is near the north marina of Willard Bay State Park. The United States Bureau of Reclamation, which constructed Willard Bay, sponsored an investigation in the early 1990s to determine if anything was left. No trace survived. Willard is likely typical, and not far away, at the Warren site near Plain City, 16 mounds excavated in the 1940s produced a similar suite of structures, artifacts, and burials. In the 1970s the farmer whose family had worked the land for over a century estimated there were once at least 50 mounds at Warren. Fremont sites excavated in the 1960s in the Bear River Migratory Bird Refuge include the Levee, Knoll, and Bear River No. 3 sites, and others known only by their state number. Excavations were conducted in Utah Valley at the Seamons Mound in the late 1960s, at the Woodard Mound at the south end of Utah Lake in the 1980s, and at the Hinkley Mounds, where 20 spectacular clay figurines were found in the late 1950s and where excavations continued in 2015. The history of the Utah Valley sites parallels the story from the Big Village at Willard.[7] It began with early interest in relic hunting and was followed by intermittent attention by archaeologists. Mounds were steadily destroyed or covered by urbanization. This is still happening.

Something else that may be hidden by urbanization is evidence of Fremont peoples using irrigation. The Utah pioneers came to rely on irrigation because they had quickly utilized the agricultural land along streams and below springs that could be farmed without the expense of irrigation. Nineteenth-century Utah settlers claim they constructed their irrigation systems along the same routes as ancient peoples. According to one archaeologist, "In several places, the survey was told that early settlers found irrigation ditches near archaeological sites," and in Ferron Creek, central Utah, "The early white settlers are said to have found irrigation ditches just above the mouth of the canyon." Another individual, "in conversations with a land-owner along Bull Creek, south of Hanksville, Utah, was told that aboriginal fields and ditches were observed when the first Europeans arrived." There are numerous Fremont sites along Hill Creek on the Tavaputs Plateau, and "a prehistoric irrigation ditch a half-mile long" was noted at one village in the 1930s. Irrigation ditches have also been found in Nine Mile Canyon.

Archaeologists discovered irrigation ditches and water control features at the early Basketmaker/Fremont site at Steinaker Gap in the Uinta Basin. That they dated between either AD 250 and 400 or AD 700 and 750 shows that even in those early days of farming, irrigation was seen as worth the effort. Not far from there, on a tributary of Cub Creek in Dinosaur National Monument, three deeply buried channels were recently found. They are more of a water-harvesting system than an irrigation canal and show the ingenuity and opportunism of Fremont farmers. The channels reflect three periods of use: AD 200–260, AD 380–470, and AD 530–1030. The channels captured ephemeral water from surrounding slickrock and directed it to a nearby floodplain—a relatively inexpensive insurance policy. An irrigation ditch documented at Nawthis Village near Salina was used sometime between AD 750 and 1300. There may be a large, deep irrigation canal at Median Village in the Parowan

Valley, occupied between AD 950 and 1020, and the excavator of Median noted similar features at a Fremont site near Nephi and at Caldwell Village near Vernal.

A prehistoric irrigation system over four miles long on Pleasant Creek, several miles above Capitol Reef National Park, was shown to Noel Morss in 1928 and relocated in 2010. The system was likely constructed in Fremont times and was also used sometime between AD 1460 and 1636. The local farmer who alerted Morss claimed the canal was ancient because it showed the lack of modern tools in the way it had been built around obstructions a modern trench digger would cut through. Although horse-drawn metal tools made such work go faster, older Utahns' know that the Utah pioneers were keenly aware of the "sweat equity" invested in irrigation. I suspect the Fremont people did too.[8]

Evidence of irrigation is difficult to find and document, but it may have been a big part of Fremont life, as it was for the nineteenth-century pioneers. Researchers who conducted experimental studies growing maize in Range Creek Canyon above Price, Utah, concluded that irrigation is mandatory for farming except in a few places with natural sources of water.[9] Indeed, the fact that the ancients and the moderns chose to live in the same places to construct irrigation systems is why Fremont settlements lie under virtually every town along Interstate 15 from Brigham City to Cedar City, and in the Sevier and Sanpete Valleys.

From AD 500 to 1300 the Wasatch Front harbored an intense Fremont presence, but the evidence remains largely hidden by nineteenth-century Utah towns and subsequent urban expansion. But a few important Fremont villages excavated in recent years have elevated our knowledge of the Great Salt Lake Fremont peoples well beyond the earlier investigations. The recently excavated sites include Wolf Village near Goshen, Five Finger Ridge near Fremont State Park in Clear Creek Canyon, and Baker Village near Great Basin National Park in Nevada.

Wolf Village, located south of Utah Lake on private land, provided an opportunity to document a site in context. Seven pit structures and two surface adobe structures excavated between 2009 and 2013 represent only a portion of the site. Wolf Village was occupied in the eleventh and twelfth centuries. One of the pit structures is the largest ever documented at a Fremont site. Nearly 25 feet across, it had the typical four main support posts supplemented by over 200 secondary posts, many along the perimeter. It had a large central hearth, over three feet across, and two subsurface roofed ventilator tunnels. The structure had occasionally been remodeled and repaired. Adobe surface structures are found widely across the Fremont world, and their documentation at Wolf Village supports the hypothesis that they were used in the Great Salt Lake area as well, although until recently they were only suspected given the fragmentary and hidden nature of Wasatch Front

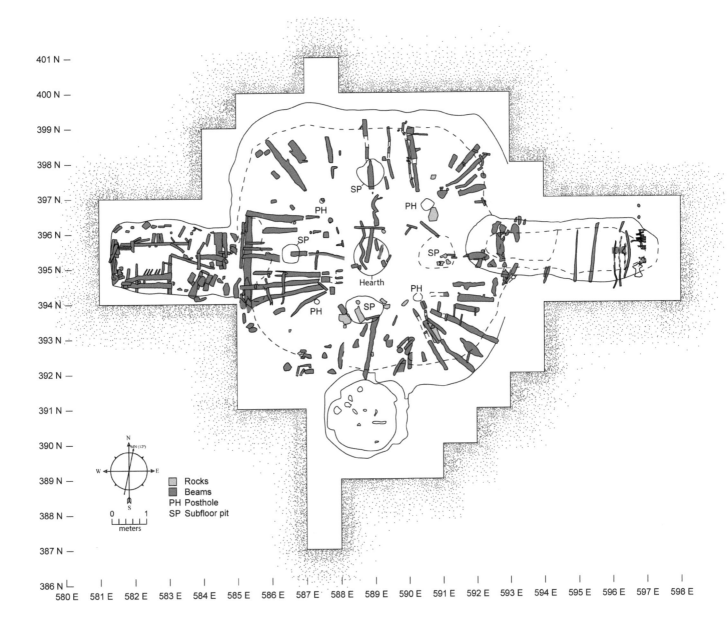

8.5 Plan view of Structure 2 at Wolf Village near Goshen, Utah. This is the largest excavated Fremont pit structure, with over 200 support posts arranged around the typical four main posts. Courtesy of James R. Allison, Brigham Young University.

sites. Most of the structures were residential, but some of the largest may have been communal. Because communal structures belong to and integrate communities, the existence of such large structures at Wolf Village provides a window into Fremont society and hierarchy. Also significant is the site's architectural variability, which suggests diversity in heritage among the occupants.[10]

Farther away, but still in the sphere of the Bonneville Basin, is Five Finger Ridge. Excavated in the late 1990s to make way for Interstate 70 through Clear Creek

Canyon, Five Finger Ridge is the largest Fremont site ever excavated using modern methods. The ridge was largely removed to make way for the highway, but its remnant is visible from Fremont Indian State Park, and the museum there describes the site. Over 80 structures were found in several clusters. A dozen pithouses could have been occupied at any one time during the twelfth century, and a conservative estimate of population size is about 100 people. There was an intense occupation in the late thirteenth century, when the population may have included several hundred people, indicating that maize agriculture persisted in some places to AD 1300 and later. A plaza, a large central structure, and an unusually large pithouse suggest communal functions and hierarchy. Much of the pottery used at Five Finger Ridge was imported from the Parowan Valley, over 40 miles away. Fremont big villages did indeed exist, and the society included far-flung associations and likely harbored a significant diversity of identity, ethnic heritage, and language histories.[11]

Baker Village is not the most westward of Fremont sites—those lie southeast of Ely, Nevada. Well-made Fremont pottery is found even in central Nevada, indicating extensive networks among skilled women potters. We have gained a sense of the western Fremont frontier at Baker Village because it was carefully excavated from 1991 to 1994. It sits at the foot of the Snake Range, the home of Great Basin National Park. The main period of occupation was from AD 1220 to 1295. Seven pithouses, a large central structure, and other surface structures around it were excavated. The site is much larger, and most of it remains buried. Its significance is the window it opens into Fremont society. It was a planned village arranged around the large central structure. The structures were aligned within three degrees of each other, and with the solstices. Evidence of long-distance connections includes pottery from the Parowan Valley, seashells from the Pacific coast, and turquoise from mines in Nevada, California, Arizona, and New Mexico. Baker is a strong candidate for irrigation agriculture because of its location on Baker Creek and the fact that farming would not be possible in eastern Nevada without it. Like Five Finger Ridge, Baker experienced a burst of occupation in the late thirteenth century, possibly because irrigation could hedge risk and help the people persist.[12]

An interminable stereotype of the Fremont peoples is that they lived as mixed farmers and foragers. Although early archaeologists recognized their affinity with the Southwest, the Fremont seem different from the Ancestral Puebloan peoples, even though they are of them. Were they true farmers? Could villages like Wolf, Five Finger Ridge, Baker, and Willard result from a foraging economy in the eastern Great Basin? Not likely.

By the 1990s stable carbon isotopes from human bone were being used to measure Fremont peoples' diets. The analysis identifies in a general way the amount of maize consumed over a good portion of a human life. Maize and similar plants accounted for 73–85 percent of the diet at four villages scattered across the Fremont world: Caldwell Village in the Uinta Basin, Nawthis Village on Gooseberry Creek above Salina, Backhoe Village in Richfield, and the Evans Mound near Summit in the Parowan Valley. The proportion of maize consumption at these villages is the same as that of Ancestral Puebloan peoples in the Four Corners area. Marginal farmer stereotype broken? Not necessarily.[13]

The human bone from museum collections used to study the stable carbon isotopes all came from Fremont villages where a fair number of burial interments were made in the floors of houses. What about the Fremont people who lived in small farmsteads or hamlets, or those who camped out on trips to visit relatives and other tribes, or those who foraged in years when agriculture fell short? What about the Fremont people who were buried in special places on the landscape? People in Indigenous societies are buried in different contexts depending on how they lived and, as some anthropologists have pointed out, depending on how they died.

Mother Nature can be a destroyer and a creator. Some remember national news of an overflowing City Creek diverted down State Street in Salt Lake City in 1983. Over the next few years, Great Salt Lake rose over 20 feet, flooding Interstate 80 and large areas west of Layton, Ogden, and Brigham City. The lake peaked in 1987 at an elevation of 4,211.6 feet above sea level—a historic period record. The water gradually receded to expose a moonscape where former stream channels were filled with sediment and the natural levees along streams were planed off.

Soon there were reports from avocational archaeologists of large numbers of human bones scattered across 30 square miles of mudflats. Desecration of the graves by relic hunters soon followed. Local members of the Utah Statewide Archaeological Society volunteered to cover the exposed burials, and they used several methods to decoy burials from souvenir hunters. The Northwestern Band of the Shoshone Nation, then based at Fort Hall, Idaho (some years later the tribal headquarters was moved to its present location in Brigham City) were very concerned about the unfolding tragedy. The Utah legislature quickly passed an act to save the human remains from destruction by ice sheets, waves, and wind—and from the inevitable desecration caused by relic collectors.

The calamity exposed the largest assemblage of Fremont skeletal remains ever found. A minimum of 85 individuals were represented, but the total was surely much higher. There were thousands of scattered bones, but many of the burials were largely intact. In one area there was a small cemetery where 11 people were interred over a span of years. They were accompanied by offerings including large grinding stones rubbed with red ochre, gaming pieces, fine bone awls, a bison horn, and an effigy of

8.6 The flooded Bear River Migratory Bird Refuge in 1985. The view is to the southwest, toward the Promontory Mountains. Photo by Steve Simms.

a duck's head fashioned out of bone. The flooding of the lake did not discriminate, and everyone who was buried in that 30 square mile area was equally exposed.

The involvement of the Northwestern Band of the Shoshone Nation was crucial to facing a natural event that turned into a cultural tragedy. Over months of meetings at Fort Hall, listening to feelings and perspectives, a collaboration resulted in a decision to remove the burials and all scattered human bones to protect them until a proper place of rest could be found.

The study of Shoshone history held some interest, but not to everyone. Some despaired. Others offered hair samples for DNA. Some pointed out that the tribe had current issues of great importance such as health care and education. Additional collaboration led to a vote by the tribal council to allow a small sample of bone from 50 individuals—something like a biopsy from a patient at a doctor's office—to be separated from the bones that were eventually transferred to the tribe. The samples were dated using AMS radiocarbon dating, the most precise method and one that requires only a few grams of bone. The bones were sampled for mitochondrial DNA, enabling tracing of maternal ancestry. Isotopes of stable carbon and nitrogen were measured to identify diet, especially maize consumption. CT scans were done on the femurs and tibias of 15 individuals and the humeri of 12, enabling an engineering analysis of lifetime activity patterns. The analysis distinguishes between local movement versus long-distance hiking, and between mobility on flat versus steep terrain. The humeri reveal the degree of upper-body effort expended over a life. Dental histories—including tooth wear and caries, as well as skeletal indications of nutritional stress—were examined for 59 individuals.[14]

This rare opportunity for study has elevated our understanding beyond a simple categorization of settled farmers and nomadic foragers. First, the dating: the deceased lived between AD 400 and 1400, but the period most represented is AD 800–1150, the height of Fremont times. Diet ranged from committed farmers consuming up to 70 percent maize, to some around 50 percent, and others only 35 percent. Any division of this population into foragers, farmers, or a mixture of both is an arbitrary boundary in a population of continuous variability.

Nor did this variation correlate with where the burials came from. At the Big Village of Willard there were two funerals for adults whose diets were largely maize, and another funeral hundreds of years later for an adult whose diet tended toward foraging. We have no way of knowing whether any of them spent their entire lives at Willard, but I doubt it given the dynamic life history we would expect of their lifeways.

The burials came from an archaeological landscape that included areas of scattered pithouses, substantial mound sites, and short-term camps. But there is no way to associate the numerous burials with spatially overlapping occupations spanning three centuries because of the erosion by the fluctuating Great Salt Lake. In the case of the small cemetery of 11 burials, 10 were very much maize eaters, but the eleventh tended toward foraging. A person from Warren Village near Plain City was a maize eater.

Taken together, the sample shows the Great Salt Lake Fremont peoples ate less maize than those at the Fremont villages studied in the 1990s and referred to previously. Whether this is due to sampling bias or is a real difference is hard to tell. The four Fremont villages with high proportions of maize—Caldwell, Nawthis, Backhoe, and Evans—are also near wetlands, and those resources appear in hearths, refuse middens, and pollen samples. Nevertheless, the people relied on maize.

There is one caveat about the Great Salt Lake burials. They all came from wetlands at relatively low elevations—4,206 to 4,212 feet. By 2001, the lake had receded to only 4,202 feet, exposing another 11 burials miles west of Willard Bay, closer to the

Promontory Mountains than the Wasatch Mountains. Many of the people buried in the wetlands died during droughts that shrank the Great Salt Lake, enlarged the wetlands, and invited occupation in places flooded in other years. Most of the burial sites in the wetlands were well below the land with farming potential, which is above 4,220 feet. Indeed, the Big Village at Willard and most farms developed by farmers in the nineteenth century and later are above 4,250 feet. In this way, the Great Salt Lake burials are a biased sample, even though it is the best opportunity we have ever had to see a diversity of Fremont burials. I suspect there really is a difference between burials recovered by archaeologists digging houses versus burials exposed en masse by Mother Nature. Thus, both samples are biased in their own ways. So what do the Great Salt Lake burials tell us?

The biomechanical analysis of lifetime activity patterns of the Great Salt Lake Fremont peoples was similar to studies done at the Stillwater Marsh near Fallon, Nevada. It revealed that Great Salt Lake Fremont males traveled long distances in rugged terrain, implying they frequently ventured out of the wetlands. For example, a favored toolstone in the wetlands was a brown chert that comes from the pass between Cache Valley and Ogden Valley, about five miles west of Powder Mountain ski resort. This would require a walk over North Ogden Pass and then north above Liberty, or from Brigham City up Box Elder Creek and south from Mantua. The female samples showed a life of hard upper-body work but less walking, and over flatter terrain. An identical pattern for males and females was found in a large burial sample from Stillwater Marsh. In both places it seems women anchored villages and camps in the wetlands, probably family groups with children and the elderly. They did the hard work of pounding roots, grinding seeds, preparing hides, and manufacturing everything from housing to tools, pottery, baskets, and fiber clothing.

The men hiked the mountains to hunt and obtain resources such as toolstone that was rare in the wetlands, but also medicines, special types of wood, antler, and exotic stones. It is significant that these activity patterns did not vary whether the person ate a lot of maize or tended toward foraging. Further, the similarity to the Stillwater sample is significant because maize farming never came to the western Great Basin.

The dental health of the Great Salt Lake Fremont peoples is consistent with a maize diet, but also with a mixed diet. The population does stand out in the number of growth-arrest lines and evidence of inflammation in the bones indicating periods of food stress for significant periods, but at lower rates than for other Fremont and forager groups in the Great Basin. Nor did the population suffer from iron-deficiency anemia. The varied diet and lifeway of the Great Salt Lake peoples paid off compared to those of other farmers and foragers.

What does the DNA say? Recall that the DNA of the Great Salt Lake Fremont peoples shows distant affinity to the Ancestral Puebloans and to the living Puebloans of the upper Rio Grande region of New Mexico: speakers of languages in the Kiowa-Tanoan family. There are differences from them as well, which is inevitable given that a thousand years had passed since the Basketmakers migrated north and reached peak Fremont populations on the Wasatch Front. The sample may also be shaped by genetic lineage extinctions that are common in small populations of humans. More interesting, the Great Salt Lake sample spanned three centuries and could represent diverse peoples. Living in the eastern Great Basin, the Great Salt Lake Fremont surely interacted with Fremont peoples descended from Western Basketmakers of the Uto-Aztecan language family. Underneath all this is the immigrant and Indigenous heritage of the Fremont peoples, and the fact that we lack genetic data on Indigenous forager populations in the eastern Great Basin or anywhere in Utah, eastern Nevada, Idaho, Wyoming, and western Colorado. The key remarks in discussions with geneticists is the homogeneity of the Great Salt Lake sample. It seems to be one biological population. The genetics are consistent across diets ranging from farming to foraging, and with lifetime activity patterns as revealed by the biomechanical study.

The biological homogeneity shows that the diversity in Fremont heritage, culture, and language history was brought together by daily life. The Great Salt Lake Fremont probably included diverse tribes and languages. Again, it is a cardinal error to presume that the history of a language and a tribal affiliation are one and the same. The Great Salt Lake burials illustrate this diversity in the variety of burial positions and orientations. Some were buried flexed and reclining on either the left or right side. Some were extended and positioned on their left or right side. Several infants were buried in unusual postures with their heads tilted as if to look across the ground surface. Burials faced all compass orientations. One appeared to be a water burial: a complete skeleton was found on its side with legs and arms splayed and embedded in fine silts at the bottom of what was then a stream channel. Some people were buried with offerings, but others with nothing. In one case, an infant was placed on the lap of an adult female. Indeed, there was a diversity of religious beliefs and practices among the Fremont peoples buried in the wetlands over a span of three centuries.

Communities among foragers and farmers such as the Great Salt Lake Fremont are pliant. Mobile peoples arrive, stay, and leave villages, creating an ebb and flow not only of population, but of mixed identities, language, and heritage. Some were just travelers and foreign. Some were adopted relatives. Some were members of families who lived elsewhere for years. These are called pliant communities. It is difficult for modern people, including archaeologists, to free ourselves of stereotypes about human behavior and organization because our culturally conditioned assumptions and categories are so routine. When it comes to communities and households, "we live in a home-centered culture where place is conceived as stationary, and the journey (or migration) is a departure from the norm."[15]

Consequently, there is a dynamic among ancient communities of interchangeable participants, with people coming and going while they traveled, or as they moved depending on the seasons. This pattern was inherent in Fremont origins as Indigenes and immigrants, as well as potential multiple Southwest migrant communities headed north.

This dynamic is also evident in interactions between the large populations along the Wasatch Front and the scattered rural Fremont hamlets in the west deserts, including the Buzz Cut Dune near Callao at the foot of the Deep Creek Mountains. There, pottery was both locally made and imported from the Wasatch Front. Toolstone came from as far away as the Tosawihi quarry north of Battle Mountain, Nevada. Great Salt Lake Fremont peoples frequented the Snake River Plain of southeast Idaho and into the Wyoming Basin, and we will learn more about that. I like to call this dynamic "the Desert and the Sown."[16] It seems to have persisted through Fremont times and, as we will discover, into recent centuries.

The founding of the Fremont culture was at least a five-century process, only becoming apparent in archaeological terms by AD 500. Another six centuries on, by AD 1150, the landscape had never been so populous. We found that villages such as Willard, Warren, Wolf, Five Finger Ridge, Hinkley, Woodard, and Baker are among many large villages that served as central places in dispersed communities composed largely of hamlets and farmsteads.[17] Surrounding these was an orbit of temporary camps for collecting roots, harvesting geese during the summer molt, conducting mass catches of suckers during the spring spawn, hunting deer along the edges of the marshes and bighorn sheep, deer, and elk in the mountains, and occasionally hunting bison in groups, as documented at the Levee site near the mouth of the Bear River and other mass exposures of butchered bison bone in the wetlands that have never been studied.

All these places were not inhabited at once; instead, the size of villages ebbed and flowed, punctuated by stops and starts. Even though Fremont peoples were settled farmers, sense of place embraced a rhythmic tempo anchored to landscape. Social networks of family, lineage, and alliances shaped the movement of people. Fremont society consisted of a sequence of hierarchies. On the lowest rung was the family and farmstead, where everyday decisions were made. In hamlets, several families of kin formed the next rung. Villages served as central places where leaders orchestrated communal seasonal activities and the rituals for guiding life and ensuring the future. Leaders were charismatic individuals—male and female—who served as stewards of the rituals and the stories. They did not so much dictate, but rather chaperoned political negotiations, trading events, and feuds. In such systems that have been studied by anthropologists, the leadership of chiefs is contextual and shared. As such, and in strong contrast to modern leadership—which is based on personality, even celebrity—leadership is faceless.[18] Stewardship of ritual is paramount, and along with kin, alliances, and charisma, it is the source of power more than direct coercion. At still larger scales, dispersed communities anchored to one or more central villages are theatres of dynamism. There is a circulation of labor adjusted to farming and foraging activities, and a circulation of kin, including blood relatives, relatives through marriage, and fictive kin. Weaving through all this is a flow of itinerate visitors and guests of potentially contrasting identities and languages. I have argued elsewhere that Indigenous life was more cosmopolitan than allowed for in modern cultural stereotypes of "Indians" or "primitives."[19]

The Fremont Wasatch Front was the most populous part of Utah. It was fully occupied. Home. Loved. Lived. The Human Wilderness was at heights not to be seen again for over five centuries, when the fur trappers and Utah pioneers entered a land that was so different, it seemed to them to be unused, wild, primal, and occupied by only a few "savages." Little did they know.

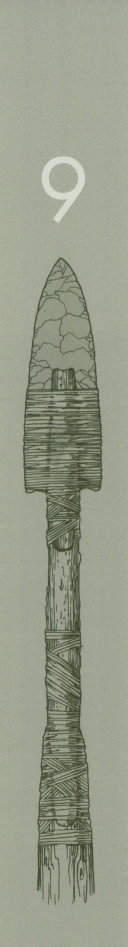

9

Upheaval

The word "upheaval" conjures images of dire straits and people craving better times, but in human history upheaval is inevitable rather than exceptional. The thirteenth and fourteenth centuries in the Great Salt Lake region were transformative. There was climate change, albeit not rapidly human driven as it is today. There were migrations from north to south and from south to north. There were changes in lifestyle, homeland, and sense of place. It turns out that the Great Salt Lake region and the Uinta Basin, seemingly unlikely places to drive history, were pivotal. This time of upheaval would shape changes among Fremont peoples. It was the time of migration of Dene peoples of Canada ("Dene" is more appropriate than the previous terms "Athabaskan" or "Athapaskan"), eventually leading to the Navajo/Apache Dene of the Southwest. Upheaval would lead to the ethnogenesis of the Kiowa of Wyoming, who would eventually migrate to the southern Plains. Upheaval would be a conduit for the long histories of the Shoshone and Ute.

For decades archaeologists have argued about stories. The Fremont farmers either became foragers or migrated to the Southwest. For some the Fremont peoples simply vanished, making it a lost culture. The sheep-raising Navajo and the equestrian Apache of the Southwest migrated there from Canada along the eastern slopes of Alberta and the Colorado Front Range. The Kiowa, bison-hunting equestrians of the southern Plains in eastern New Mexico, are a mystery. Kiowa beliefs passed down over generations say they came from Yellowstone, and while they exhibit cultural affinity with Plains Dene speakers, they share a Kiowa-Tanoan language history with Puebloan farmers of the upper Rio Grande in northern New Mexico.

There are reasons to suspect that some Fremont peoples in the Great Salt Lake area and Uinta Basin used their presence and relationships in Idaho and Wyoming as a springboard to migrate north and eventually take part in Kiowa ethnogenesis. Fremont peoples who instead migrated to the Southwest could potentially have joined Kiowa-Tanoan or Hopi speech communities, or, as some argue, the Keresan speech community. Keresan is distinct from Kiowa-Tanoan and Uto-Aztecan languages and is suspected of being relevant to the Chacoan world. It is found in some historic Rio Grande pueblos, including Acoma, Cochiti, and Zia in northern New Mexico. Not all Fremont peoples had to do the same thing.

A meandering diversity of interactions and ancestry may very well be the same for the Shoshone and Ute. The most common story is they arrived late in a changing Fremont world and replaced them as part of a thing called the Numic Spread. Others question whether the Numic Spread was recent or long ago, a single event or a process with multiple transformations, old and recent.[1] The relationship between the Numic branch and earlier forms of the Uto-Aztecan language family is rarely explored even though some linguists and archaeologists believe that Uto-Aztecan languages were present in the Great Basin at least 6,000 years ago and as many as 8,000 years ago.

Archaeology is changing through a collaboration of the natural sciences and physical sciences, offering technical analyses unheard of only decades ago. It is changing through discoveries in cultural anthropology and the distinctive analyses of anthropological linguistics. It is also changing because there is more of an ear for the voices of Indigenous Americans who tell their own histories. A multifaceted history of a polyethnic, multilinguistic, dynamic, and cosmopolitan Native America seems approachable and worthwhile. This turn of inquiry contests two egregious narratives about Native Americans and Indigenous peoples in general. First is the expectation that Indigenous peoples must remain in place lest their identity be threatened. Second is that they must stay the same, never changing from the roots of their origin lest they lose authenticity. These notions are yet another facet of the Biblical Model, and it has long been imposed upon non-Western peoples everywhere in the world. It is partially a consequence of the Pristine Myth. Yet considering analogies from anthropology and history, we find that ethnogenesis may be part of all the stories during a time of upheaval.[2]

Tracing language and ethnicity is a rare opportunity in the study of ancient history. The ethnicities, languages, and tribes of the explorers, pioneers, and settlers from Paleoindian through Archaic times remain murky in the depths of deep time. But in the period of upheaval over the last millennium, there is greater opportunity to pursue such realities.

It is easy to point out the difficulty and dangers of identifying ethnicity, identity, and language using material culture such as pottery and arrowheads, the most common objects. Artifacts such as basketry, footwear, and items with symbolic content, such as incised stones and gaming pieces, offer greater potential to see affinity, but some of these items are found far less frequently. I recall a study of Southern Paiute arrows collected during the John Wesley Powell expedition on the Kaibab Plateau in Arizona and nearby areas and curated at the Smithsonian. Comparison of the arrows with known Southern Paiute bands revealed that the differences among bands could be detected in the painted designs on the cane arrow shafts. The stone arrow tips themselves, however, revealed nothing about band affiliation, nor did they distinguish between Southern Paiute, Ute, and Shoshone. Archaeologists have a lot of arrow points, but precious few arrow shafts.[3]

Rock imagery surely represents common ideological values, but these can spread through direct migration of people or by others adopting the ideology. Christian symbolism spread across Europe over a thousand years ago, traversing a diversity of ethnic identities and language histories. Yet we cannot use the Christian cross to delineate tribes and languages. In the same way, it is dangerous to identify tribes and languages across variations in lifeways atomized as either farmers or foragers. Apaches and Navajos contrast markedly in lifeways and identity yet share a language history.

One key is to remind ourselves of the distinction between ethnicity/identity/tribe and language history. They are not the same. American identity arose in colonial America, yet modern American material culture, lifeways, and perceptions are worlds apart. Our English language took form in England but is a member of the vast Indo-European language family that spans Eurasian cultural diversity over thousands of years.[4] Our identity as Americans is independent of our language history and now includes Spanish and diverse languages of people from around the world but who strongly identify as Americans.

With caution in mind, we see the power of story in tracing language history and investigating an ethnically complex and dynamic Native America. This broader quest offers a path to investigate the multifaceted fate of the Fremont peoples, including migration north of Kiowa-Tanoan speakers and migration south of both Kiowa-Tanoan and Uto-Aztecan speakers who found new homes and identities among a diversity of speech communities in the Southwest. We might be open to a resilience among Fremont farmers—some who continued to farm, and some who continued as foragers in a world of Shoshone and Ute-Numic speakers. We can look under the labels and see the emigration in the thirteenth century of Dene speakers from Canada to northwestern Utah, where migrants encountered a Fremont world in upheaval. Some Dene migrants stayed only a few decades before continuing to the Southwest, either via the Plains and then south along the Colorado Front Range or through the Rocky Mountain parklands, or via a western route from the Wasatch Front east to the Uinta Basin and south along the Colorado–Utah border. They were part of the vast Dene migrations, which led to the Navajo and Apache peoples becoming part of a linguistically and ethnically complex Puebloan world. We can explore a persistence in Dene presence in Utah as some migrants settled and interacted with the Wasatch Front Fremont people and stayed on, especially in Utah Valley. We can be open to exploring the deep history of the Uto-Aztecan languages in the Great Basin, changes in those languages, and the descendant genealogy of the Shoshone and Ute.

Ethnogenesis—the changing of ethnic identity, kinship, associations, and lifeway—is neither automatic nor incessant, but a material process subject to the tyranny of circumstance upon real lives—especially during times of migration and change. Upheaval.

Fremont populations grew in the eleventh and twelfth centuries on the back of maize agriculture, and they likely used irrigated maize agriculture that required an investment of labor to build and manage. Wasatch Front populations also benefitted from abundant wild foods in the wetlands and mountains. The linguistic diversity that was part of the origins of Fremont peoples persisted and shaped their interactions. Great Salt Lake Fremont suggests heritage with Uinta Fremont, Sevier Fremont, and foragers of the eastern Great Basin—ancestors of historic Shoshone and Ute.

Great Salt Lake Fremont presence was widespread over southeastern Idaho. They hunted bison at Rock Springs in the Curlew National Grasslands west of Malad. They hunted bighorn sheep at Standing Rock Overhang in Weston Canyon northwest of Cache Valley. Fremont pottery is found at Wilson Butte Cave and Pence-Duerig Cave north of Twin Falls, at a host of lesser-known sites, and in private collections. The Great Salt Lake Fremont peoples obtained most of their obsidian from southeastern Idaho, especially the sources near Malad. Evidence from several places suggests that during Fremont times there was also an early presence of Uto-Aztecan Shoshonean groups in eastern Idaho, suggesting diversity in the speech communities of people using the region.[5]

Fremont populations reached their peak in the AD 1100s, and then there was a several-century period when lifeways diversified and people migrated. This change is often attributed to a drought, and indeed there was a severe drought several decades long in the mid–AD 1100s. But Fremont peoples had experienced droughts before. A drought in the AD 500s was worse than the one in the 1100s, but populations were still small enough to adjust. Additional droughts occurred in the AD 600s and 700s, and a long drought from AD 790 to 830 surely must have affected people's lifeways.

What happened to the Fremont peoples was something economists recognize widely through history. Periods of stress that don't collapse a society spur

9.1 Natural landscape routes shape pedestrian migration. This map shows major routes relevant to the migration of Dene peoples from Canada to the Southwest. Routes of the Fremont peoples' migration during that time are also shown, with the Great Salt Lake Fremont moving north across the Snake River Plain to Yellowstone, and the Uinta Basin Fremont north to Wyoming along the Green River and east into the Wind River basin. Fremont peoples also migrated to the Southwest. Peak migration was likely in the AD 1300s, but migrations spanned AD 1100 to at least AD 1500. Cartography by Chelsea McRaven Feeney.

intensification as people hope to sustain a familiar way of life. Such efforts carried the Fremont peoples through a long but not particularly severe drought from AD 930 to 1010. Even with those efforts, migration occurred on local scales. A feature of migration throughout history is return-migration when heritage lures people back to places familiar to collective memory. The Cub Creek area in Dinosaur National Monument is an example. The region had been occupied since AD 300 by people with a Basketmaker style of settlement, like the Steinaker Gap site northwest of Vernal. The uplands of the Cub Creek area feature small, dispersed settlements and farms with maize processing apparent in roasting features. Between AD 750 and 1050, there was growth, and villages were built in the lowlands along Cub Creek, probably using irrigation. This period of intensification was a time of predictable rainfall interspersed with brief droughts. It was manageable. But after AD 1050 there was a decades-long period when rainfall became less predictable. The people could not plan and invest. The occupation of the uplands continued, but investment in lowland villages decreased. The region continued to be occupied until the AD 1300s, but there may have been local out-migration; some of the rock imagery suggests that some fraction of the population may have returned to the Southwest, including Hopi. Local adjustments like this were likely common rather than wholesale regional abandonments.[6]

Stepping back to the Fremont world writ large, up through AD 1150 the Fremont peoples' way of life persisted and grew as they continued building more infrastructure, cooperating, and working harder. Indeed, populations grew the most between AD 900 and 1150. Like efforts in the twenty-first century to sustain economies and lifeways despite the inexorable march of climate change, immigration, and conflict, it is those on the margins who suffer, while those with means remain relatively unscathed—until upheaval sets deeper change in motion.

Climate modeling and tree-ring records from the Tavaputs Plateau above Price, as well as from Nevada, Oregon, and New Mexico, have revealed that a severe drought occurred between AD 1140 and 1160, a time of peak temperatures as well. After AD 1150, temperatures became volatile and trended lower for the next several centuries, shortening the growing season. Precipitation differences between years also became volatile and would have created uncertainty. Additional droughts occurred around AD 1240, followed by a severe drought between AD 1270 and 1300, by which time the growing season had already shortened significantly. There is also evidence that winter precipitation decreased, meaning less snowpack, which was crucial to Fremont irrigation. A decrease in summer moisture could have been fatal for Fremont peoples who dry-farmed. The summer monsoon necessary for bringing in a maize crop was always an Achilles heel for the Fremont because the monsoon weakens as one farms farther and farther north of the Colorado River.

The climate from the mid–AD 1100s to 1300 brought increasing pressure on Fremont peoples: not enough water from snowpack, a shorter growing season, wild swings in rainfall from year to year, and long periods of drought that shrank Great Salt Lake. Population declined as people had to rely more on foraging. Rather than seeing the Fremont culture as collapsing due to a single event with a single date caused by the single force of a drought, upheaval came to the Fremont over a long span of time and through a conspiracy of forces.

One consequence of climate change is migration. We are experiencing that in the twenty-first century. Climate change causes food and water shortages in some places. This spurs migration to places not under the same pressures, which leads to conflict. Migration and conflict are now occurring on massive scales all around the world. Through such times people may remember their roots, but their lives change, they move long distances, they learn new languages, and they identify with new things. There is a disconnect between the world we are living in and the past we imagine. The Pristine Myth rears its head again as it casts Indigenous peoples as unchanging and frozen in time, as if they are museum pieces. Nothing could be farther from the truth. Fremont peoples would be caught up in continental-scale diasporas and ethnogenesis that occurred over the several centuries that climate scientists know well as the transition from the Medieval Climatic Anomaly to the Little Ice Age.[7]

The origins of the Uinta and Great Salt Lake Fremont peoples are found in the Kiowa-Tanoan speakers of the Eastern Basketmaker culture, and those relationships may also be part of their fate. An affinity between the northern Fremont and Plains peoples was recognized in the 1930s and persisted as evidence mounted. Fremont pottery is found in southeastern Idaho and at dozens of sites in western Wyoming, albeit in small quantities, but then foragers only use pottery when it fits their lifestyle.[8] Connections of Great Salt Lake peoples with the north are also seen in the movement of obsidian, which mostly came from southeastern Idaho.

Rock imagery suggests shared ideological themes. Shield figures common to the Plains are found on the Tavaputs Plateau, in the Uinta Basin, and along the Wasatch Front. Shield imagery also occurs on the eastern Snake River Plain, which was frequented by Great Salt Lake Fremont peoples. Southwest Wyoming harbors a significant amount of Fremont rock imagery so distinctive that it indicates the presence of groups of Fremont peoples, probably from the Uinta Basin. These places are along the Green River, south of the town of the same name and east past Rock Springs.

Even farther into central Wyoming, Fremont rock imagery featuring fringed shields, feathered staffs, and bear figures shows uncanny affinity to the Castle Gardens Style of rock imagery in the Wind River basin of central Wyoming. The style

9.2 Castle Gardens, in the Wind River basin near Shoshoni, Wyoming, is a sacred landscape. Hidden within a rolling, featureless sage plain, this colorful gash becomes apparent only when a traveler reaches the rim of the draw that harbors abundant rock imagery. Photo by Steve Simms.

is less directly Fremont than the imagery in southwest Wyoming, but it dates to the heart of the Fremont period, between AD 1000 and 1250, and some images that date to AD 1450 to 1700 could represent the migration and subsequent persistence of Fremont peoples.

The Fremont rock imagery in the Great Salt Lake area is more subdued, but common. It is often placed on rock such as gneiss, making it difficult to see. Images are often individual rather than grand murals, as at places in the Uinta Basin. Avocational archaeologists who hunt rock imagery know there is a great deal of it in the Great Salt Lake area, even though its subtlety causes it to be overlooked.

A spectacular example of anthropomorphic shield imagery is locally known as the Red Man of Timpie, near Grantsville. Connor Springs, west of Corinne, is a medley of themes and styles, including the Great Basin Curvilinear Style and Fremont motifs. The rock imagery there is protected on the private land of ATK Thiokol Corporation. More than 200 incised prayerstones were found in the

9.3 Example of shield motifs at Castle Gardens that evoke Fremont as well as Plains imagery and stories. Photo by François Gohier.

Connor Springs and Blue Hills area, but these are all in private collections. (We will discover more about prayerstones, incised stones sometimes referred to as "portable rock art.")

Connor Springs is an example of a sacred landscape, and not far from there, on the east side of the Promontory Mountains, a cache of painted bones, some in leather sheaths, were excavated from a cave by an amateur collector between 1930 and 1950. Seven specimens, including five bison scapulae and two ribs of either bison or elk, were painted with geometrics, anthropomorphs, and zoomorphs in black designs that resemble Fremont rock imagery motifs. All were laid together in a grass-lined pit along a side wall of the cave, a situation indicating a commemorative offering.

Utah Valley also harbors a sacred landscape in the Lake Mountains west of Utah Lake. Rock imagery there ranges from very old to Fremont motifs and is protected by the Smith Family Archaeological Preserve. As one proceeds south of the Great Salt Lake region, the Fremont styles hold more in common with Ancestral Puebloan imagery and the Western Basketmaker, Uto-Aztecan heritage of Fremont. The Great Salt Lake and Uinta Basin areas can be seen as borderlands.[9]

9.4 The Red Man of Timpie, one of many shield figures around Great Salt Lake, overlooks the south shore near Grantsville. Courtesy of Randy Langstraat.

Natural travel routes available to Great Salt Lake Fremont peoples follow the Snake River across the eastern Snake River Plain, known to them for centuries, possibly from following bison. Fremont-style pottery is known along this route and even occurs at Reas Pass, which culminates the migration as it traverses the Continental Divide before a mere 10-mile descent to the Yellowstone Plateau. Peoples of northeastern Utah and northwestern Colorado had long followed the natural routes through Browns Park and north along the flatter stretches of the Green River, mesas, and drainages all the way to Rock Springs and Green River, Wyoming. Fremont presence and interaction were strongest in the Wyoming Basin, which stretches diagonally across southwest Wyoming and into northwest Colorado. Migrants could then proceed north toward the upper waters of the Green River with several options for reaching Yellowstone. An alternative would have been for travelers to head northeast over South Pass, skirting the southern flank of the Wind River Range into the Wind River and Bighorn basins. The dating suggests centuries of episodic interaction, resulting in distinctive rock imagery and introducing small amounts of pottery and basketry to add to those already being made there.

9.5 Great Basin influence is evident in the staggering diversity of imagery on boulders at Connor Springs. Photo by François Gohier.

9.6 Anthropomorphs and cupules adorn only the top of Coulter Rock, above Willard, Utah. The imagery goes unnoticed until one climbs the rock. Photo by François Gohier.

These northward migrations were not likely coordinated waves of advance, but rather piecemeal with return-migration, and taking place on scales of human generations. As farming options declined, landscapes to the north became opportunities for people with existing social networks given that some Fremont peoples had long been frequenting parts of Idaho and Wyoming. If there is a unifying theme to the migrations, it may be a shared language history among the northern Fremont. As to ethnicity and identity, they may best be described as diverse in the absence of being able to identify such things with any precision.

Northward migration was not the only Fremont response to changing times. Fremont peoples on the Colorado Plateau in central Utah and in the Great Basin of western Utah derived from the Uto-Aztecan-speaking Western Basketmaker peoples. In the borderland zone near Escalante, Utah, Ancestral Puebloan and Fremont groups had alternated spasms of settlement over several centuries. The geography and common language history along this borderland eventually pulled people south of the Colorado River.

At Five Finger Ridge in Clear Creek Canyon, on the edge of the Bonneville Basin, farming persisted after AD 1300, showing that the end of the Fremont culture was fragmentary, not an event in AD 1150. The occupants of Five Finger Ridge also held ties to the south. Baker Village below Great Basin National Park occupies the western borderland of farmers and foragers in eastern Nevada. The period of greatest Fremont occupation at Baker Village was AD 1220–1295, persisting through much of the severe drought between AD 1270 and 1300. Baker may have survived because of an investment in irrigation agriculture, without which the village could not have existed in the first place. By that time, the residents surely were in association with Great Basin foragers speaking the Uto-Aztecan languages of Ute and Shoshone—the Numic languages.

In a few other places—such as the Piceance Basin in northwestern Colorado, the Tavaputs Plateau, and Capitol Reef—pockets of Fremont descendants persisted through the AD 1500s and on in a world of Numic-speaking foragers.[10] In the spaces between the dwindling central place villages were surely remnant Fremont peoples who returned yet again to foraging in a milieu of language diversity. How this relates to peoples, ethnicity, and identity we may never know precisely, but the situation was ripe for the process of ethnogenesis in a context of changing sense of place.

The next phase of the story turns to caves in the Promontory Mountains looking west across the northern arm of Great Salt Lake. Expansive grasslands existed north of the lake, as well as east of the Promontory Mountains, reaching past Connor Springs to Corinne and the Bear River. The Promontory Caves were first excavated in 1930 and 1931 and interpreted as neither Fremont nor Shoshone but as a "temporary" occupation of "Athapaskans" (now known as Dene) "on their way south." The occupants of the caves interacted with Great Salt Lake Fremont peoples. Excavation at the Promontory Caves from 2011 to 2014 and new analyses led to similar conclusions, but the new work takes the story into how the migrations played out in human terms during this period of upheaval in the thirteenth century and beyond. The spectacular preservation and range of objects found in the caves, along with precise dating, enable questions to be investigated that are typically unavailable except to speculation. The work offers a peek beyond language history into identity. The notion that Fremont culture included many peoples was proposed decades ago. So was the critique of a propensity among archaeologists and arrowhead collectors to obsess over archaeological cultures and typologies, a habit that tends to conflate pottery and arrowhead types with peoples despite a denial that no such thing is being done. As one famous archaeologist said decades ago, "You don't have to be Swedish to drive a Volvo."[11]

Questions of identity and ethnicity remain difficult to approach. Tracing language history appeals to the discipline of anthropological linguistics. Ancient and modern DNA studies trace gene flow, but there is no strict relationship of genes with language or ethnicity. One gem of the work at the Promontory site is that it provides the opportunity to see the interplay between identity, migration, and language. In so doing, it illuminates the other changes that occurred in the Great Salt Lake region and beyond during this time of upheaval.[12]

Dene migrants occupied the Promontory Caves from AD 1250 to 1290—two generations. Estimates place the population at about two dozen or fewer in the larger of the two caves. They focused on hunting bison. They made efforts to interact with the local Fremont people. Their distinctive pottery sometimes shows Fremont characteristics, an indication that Fremont women worked with Promontory women potters. More than 250 moccasins were found in the old and new excavations of the caves, indicating the Promontory Caves were a moccasin fabrication and repair shop. Most of the moccasins are made of bison hide, and DNA analysis shows overwhelmingly that female bison hides were preferred for their higher quality and because they were more workable.[13] Many of the moccasins were for children. When moccasins were repaired, commonly worn-out soles, less-worn sections such as the cuff were recycled into new moccasins. Ethnohistory reminds us that moccasins could be made by women, men, and children. The Dene occupants of the caves made a distinctive style that is found in western Canada, their region of origin, and that style is also found in the Southwest among Apachean Dene populations—where they ended up. The Dene moccasins differ markedly from the two types of moccasins made by Fremont peoples, some found in the Promontory Caves, but also in other

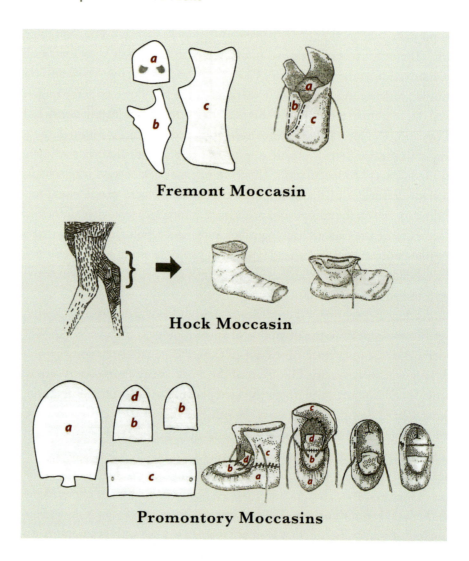

9.7 Contrasting styles and manner of fabrication of Fremont, Hock, and Promontory moccasins. From Ives 2014. Courtesy of Jack Ives, University of Alberta.

Great Salt Lake and Utah caves. The Promontory moccasins also differ greatly from Shoshone and Ute styles.

The small population at the Promontory Caves is a microcosm of continental-scale migrations of Dene from northwestern Canada to the south, ending up in northern New Mexico and Arizona as early as AD 1300.[14] The forces that set the Dene migrations in motion are part and parcel of continental trends beginning with the settlers of the Archaic. All over North America, foragers parted out the land, grew populations, and developed societies that ultimately led to the adoption of agriculture, culminating in a fully occupied continent with places such as the Mississippian culture city of Cahokia and the Ancestral Puebloan center place of Chaco by the eleventh to thirteenth centuries. No part of the continent escaped the process, which also included peak populations among the foragers of California and, as we found previously, even among the Great Basin and Intermountain settlers.

Dene peoples in the Canadian subarctic of British Columbia and Alberta experienced their own demographic shift beginning over 2,000 years ago. Trends toward increased territoriality and resource stress from growing populations fostered specialization in salmon and caribou, but virtually all other available resources were used. The process unfolded over centuries. The White River ash eruption in eastern Alaska in AD 850 disrupted caribou herds, and like so many times in history, an event like that can trigger a change in process that had been brewing for a long time. The Dene of the subarctic were accustomed to the severe stresses of making a living in such an environment. They developed extensive social networks, and they employed mobility and a flexible technology. They adopted useful practices, technology, and ideology from neighbors even as they maintained their identity. These things became hallmarks of the Dene migrations to the south.[15]

9.8 The distinctive pleated Promontory moccasin. Photo by Alyson Wilkins. Courtesy of Natural History Museum of Utah.

Several lines of evidence attest to the far-flung interactions of Dene migration. A distinctive D-shaped bifacial scraper called a *chi-tho* is common in Canada. These are also known from Promontory archaeological sites, especially in Utah Valley, and one was found at the Levee site, a Fremont occupation on the Bear River delta. This tool is otherwise unknown to the cultures of the Great Basin. A variety of gaming and gambling artifacts were also found in the Promontory Caves, including cane dice, oval bone gaming pieces, and fiber-wrapped hoops. These are known on the Plains in Wyoming and Montana, and in British Columbia and Alberta. They differ markedly from Fremont gaming pieces found in the Great Salt Lake area. Influence went north as well. Within a narrow corridor of the spectacular Grotto Canyon, nestled in the mountains of southwestern Alberta, is Fremont style rock imagery featuring anthropomorphs with staffs and headdresses and an image of a Puebloan flute player.[16]

A powerful symbol of expansive travel during these times is also found in moccasins. The hundreds of moccasins found in the Promontory Caves show how

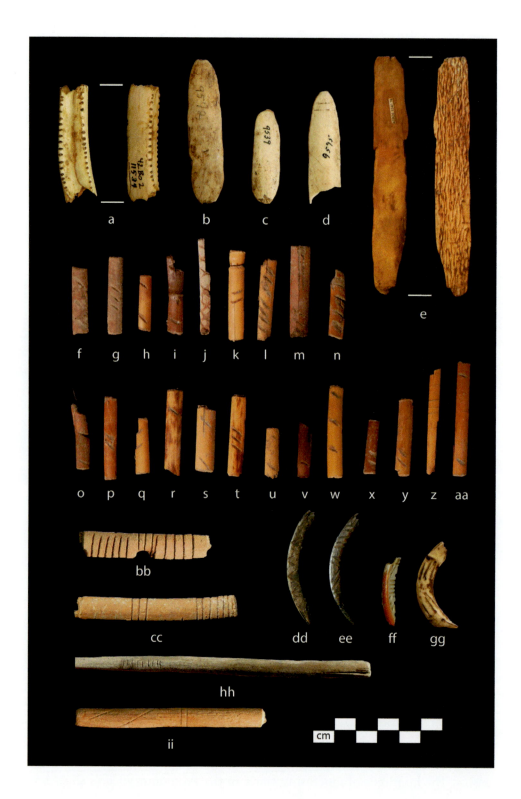

9.9 Dene style gaming pieces from the Promontory Caves manufactured of bone, cane, wood, and tooth. These are used for hand games (*top row*), dice games (*second row*), and stick games (*hh–ii*). All are from the collections of the Natural History Museum of Utah except for items *dd–ff*, which are from the John Hutchings Museum of Natural History, Lehi, Utah. From Yanicki and Ives 2017. Courtesy of Jack Ives, University of Alberta.

9.10 Fremont style gaming pieces from the Great Salt Lake wetlands near Willard Bay contrast with those from the Promontory Caves. Photo by Laura Patterson.

important they were. They were made there, and many were repaired. Franktown Cave, located south of Denver, Colorado, is on the eastern prong of Dene migration from Canada to New Mexico. It is a Promontory site associated with bison hunters who occupied the cave between AD 1180 and 1280, partially contemporaneous with the Promontory Caves in Utah. Analysis of stable carbon and nitrogen isotopes in bison hides can identify general areas where the animals lived. There are significant contrasts in the isotope signatures of grasslands in the western Plains and those of the eastern Great Basin. One of the moccasins found in the Promontory Caves had been repaired, likely because the sole had worn away. The hide cuff piece used to attach a new sole made of local bison from Promontory was from a type of bison found on the Plains grassland that occurred around Franktown Cave![17] Surely as the people covered hundreds of miles, they wore and repaired many moccasins. The cuff piece was likely transferred to several new soles before its final discard in Utah. Of course, this kind of movement by foot was centuries before the domesticated horse would be introduced to the Americas by the Spaniards.

The combination of long trips, shared rock imagery symbolism, the spread of tools particular to faraway places, and the array of gambling pieces befits migrants encountering new peoples. Social relations needed to be established and new members recruited, often by bringing in local women, with kinship ties following be they blood, marriage, or fictive. All are essential to the journey.[18]

Southeastern Idaho and western and central Wyoming were landscapes of interaction among Fremont peoples and Numic-speaking groups prior to the arrival of the Dene. It is the interaction of Dene migrants with Great Salt Lake Fremont peoples in the thirteenth century that is relevant to the ethnogenesis that culminated in Kiowa origins in the Yellowstone area. As the Fremont speech community with

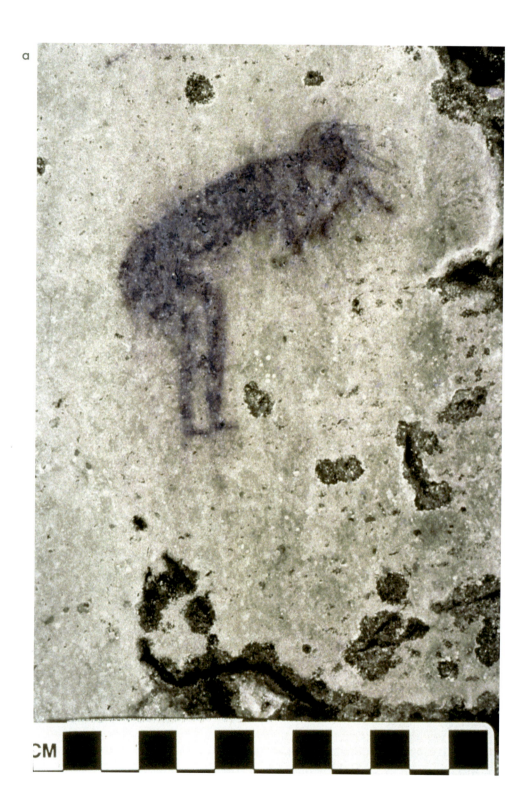

9.11a–d Rock imagery from the sacred landscape of Grotto Canyon, Alberta, evokes interaction with Fremont and other Puebloan peoples. The imagery is very faint at the Grotto Canyon site. These photos include (a) a Puebloan flute player, and (b and c) detail images of Fremont style anthropomorphs with headdresses, staffs, and rattles. A composite drawing (d) shows the spatial relationships of the images. From Magne and Klassen 2002. Courtesy of Martin Magne; also Applied Photographic Research, James Henderson, and the Alberta Archaeological Association.

b

a Kiowa-Tanoan language history fragmented and went north, transforming from farmers into foragers in landscapes they had some familiarity with, they enhanced ties with Plains Apachean Dene peoples. Out of the interactions between contrasting speech communities, Dene and Kiowa-Tanoan, the Plains Kiowa took shape in the Yellowstone area beginning in the sixteenth or seventeenth century. The Kiowa have long been known to have had relationships with Plains Apache peoples, and these are stressed in their origin stories.[19] The stories of the Kiowa-Tanoan-speaking Eastern Basketmakers, the Uinta and Great Salt Lake Fremont peoples, the Promontory Dene, Numic speakers, and the historic Kiowa are of a single cloth.

During the occupation of the Promontory Caves by the first migrants, more Dene arrived around AD 1275–1295. Even as some Dene continued to migrate south over the decades, others settled and continued the Promontory presence along the Wasatch Front, and especially in Utah Valley, for another several hundred years,

c

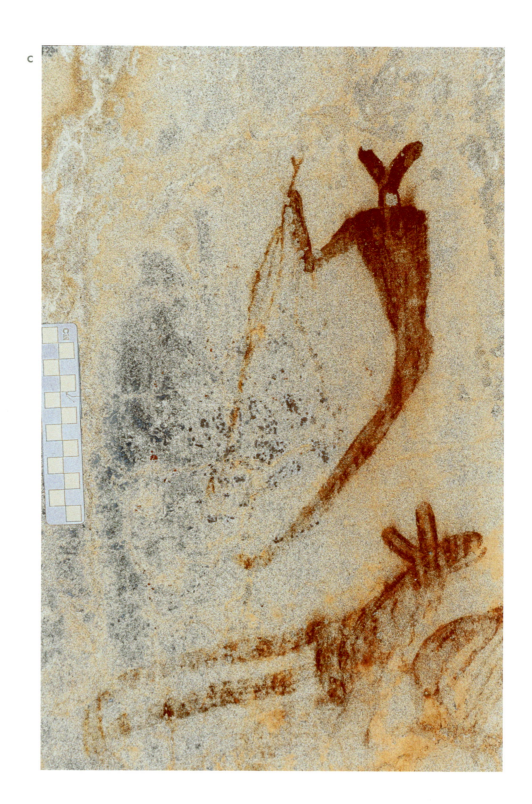

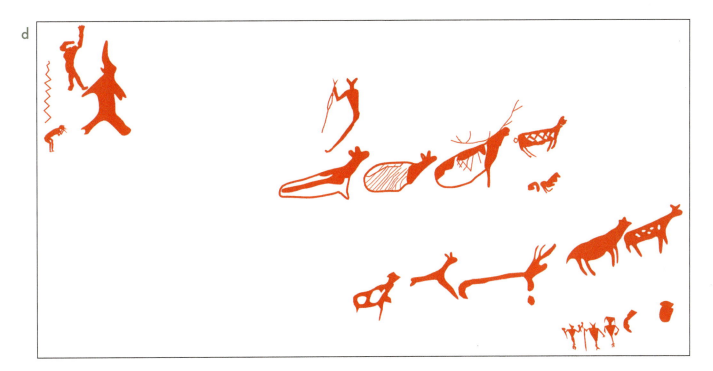

d

to about AD 1600. There is some evidence that bison numbers declined as climate change ushered in the Little Ice Age. The period between AD 1300 and 1400 seems to have been wet in the eastern Great Basin, but that may have been accompanied by a cooling trend and the continued absence of the summer monsoon rain that had been essential to Fremont farmers in the preceding centuries.[20]

Lifeways turned to more generalized foraging, as they had for the settlers of the Archaic before farming. During this later period of the Promontory occupation, between AD 1300 and 1600, many Fremont peoples migrated out or shifted to foraging while others hung on to farming. All this occurred in a milieu of the ancestors of the historically known Shoshone and Ute, speakers of the Numic languages. I suspect the Numic speakers had been a part of the Fremont mix for a long time.

10

Descendants

The living Native American tribes of the Great Salt Lake region are the Shoshone, Goshute (a dialect variation of Shoshone), and Ute. Their ancestors were present in the Great Basin region during the time of the Archaic settlers and through the time of upheaval. Indeed, they signify a chronologically deep language history in the western United States. A great deal of ethnography and history has been written about the Shoshone and Ute because the Great Basin was the last wild frontier in the lower 48 states. Scholars of the late nineteenth century, including John Wesley Powell, documented Indigenous languages, and one of the first comprehensive classifications of North American Indian languages was published in 1891. By the early twentieth century, anthropologists were pursuing the opportunity to record Native life as it was before the immigrant Euro-Americans arrived. There are eyewitness accounts, interviews with the elders, ethnographies, diaries, photographs, sketches, and paintings documenting the last two centuries of Native life—the organization of their societies, their perceptions, and their beliefs. The ethnographic history of the Ute and Shoshone is rich.[1] It is also a seduction tempting us to simply impose this history onto the past. Doing so would be an injustice. The Shoshone and Ute did not arise in the last few centuries but are descendants of a diverse language community in the preceding millennia.

Like the history of the Fremont and Dene peoples, Shoshone and Ute history can be known more comprehensively than that of most settlers of the Archaic, let alone the history of the explorers and pioneers of remote antiquity. The ancient Shoshone and Ute can also be known in terms of their language history, with the usual caveats. First, language history and people/tribe are distinct things. Second, language, culture, and ethnicity are not bounded things, but reflect ongoing processes of change. We can explore the descendants of those who lived before to discover the role of the Shoshone and Ute over the millennia.

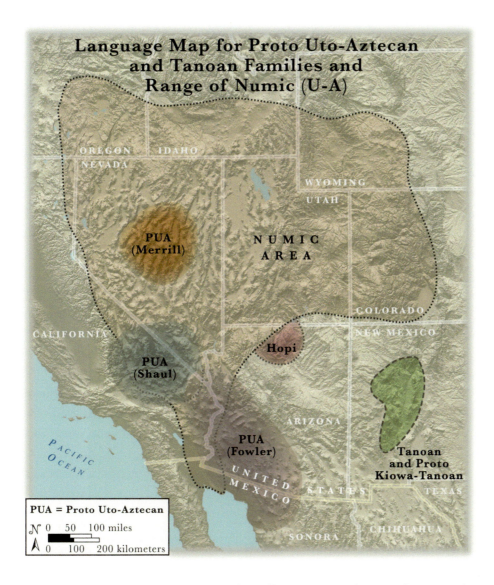

10.1 Historic locations of the Uto-Aztecan and Kiowa/Tanoan language families and the locations of speakers of their hypothesized ancient proto-languages prior to diversification. The historic location of Hopi (a Uto-Aztecan language) is shown, as is the historic period distribution of Numic languages (a branch of Uto-Aztecan). Linguists have proposed several possible homelands for Proto-Uto-Aztecan (PUA), including Catherine Fowler, William Merrill, and David Shaul (see note 10.2). Cartography by Chelsea McRaven Feeney.

The Shoshone, Goshute, and Ute tribes of history in northern Utah are members of the Numic subfamily of the Uto-Aztecan language family. The name "Numic" is derived from the cognate word for person or human: in Shoshone, *newe*, and in Ute, *nuche*. The Numic languages span the northern Colorado Plateau, the Great Basin, and southern Idaho, as well as the western half of Wyoming. They include the Central Numic languages of Shoshone, Panamint, Timbisha, and Comanche; the Southern Numic languages of Southern Paiute, Chemehuevi, and Kawaiisu; and the Western Numic languages of Northern Paiute and Mono. The Numic subfamily—along with Hopi, the Takic subfamily of southern California languages, and Tubatulabal of the southern Sierra Nevada—are all Northern Uto-Aztecan.

It is distinguished from the Southern Uto-Aztecan subfamilies and languages of peoples in Mexico who eventually became maize farmers. The language of the Aztecs, Nahuatl, is Southern Uto-Aztecan.

Linguists employ differences and similarities in speech among these subfamilies and languages to identify a common ancestor language—a conceptual Mother language. Proto-Uto-Aztecan consists of common terms that span the lexicon and over time diverged into new forms spoken in new places. For over 50 years linguists positioned Proto-Uto-Aztecan in western Arizona and northern Mexico. More recently, it has become evident that the Great Basin may be crucial to locating this common ancestor Mother language. This is because pinyon pine, a resource crucial to the economy of Great Basin foragers, did not inhabit the central and northern Great Basin until about 8,000 years ago in northeastern Nevada, after 6,000 years ago in central Nevada, and later in western Nevada. Pinyon pine occupies a thermal belt on the lower flanks of Great Basin mountains and was unable to spread north of southern Nevada during the Pleistocene ice ages. Reconstructions of Proto-Uto-Aztecan have been unable to find a biological term for pinyon pine or pine nuts, yet if the traditionally proposed homeland of this ancient common ancestor was Arizona and northern Mexico, where pinyon pine did live, a biological term should be expected. The same situation exists for the biological term for oak trees. Thus, the Proto-Uto-Aztecan speech community had to exist in the central Great Basin prior to the migration of pinyon from the south between 6,000 and 8,000 years ago.[2]

Geography and lifeway shape how language changes and how fast. Speech among people diverges as distance increases and frequency of interaction decreases. Yet among the foraging Settlers of the Archaic we found that territorial ranges can be enormous and evolve over the life history of individuals. This causes language to change more slowly and in small increments over geographic space.

We also found that kinship systems among foragers throw the net widely, gathering lineages together. Analysis of semantic shifts in Numic kinship terminology suggests the presence of regional marriage networks. Anthropologists suspect that bilateral cross-cousin marriage was common in the Great Basin, as it is among other low-density foragers in the deserts of the world. "Bilateral" means descent can be traced in male and female lines, and cross-cousin marriage ensures that males and females from different lineages will be brought together.[3]

This form of marriage and descent in the context of large foraging territories slows the rate of language change and blurs the boundaries among variations in speech across the landscape. Subtle differences in speech over large areas result in one not being able to understand as well the farther one travels from one's routine places. Instead of moving across a defined border where the language changes abruptly—

think crossing the border from France to Spain—the change is gradational. Linguists call this a dialect chain or dialect continuum and refer to the Numic languages in this way. It is best to think of the boundaries between speech communities as being a transitional space, a borderland, and this space must be measured in terms of 100 miles or more, which is very different from how we conceptualize borders as a line in the sand—sometimes even marked by an imposing wall.

Ancestral predecessors of the Numic languages may have diverged in the Great Basin 6,000 or more years ago. Thus, an ancestral speech community of the historically known Shoshone and Ute existed in the Great Basin during the time of the Archaic settlers. This early speech community would make many transformations before becoming the Numic languages recorded by linguists in the last century or so. Just as the Kiowa of the historic southern Plains can trace a language history from the upper Rio Grande of New Mexico, north through Utah and Wyoming, and back to the Southwest over nearly two millennia, the Numic languages similarly transformed and were spoken in different places. There is no homeland. The Biblical Model is not helpful.

Hopi language history is also important because it began to diverge from other ancestral Northern Uto-Aztecan languages about 3,000 years ago as the farming of maize, beans, and squash arrived in northern Arizona. The adoption of farming changed their world and laid the groundwork for the Western Basketmaker and Fremont peoples. Eastern Basketmaker immigrants, largely of a Kiowa-Tanoan language history, migrated north through eastern Utah and western Colorado, encountering either people of an unknown language history or ancient Uto-Aztecan speakers, whether they were ancestors of the Ute and Shoshone or ancestors of the Hopi. By AD 500 and after, these immigrants and Indigenes became Fremont farmers.[4]

To be sure, there are differences between the regional presence of ancestral Ute and Shoshone speech communities and the Fremont peoples'. In particular, differences in material culture included the ethnically sensitive markers of textiles, basketry, footwear, and rock imagery. Projectile points are tricky to use, but the most common arrow point used by Fremont peoples is called a Rosegate point, along with some regional varieties of arrow points. Yet Rosegate points were not exclusive to Fremont but common across the Great Salt Lake region among non-agricultural peoples. Another common arrow point is the Desert Side-notched. It spread from Mexico to Canada after about AD 1000 and was used by speakers of dozens of languages spanning the Uto-Aztecan, Dene, and Kiowa-Tanoan language families. While much can be done with projectile points to mark time, and they are incredibly common, it is best to stick with the good advice that stone points don't speak languages, and they don't define peoples. Stone points are technological styles and traditions that span cultural diversity rather than define it. We certainly saw that in the case of the Promontory Dene culture migrating from Canada to Utah and the Southwest in the time of upheaval to eventually become part of the mosaic of languages, identities, and ethnicities of the Puebloan world. Interaction involved both cooperation and conflict, not boundedness.

Given that the Fremont speech communities appear culturally distinct from the Numic speech communities, and given the larger populations generated by farming societies, the Numic presence was likely peripheral, but this does not mean isolated. The concept of borderlands implies interaction—the transport of foods and materials, recruitment of group membership through trading partners, friends, collaborators, marriage, childbearing, adoption, and capture. Ideology can also span borderlands through common understandings and perceptions of the spiritual world expressed in ritual and symbols.[5]

Ancestral Ute and Shoshone settlers of the Late Archaic occupied places where maize farming was difficult or impossible, such as eastern Nevada, far western Utah, southern Idaho, and western Wyoming. Interaction is evident in the use of pottery by Great Basin foragers by AD 1000 in places where sufficient settlement stability or redundancy in the use of places made pottery useful. Foragers near Elko, Nevada, made Fremont pottery using local materials and also imported a small number of vessels directly from central Utah. Foragers in the high, cold, and dry Grass Valley of central Nevada made pottery with Fremont characteristics. Fremont-style pottery, imported or locally made, is found at dozens of sites in western Wyoming, especially in the Wyoming Basin. These instances speak to the life history movement of women who spread the technological heritage of pottery making among forager groups of likely diverse ethnicities and language histories.[6]

An even deeper ancestral presence of foragers is evident in coiled basketry. The style of coiled basket found among Numic speakers of recent history was also made at places such as Dirty Shame Rockshelter in southeastern Oregon between 510 and 235 BC. The continuity between historic and ancestral Numic may be a thousand years earlier than the interaction evident in pottery that is apparent by AD 1000. These same basketry traditions that link to the historic period are also found in northern and central Nevada and southern Idaho.[7]

Southern Idaho and Wyoming also exhibit continuity. The Wahmuza site overlooking the Fort Hall Bottoms on the Snake River north of Pocatello began to be used 3,500 years ago and exhibits continuity in material culture all the way to the historic period, when it was a Northern Shoshone village. Other sites in southeastern Idaho suggest the same. Continuity is also seen in the use of obsidian in southeastern Idaho, the Wyoming Basin, and north to the Yellowstone Plateau extending

10.2 The Dinwoody rock image tradition of the Wind River and Bighorn Basins of Wyoming features elaborate interior line anthropomorphic and zoomorphic images possibly associated with visions and shamanic experience. The tradition began at least 3,000 years ago and continued during the Shoshonean historic period, indicating continuity in symbolism and practice. Photo by François Gohier.

as far back as 5,000 years. Of course, something like toolstone, which was used by everyone, could be used by people of diverse language histories. To imply that continuity means the Shoshone and Ute, the Numic languages, have been in the region for 3,500 or even 5,000 years would be an oversimplification. Such an assertion unnecessarily freezes the living Shoshone and Ute in time as passively changeless rather than active agents. The ancestors must be included in the understanding, not just the descendants. Nor does such a conceptualization mesh with the deep Uto-Aztecan language history.

Southeastern Idaho exemplifies the concept of a borderlands used by ancestral Shoshonean foragers and Great Salt Lake Fremont peoples, the latter traveling on bison hunts, logistic forays, or living the foraging life on the fringes of the farming world. A range of plain utilitarian pottery found in Idaho was made by Fremont, Shoshone, and Ute peoples.

The Dinwoody rock imagery tradition of Wyoming has clear Great Basin affiliations yet was practiced continuously for the last 2,000 years. That Dinwoody rock imagery also shows Great Plains affiliations exemplifies the dynamic ethnic and linguistic mosaic that was ancient Native America.

Southwest Wyoming experienced population growth and economic intensification during Fremont times, including substantial housing, earth ovens for roasting edible roots, storage, and the exploitation of virtually all food resources. James Creek Shelter west of Elko, Nevada, experienced a growth spurt during Fremont times between AD 700 and 1200. Rosegate arrow points, the kind typical among Fremont peoples but used by many others across the West, were present as the shelter became increasingly residential, not just a foraging stopover. The foragers of the Great Basin and Intermountain West were caught up in the same economic intensification and consequent population growth as the Fremont and Ancestral Puebloan farmers.[8]

The divergence of the Numic languages cannot be conceptualized as a single historical event or a single population replacement. These are processes. Language change is inexorable, shaped by migration of individuals and groups. As we found with the Dene migrations, ethnicity and identity can persist as migration and interaction among people shape language change. The story of the Numic languages and the Shoshone and Ute languages of the Great Salt Lake region is one of continuity. What began with the settlers of the Late Archaic proceeded as an ebb and flow, with periods of growth and decline, and interaction with people of diverse language histories. The transformations were driven by circumstances such as the severe drought from 2700 to 2300 BC, when groups dispersed from the driest portions of the Great Basin. Populations rebounded during a wetter period from 150 BC to AD 100, the same time Basketmaker immigrants were bringing maize north of the Colorado River. Another favorable period for ancestral Shoshone and Ute Great Basin foragers was AD 250 to 500, times that were also good for the Basketmaker/Fremont farmers in Utah. The Numic foragers of Nevada, Idaho, and Wyoming faced the same ups and downs as the Fremont farmers.

A testimony to the degree of long-term continuity, even in the face of language change and ethnogenesis, is found in the symbolic world. We learned previously about Native American maps embodied in ritualized stories anchored to places. The stories are libraries that have been passed down through generations. The repetition maintains the power of places and invites commemoration. In Numic speech communities, power—*puha* to Shoshones, and *puwavi* to Utes—is a fundamental concept recognized by all. Power can be found in any natural object, including plants and animals, topographic features, water, thunder, clouds, wind, and even stones. Power enables any of these things to become human because the earth is a living being. Power is not pervasive, nor random, but unevenly distributed. It must be nurtured through ritual, commemoration, and responsibility lest it become diminished or even lost. Of course, we know these things from the ethnographic and historic records of the Shoshone and Ute peoples, and from comparisons made by anthropologists with other cultures around the world.[9] To step into the ancient past, we must appeal to archaeology.

While rock imagery is the most evident avenue into the ideological, there is another body of material culture that is far more abundant than is commonly known: incised stones. Often unceremoniously referred to as portable rock art, incised stones have been fashioned since the time of the explorers and pioneers, 13,000 years ago. Thousands of incised stones are known from the Great Basin and Intermountain region, and their distribution forms an uncanny alignment with the range of Numic speakers not only in historic times, but the ancient times of Uto-Aztecan speakers across Nevada, the west deserts of Utah, southern Idaho, and western Wyoming. In yet another example of learning from the voices of Indigenous peoples, incised stones are given life because we now know they are associated with ritual, commemoration, and responsibility. They are associated with prayers, hence the more appropriate term "prayerstones." Understanding this phenomenon offers a window into continuity and transformation over millennia.[10]

Prayerstones occur in geographic concentrations, perhaps associated with persistent sacred landscapes. There is geographic variation in style, but unity over a vast span of terrain from the Sierra Nevada of California arcing northeastward across Nevada, northern Utah, southern Idaho, and all the way to the Bighorn Mountains of Wyoming. Motifs include curvilinear engravings, arrangements of linear incisions, and geometrics. In some areas a stone may have been preshaped to create a three-dimensional effect. There is also specific symbolism, especially in the Great Salt Lake area, such as the weeping eye motif and anthropomorphs with various shirts, skirts, and jewelry.

Prayerstone designs often parallel those in the most common rock imagery of the Great Basin, the rectilinear and curvilinear abstract styles known as the Basin and Range Tradition. These can be circles (sometimes connected or concentric), wandering lines and rectilinear motifs of dots, geometrics, grids, and hatching. Prayerstones later in time may correlate with the Great Basin Scratched Style, which was made between 1,000 and 3,000 years ago. The extensive geographic range of these styles attests to the scale of the social and ideological networks involving communities of shared beliefs regardless of ethnic identity or language across the dialect chain.

Some of the earliest prayerstones in the Great Salt Lake area are from Danger, Hogup, and Camels Back Caves. The oldest one dates to nearly 7,000 years ago, but most are younger than 6,000 years, through the history of the Numic speech community. Prayerstones continued to be used, and in 1880, 19 prayerstones were emplaced in a wickiup as part of a healing ritual in Grass Valley, central Nevada. Their use continues in the present.[11]

Prayerstones are not randomly distributed, and the concept of ritual emplacement is important to understanding their use. Prayerstones are often found in caves, most strikingly along the back walls, sometimes in groups and sometimes with other objects. But isolated prayerstones—single stones or clusters in discrete places—have

10.3a–d Prayerstones of the Great Basin Incised Style from around Great Salt Lake. The black stone is from the Vernon area and features the weeping eye motif. The two tan/brown stones exhibit common themes of hatching and horizontal lines juxtaposed against vertical lines. The five light gray to white stones are from a private collection and exhibit the unfortunate practice of someone recently coloring the incisions to make the designs more visible. Photos by Diana Call and Laura Patterson. Courtesy of Diana Call and Mark Stuart.

d

often been found as well. Avocational archaeologists know that if a prayerstone is found, others are likely to be in the area. In the Great Salt Lake Desert prayerstones are known from Promontory Cave, Hogup Mountain, the Lakeside Mountains, Grassy Mountain, Adobe Rock, Vernon, the Old River Bed Delta, and Connor Springs–Blue Creek.[12] Many are found on campsites where a variety of activities took place. They were left inside houses, alongside trails, near springs, near rock imagery, and around or in dramatic topographic features where they might be placed on a ledge or in a crack. Indeed, hundreds of prayerstones from the Great Salt Lake region are known to be in private collections, making them far more common than in any other place in the Fremont world.

Not all places have prayerstones, and the concept of emplacement is exemplified at the Graptolite Summit in the Toquima Range of central Nevada. Graptolites are fossils of 400-million-year-old plankton colonies embedded in limestones and shales. The Graptolite Summit is an iconic place for geologists and fossil hunters. The ground is littered with untold numbers of graptolite fossils, which are shiny in contrast to the limestone in which they are embedded. The fossils take on many patterns that look like pencil etchings, feathers, and geometrics. Among the millions of pieces of limestone are prayerstones. They are of simple design, often attempts to mimic the fossils that are so common. The individual stones are unprepared except

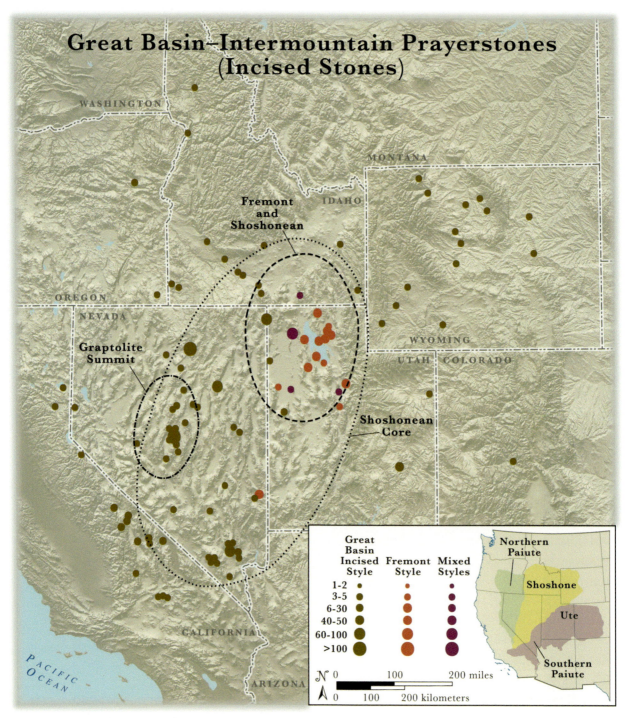

10.4 Distribution and style areas of prayerstones spanning a cultural landscape from Nevada to Wyoming. Based on Thomas 2019. Cartography by Chelsea McRaven Feeney. Courtesy of David Hurst Thomas, American Museum of Natural History, New York.

for incisions and fine crushing with a sharp tool. Their manner of fabrication itself seems ritualized.

Over 600 prayerstones are known from a 1,500 square mile area that includes the Toquima Range, the Monitor Range, and the Simpson Park Mountains—one-fifth of the prayerstones known from Nevada.

Graptolite Summit is a sacred landscape, as are the Melon Gravel left by the Bonneville Flood in the Snake River canyon; the Connor Springs rock imagery north of Great Salt Lake; the McConkie Ranch rock imagery near Vernal; and Castle Gardens in the Wind River basin of central Wyoming. All are places of power. Excavations at the nearby Gatecliff Shelter recovered over 400 prayerstones created over the last 5,500 years. Ninety-six of them were emplaced as a group near a hearth at the rear of Gatecliff Shelter over 3,500 years ago. It is not known if they were emplaced all at once, but the practice of commemoration suggests repeated visits to the cave over years, decades, or a human life. Prayerstones are part of the world of power, the stories, and sense of place. Shoshone and Southern Paiute elders describe them as offerings, as spiritual favors, emplaced to show respect and to give thanks. The practice of making offerings is part of the nurturing of power through ritual and respect. Prayerstones continued to be placed in the upper strata of Gatecliff Shelter after AD 1400, connecting it to the time of the historic period Shoshone in central Nevada.[13]

Prayerstones are so common in the Great Salt Lake region that decades ago archaeologists saw them as a key distinction of the Great Salt Lake Fremont peoples.[14] They exhibit Fremont rock imagery motifs such as decorated anthropomorphs with necklaces, weeping eyes, and feather-fringed staffs, but also geometrical designs reminiscent of Great Basin foragers. Prayerstones may be a form of expression preferred in the Great Salt Lake region given that the geology of the Wasatch Front does not accommodate rock imagery, unlike the sandstones so common across much of Fremont country.

That Great Salt Lake prayerstones employ a mix of motifs suggesting use by Fremont, Promontory Dene, Shoshone, and Ute peoples given the apparent cultural and linguistic diversity in the region where Utah, Nevada, Idaho, and Wyoming meet. Diversity within the Great Salt Lake region is also driven by the stark difference between the fertile, watered, climatically milder Wasatch Front and the high, cold, dry sage steppe; the salt flats; and the pinyon juniper–clothed mountains to the west.

Prayerstones are found less frequently on the Colorado Plateau than Fremont figurines modeled of clay and a more overt expression of rock imagery. The

10.5 This bifacial scraper, called a *chi-tho*, is an ethnographic example from the Northwest Territories, Canada, and dates to the 1930s. It was made and used by Madelaine Dryneck, a Tlicho Dene. This image shows the wrapping, which could be made of cloth or hide, that served to protect the hand during use. Hundreds of these are known from the Wasatch Front, especially Utah Valley. Courtesy of Prince of Wales Northern Heritage Centre, Northwest Territories, Canada.

connections to ancient Shoshonean ideology seem more apparent around Great Salt Lake than on the Colorado Plateau, where the Indigenous roots of Fremont peoples do not seem to be Numic as we know them in historic times. But then, the Indigenous roots of the Fremont are diverse. The rock imagery of the Archaic foragers on the Colorado Plateau that precedes that of the Fremont seems to contrast with the Great Basin styles by exhibiting layers of graphics and anthropomorphs with short horizontal arms and interior decoration. Some see the Indigenous Archaic foragers of southeastern Utah as related to the ancestral Hopi before the adoption of farming. Some note the similarity of pre-Fremont Archaic rock imagery in eastern Utah with the interior line style of Wyoming, suggesting deep Archaic roots between the Colorado Plateau and the northern Rockies and far western Plains. This connection carries forth, as we found with the Kiowa-Tanoan history linking the areas during Fremont times, and a similar set of connections between Ute rock imagery on the Plains and in eastern Utah after Fremont times.[15]

The diversity harbored in the Great Salt Lake region increased in the thirteenth century as farming became less common. Over the next two centuries Fremont people who gave up on farming not only migrated north but also south, joining speech communities potentially as diverse as Kiowa-Tanoan, Hopi, and the linguistic isolate of Keresan known since the times of Chaco. Those who stayed on became part of the world of ancestral Numic foragers who had been in Nevada, Oregon, Idaho, and Wyoming for thousands of years.

We also must allow for the continuance of some farming through it all. Fremont and Numic peoples had shared a pottery tradition since AD 1000, so the knowledge of farming was old and widespread, even if the places and times to pursue it became less favorable after AD 1300. Thinking about *the* Fremont as a bounded unit obscures the human tenacity and cultural resilience leading to a persistence of farming in some places all the way to historic times.

Add to all this the Promontory Dene migrants who passed through to the Southwest to become part of the Puebloan world. The archaeology of the Great Salt Lake region shows that the Promontory culture persisted and would ultimately become part of a Numic world by AD 1600. A distinctive Dene tool, the *chi-tho*, is a D-shaped bifacial scraper used on hides of large animals such as bison. Although it was found at the Promontory Caves, the *chi-tho* is common in collections from Utah Valley, where it symbolizes those Promontory people who persisted and maintained their identity in Numic Utah.

As farming became less frequent, life along the Wasatch Front from AD 1300 to 1600 became focused on the streams and wetlands. Promontory villages occupied the lower reaches of every stream that flows into Utah Lake and Great Salt Lake. This is best documented in Utah Valley by excavations at the Goshen Island South, Heron Springs, Sandy Beach, Little Dry, and Spanish Spit sites, as well as other less studied sites known only by their site numbers.[16] East of Great Salt Lake are the Injun Creek, Orbit Inn, and Salt Lake Airport sites, occupied between AD 1300 and 1550. All yielded abundant food refuse, small tule structures or wind breaks, food storage pits, varying amounts of pottery, and debris from the constant manufacture of stone tools. The higher elevations in the Wasatch, the Oquirrhs, and the Wasatch Back were surely used, but the locations of sites remain largely unknown.

The location of villages and temporary camps followed the opportunities. The spring spawn of suckers. The mass collection and processing of roots and seeds from summer to fall. The summer molt of geese when they were somewhat flightless and could be driven and clubbed. The near continuous hunting of all manner of small mammals such as muskrat and rabbits.

Technology included rafts made of cattail to transport foragers deep into the marshes. The rafts could hold people or simply be used as barges to carry both the take, such as eggs harvested from shorebird nests or the ducks pulled under water by submerged hunters using hollow bone snorkels. The rafts carried gear such as harpoons, nets with stone sinkers, duck decoys, bows, and plenty of arrows because many would be lost among the tules. The pattern of settlement and the foraging life during the centuries from AD 1300 to 1600 is strikingly like what was seen by the Spanish Domínguez-Escalante Expedition when they encountered the Ute people near present-day Spanish Fork in AD 1776.

The period between the Promontory Dene occupation and the arrival of the Spanish explorers spans nearly nine generations. There seems to have been a change after AD 1600. Rather than marking the arrival of Numic speakers, this change likely marks a new chapter in a long Numic history. The same arrow points that had been used for centuries persist, but there are variations that may reflect a diversity of peoples. The Fox site, a major fishing spot for suckers on the Jordan River in Utah Valley, dates to AD 1650 and may mark this transformation. The arrowheads found there are of the same type, the Desert Side-notched, used widely around Great

10.6 A common tool at sites in Utah Valley after AD 1600 is the so-called Shoshone Knife. These have a long tradition in the region spanning the last 3,000 years.

Salt Lake and across the West. Yet the arrowheads at the Fox site are twice the weight as the same type of points from the previous Promontory period. They were either made for a task specific to the Fox site or reflect a diversity in heritage within groups of people associating for cooperation, conflict, or a vacillation between the two. The Fox site, like other Utah Lake sites, contained no pottery. Indeed, pottery seems to be less common after AD 1600, although there is so much pottery found on the surface and hence poorly dated that it is difficult to say if and when it ceased to be used. Practical things such as pottery tend to be used opportunistically rather than through blind cultural allegiance.

Also, a distinctive stone tool appeared, not only along the Wasatch Front, but in Idaho, Wyoming, and northern Nevada. This tool is known from the important Wahmuza site north of Pocatello, the place that marks an ancestral Shoshonean presence but continued to be used in the AD 1700s. These unique tools—which could be anything from harpoon tips to thrusting spears to knives and are commonly, and unfortunately, referred to as Shoshone Knives—are surprisingly common. The reason for the name is that in the few cases where these tools have been dated, they are late, with a range between AD 1250 and 1750. They are found at animal kill sites and campsites, and as isolated finds. This new form of tool indeed represents a heritage even though it cannot be traced to a point of origin. Rather than reflecting something linear, it indicates a landscape scale of interaction. We lose that understanding if we merely dub them Shoshone Knives, as if it is a nameplate to be worn on the chest.

Yet again, we find that history is not a simple sequence of discrete events. Immigration and ethnogenesis are obviously not that simple in the modern world. A desire for a simpler past, when we imagine people sticking to being their people, successfully unchanged and living within strict boundaries of identity and behavior, is an irresistible seduction—the Pristine Myth about Native Americans and the Biblical Model of humanity. Such delusions leave us with an unreasonable and probably untrue story of humanity and the past.

What we will find are changes after AD 1600 that would dramatically shape the last few centuries of Native America. The nine generations between AD 1600 and AD 1776 had to deal with the consequences of unforeseeable and unmanageable forces. It was indeed a time different from the one before.

Indigenes Meet Travelers

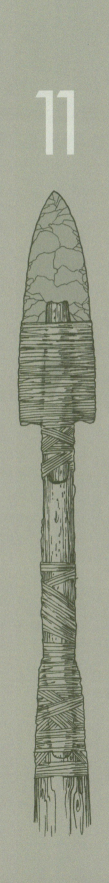

11

The Domínguez–Escalante Expedition of 10 travelers struck north out of Santa Fe, New Mexico, on July 29, 1776. Silvestre Vélez de Escalante was 26 years old, about 10 years younger than Francisco Atanasio Domínguez, who was the leader of the expedition. Both were Franciscan friars utterly devoted to the church, and the conversion of "the Indians" to Christianity. A third principal member of the expedition was Bernardo Miera y Pacheco, older than Domínguez and Escalante and a veteran of Southwestern and Mexican expeditions. Miera was the cartographer, and the map he produced is a remarkable rendition of the region. Along with Miera's map, the journal written by Escalante, but known to him and Domínguez as "our journal," ensured the legacy of the Domínguez–Escalante Expedition. Escalante had a reputation as a good writer, and his journal is a poetic representation of the landscapes, the Indigenous peoples, and the explorers' adventures.[1]

Their entourage was small by Spanish standards, reaching only a dozen early in the expedition and then varying in size as they acquired and lost Indigenous guides along the way. They were unaccompanied by heavily armed soldiers, wagons, and servants. There is little mention in the journal of the equipment and organization of the expedition. There must have been firearms and a small herd of cattle, and it is clear their larder was insufficient to endure the mountains and high cold deserts they encountered, especially departing midsummer. The stated goal of the expedition was to find a route linking Santa Fe with Monterey, California, although another clear interest was the discovery of sites suitable for future Spanish settlement.

Domínguez and Escalante were not the first to explore western Colorado. That feat goes to Juan María de Rivera. An experienced trader, his second venture north of Santa Fe in 1765 took him as far as Delta, Colorado, and the Gunnison River. Rivera carved his name into a rock face in Roubideau Canyon that is visible today,

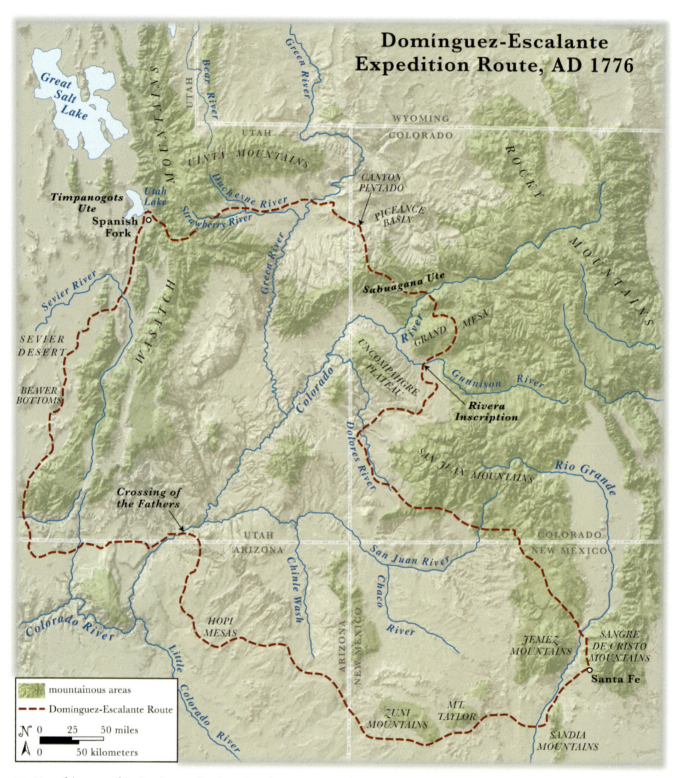

11.1 Map of the route of the Domínguez–Escalante Expedition in AD 1776 showing points of interest relevant to the route and discussed in the text. Cartography by Chelsea McRaven Feeney.

but his effort was nearly lost to history because he did not produce a substantial written record or a map.²

Our interest here in the Domínguez–Escalante Expedition centers on the guides and the routes taken through landscapes the expedition encountered. The journal includes many comments on the route, complaints about the difficulty and the lack of clear trails, and frequent frustration with the choices made by the guides. Two suspicions about the guides emerge: Some of them might be familiar with vast landscapes far from home, but their knowledge about specific routes seems vague or secondhand unless it is close to home. A third suspicion is that trails across landscapes used only seasonally and not located near villages can be faint to nonexistent. This seems especially pertinent to the uplands and rough country where trails seem to be routes through the wilderness rather than trodden pathways as present-day people might think of them.

Early in the journey two guides, who both accompanied the Rivera exploration a decade earlier, lead the way. They seem to know the route, but the specifics elude them, indicating it had been too long since they had seen the places, which is consistent with the notion that the trails were routes rather than well-worn pathways. In the journal, Escalante recounts the difficulty and the bushwhacking, frequently commenting about bad going. He complains about the guides' apparent lack of knowledge of the path. It is as if the Native guides knew *the map* that, as we learned, was conveyed through the stories passed down through generations, but they lacked the routine familiarity to know the details.

We found previously that the territories of foraging societies are large, and people could travel far—over the course of years, decades, and a human lifetime. But we mustn't think of them as commuters because frequent transit across such large landscapes is constrained by the temporal demands of foot travel except for the few living the trader lifestyle. Route-finding becomes improvised in the absence of frequent transit, and I have certainly learned this through years of solo hiking in places with no trails. Are we glimpsing notions of place? By focusing on the routes and the expedition's Native American guides, we can enliven the topics of long-distance connections, the tempo of mobility, and other things we have visited repeatedly in our excursion through ancient life in the Great Salt Lake region.

By the time the expedition reached the Gunnison River near Delta, Colorado, they hoped to find a new guide, yet up to this point they had encountered few Native Americans. This was about to change because by AD 1776, the equestrian Utes had a significant presence in northwestern Colorado, as did the Shoshones, known to the Spaniards as Comanches. Somewhere along the Gunnison River, the group encountered a Ute named Red Bear, immediately changed his name to Silvestre,

11.2 Fremont style shields and figures at Canyon Pintado, Colorado. The imagery is typical of northeastern Utah, northwestern Colorado, and western Wyoming, likely along natural travel routes. Photo by François Gohier.

and were led to a large encampment of Utes high on Grand Mesa, southeast of Grand Junction. Silvestre turned out not to be of the local band of Utes, known to the Spaniards as the Sabuagana (also known as the Uncompahgre). Remarkably, Silvestre was Timpanogots (also known as Timpanogos), a Laguna (Lake) Ute. His ties were to the Utes of Utah Lake, who seasonally ranged between Utah Valley, the area of the Strawberry River, and east along the Duchesne River. Escalante also refers in the journal to half a dozen other Lagunas in the Sabuagana Ute camp. One of them, a boy whom the Spaniards named Joaquin, accompanied the expedition not only to Utah Lake, but through the entirety of the journey back to Santa Fe.

Silvestre guided the expedition across the Colorado River near De Beque, Colorado, then up Roan and Carr Creeks toward Douglas Creek and across the Piceance Basin. As noted in the journal, they passed by the spectacular rock imagery at Canyon Pintado, which speaks to eastern Fremont and Wyoming affiliations. The region also has Fremont residential sites that persisted to AD 1550, long after the presumed demise of Fremont.³ The expedition continued west and crossed the Green River at a natural ford a few miles north of the modern town of Jensen, Utah. Silvestre seemed a willing guide, and surely more capable than the Spaniards, but the path along the Duchesne and Strawberry Rivers brought frustration.

Escalante complained about the bad choice of routes, too many river crossings, impassable terrain, injured horses, and being taken through impenetrable stands of willows, chokecherry, and scrub oak. In turn, Silvestre seemed frustrated with the Spaniards' slow pace, even though the pack animals were loaded with gear and supplies. He would sometimes get ahead of the group. One might think that there would be recognizable trails, and even though the Utes of Utah Valley did not have horses in 1776, Silvestre had lived among Colorado Utes who did. Thus, he should have been familiar with the differences between foot and horse travel. In the journal, Escalante remarks that the route often lacked any apparent trail.

Silvestre guided the small expedition upward into the high sage barrens now inundated by Strawberry Reservoir. By then it was mid-September, when freezing nights are common at Strawberry. Silvestre did not take the group northwest along a natural route up Strawberry Creek toward Daniels Pass and the short descent to Heber, the Provo River, and Utah Valley. Instead, he took the party down Diamond Fork to the Spanish Fork River and Utah Valley. Silvestre may have made this choice after seeing smoke and suspecting the fires came from members of his own band out hunting. It may also be that Silvestre was from the southern end of Utah Lake, and this caused him to seek the area of Spanish Fork. Indeed, Silvestre seems to have become more certain of himself and the route after passing the Strawberry area.

Domínguez and Escalante's journal makes it clear Silvestre was a good guide. He knew the stories and the map. The travel of individuals across landscapes spanning over 300 walking miles from Grand Mesa, Colorado, to Utah Lake must be seen as episodes on the scale of life history. Silvestre likely did not routinely walk from Utah Lake to Vernal and beyond, but over the course of years, he and others did just that—at least once. Some of the people knew the way on larger scales, but the scale at which they knew every step of the way was much smaller. The Indigenous experience was at once geographically expansive, reflecting the cumulative experiences of travelers over human generations, and also local.

Domínguez and Escalante's account of life at Utah Lake is a centerpiece of the journal. They marveled at how populous the area was yet reported no numbers. They observed Timpanogots villages all around the lake, and especially on the delta of the Provo River, the same area where archaeologists discovered habitations dating to Fremont and Promontory times. Miera plotted the location of numerous villages on his map, although it is not known how many people lived in each or which ones were in active use. The economy focused on fish and the abundance of the wetlands. Indeed, the food-named group of the Utah Lake Ute was Fish Eaters according to the equestrian Utes of western Colorado.[4] A parallel exists with the well-documented lakes of the western Great Basin, the Northern Paiutes at Pyramid Lake, and the Shoshones and Paiutes at Walker Lake, Nevada. There people lived in sizable villages and had multiple levels of leadership, yet there was fluidity in band membership and residence.

In the journal, Escalante refers to many Timpanogots chiefs at Utah Lake and a degree of hierarchy in the influence of some over others. He also mentions "wattle huts of willow," typical of Native American villages in wetlands across the Great Basin. While all spoke the Yuta language, Escalante heard noticeable variations in speech and in the pronunciation of individual words. This speaks to diversity in the language histories of people living together—something our story finds repeatedly in the long Indigenous history. Escalante also remarked that many of the men were fully bearded. In fact, the practice of growing beards or not varies widely among Native Americans across the continent, but the comment again signals diversity.

Escalante used the term "pueblo" to refer to the Utah Lake villages, but those villages were nothing like the stone and adobe pueblos of New Mexico. It is telling that he also referred to a long-abandoned Fremont ruin east of Myton in the Uinta Basin as a pueblo. He observed that it was round, thus different from the pueblos of the Southwest he knew, and he noticed that it had decayed into a low mound. This is typical of abandoned Fremont sites. Escalante simply used the Spanish word for "town" to refer to all occupations. It is thus significant that he compared Utah Valley to the many pueblos near Santa Fe. The term "pueblo" is a misstatement, but it signals how Utah Valley struck him as a place with a substantial human presence akin to the Southwest. Escalante also extolled the potential of Utah Valley to support future Spanish settlements. He and Domínguez were clearly more impressed with this place than any other they encountered on the expedition.[5]

The Utah Lake Utes did not have horses, and this speaks to lifeway diversity among the Ute speech community. The people obviously traveled among diverse groups and adjusted to the dialect chains that brought less intelligibility with increasing distance. In the journal Escalante implies that relationships of the Utah Lake Utes with their equestrian neighbors, both Utes and Shoshones, were based on accommodation and avoidance more than outright conflict. Apparently, the Utah Lake Utes withdrew from the Strawberry and Duchesne Rivers not long before the arrival of the Spaniards because of fear of attack by the horse-mounted Colorado Utes. The Laguna Utes at Utah Lake also had concerns about horse-mounted Shoshones along the northern Wasatch Front, but it seems contact was infrequent.

One can only wonder if the asymmetry in power between groups with and without horses was a circumstance that caused less interaction.

Firearms are another potential source of asymmetry in power. No mention is made of Natives in possession of firearms, neither equestrians nor those at Utah Lake. But then neither does Escalante mention firearms possessed by the Spaniards, even though one must assume they had them given the two bison killed before arriving at Utah Lake and the horses they killed to survive starvation on the return to Santa Fe.

Their stay at Utah Lake lasted only four days before the party continued south along the route of Interstate 15 through Nephi and Scipio. Their guide Silvestre remained behind in Utah Valley, while the boy Joaquin was joined by José María, a Laguna who guided the party south toward Delta, Utah. The matter of finding water and pasturage for the horses became critical as the expedition navigated the saline wetlands of the Sevier Desert. They were northwest of Pahvant Butte when they noted shells, implying the Sevier Desert had seen wetter times. It had seen just that many times since the end of Lake Bonneville.

After leaving Utah Valley, the party encountered camp after camp of Native Americans, at some point traversing the dialect continuum between Ute and Southern Paiute. Little mention is made of it, but by the time they reached Black Rock, overlooking the Beaver Bottoms north of Milford, their Laguna guide José María had left the party without notice. At that point he was far from his country, and Escalante observed that after José María's departure, the party had no one who knew the country ahead even from hearsay. They had no one who knew the stories.

Domínguez and Escalante seemed to realize there was no practicable route west toward Monterey. The Utes they encountered in Utah Valley and along the Sevier River seemed aware that fewer people lived to the west. We have seen this contrast before between the Wasatch Front and the western deserts of Utah and Nevada. This dichotomy may also mark a language transition, as suggested for Fremont times. Even after the demise of Fremont agriculture, a certain void seemed to persist between the well-watered Wasatch Front and the rugged, often waterless mountains of Utah's western deserts.

As for the Domínguez–Escalante Expedition, a route west across Nevada at this latitude would have been treacherous and largely waterless, and success would only bring the party to the massif of the Sierra Nevada. To reach Monterey from the latitude of Delta and Milford was an impossible quest.

The expedition continued south toward Cedar City, encountering small groups of Southern Paiutes along the way. When they reached Toquerville, the party encountered Southern Paiute maize farmers. These farmers of the St. George Basin

11.3 *A Timpanogots Village*, by Eric S. Carlson. This depiction shows a village on the Provo River delta with Mount Timpanogos in the background. The village is on a natural levee along one of the many stringers of the lower Provo River. It was spring, but the mountains were still laden with snow. The *cumu-paku* (suckers) were spawning. Taken in nets as shown here, or with weirs, traps, and by hand, the fish were filleted and hung on racks to dry. Other *paku* were also taken, including *saa-paku* (whitefish) and several varieties of *ata-paku* (trout). Tule

rafts facilitated foraging in the wetlands for muskrat, duck eggs, and such. Villages could consist of a dozen or more houses made of reed mats fastened to a willow frame. The plaza among the homes was a place of communal activity for processing fish, drying roots, and preparing skins, just to name a few activities. Utah Valley and the rest of the Wasatch Front were populous for many centuries, and the Spaniards compared it to the numerous Puebloan peoples around Santa Fe, New Mexico. Courtesy of Eric S. Carlson.

were an isolate in a sea of Southern Paiute foragers in the deserts and the surrounding high plateaus of southwestern Utah and northern Arizona. Southern Paiute farming is a topic we will return to.

Once past the Virgin River, the Ute guides had increasing difficulty communicating with the Southern Paiutes—the dialect chain was straining. From the area of Hurricane, Utah, east along the Vermilion Cliffs, across the Colorado River at the Crossing of the Fathers (now under the waters of Lake Powell), and on into Arizona, the party repeatedly encountered small groups of Southern Paiutes. Most were reluctant to engage, even fleeing the strangers. The timidity of Natives along this stretch of the route contrasts with what the Spaniards had encountered on the trip up to this point. The atmosphere of tension caused Escalante to comment that the Southern Paiutes were afraid of and enemies of the "Moquis," whom he associated with the Navajo/Apache, although the term "Moqui" can also refer to the Hopi during the early historic period. Throughout our journey into the deep past, we have talked of interaction among groups of contrasting peoples and languages, with the reminder that peace and conflict are two sides of the same coin. Both inevitably forge consequences in behavior, culture, and language.

The Domínguez–Escalante Expedition epitomizes a long-held myth in the making of America—the myth that efforts like theirs marked discovery of or first contact with Native American peoples. The expedition did indeed explore the northern Colorado Plateau and eastern Great Basin, documenting the experience with a wonderful map and a rich journal. But by then over two centuries of contact had already changed Native American cultures and lifeways. Contact is not an event. Pristine is not a state of being. The Great Salt Lake region was not immune. Indeed, the large populations along the Wasatch Front during Fremont and Promontory times through AD 1600 signify an America that was far from a wilderness populated by a few scattered and inconsequential "savages." It may have seemed like wilderness to the Spaniards—as it did to the English on the Atlantic coast and the French in eastern parts of what is now Canada—but that unfortunate albeit romantic myth remains alive today. On the contrary, America was a Human Wilderness and had been for many millennia. By the time Domínguez and Escalante arrived, Indigenous peoples' lives had been altered by multiple forces: European diseases of density, the domesticated horse, and trading relationships involving everything from furs and hides to guns and human trafficking. All these things altered the behavior of Indigenous peoples, displaced people into new territories, and shaped the processes of identity and ethnogenesis. These changes typically rippled through Native American societies and populations long before face-to-face contact with Europeans and later Euro-Americans. The process of Indigenes-meet-travelers occurred on different scales of time and space. The process was not linear, and it was not monolithic.

The largest-scale effect of European exploration and colonization of the Americas was depopulation caused by diseases such as smallpox, measles, malaria, influenza, and scarlet fever. Urbanization in Eurasia was early and pervasive relative to the Americas, and co-evolved with large numbers of domesticated animals such as pigs, cattle, sheep, and goats. These were absent in the Americas, and urbanization was late and restricted to portions of South America and Mesoamerica. Populations in the Eastern Hemisphere developed resistance to diseases of density and animal domestication, and the susceptibility of Native Americans to those diseases testifies to the long isolation of the two hemispheres. If people traveled between them millennia ago, they were few and were either culturally absorbed, killed, or died from the struggle to survive.

The death toll among Native American populations from Eurasian diseases is difficult to muster, but as many as 100 million Native Americans may have died in the first 150 years after the Columbian date of AD 1492. The high end of this estimate may be overreach but would amount to a 95 percent depopulation. Even if the true number is only 50 percent or 70 percent, it deserves the monikers of The Great Dying or American Indian Holocaust.[6] On a macroscale, the impacts of this debacle were planetary, with some recent studies suggesting that the removal of so many people from an entire hemisphere caused significant reforestation of lands cleared by Indigenous management, a consequent increase in carbon sequestration, a decrease in atmospheric carbon dioxide, and a decline in temperature that contributed to the coldest part of the Little Ice Age.[7] Consequences on such a scale are largely attributable to the huge Native American populations in Mesoamerica, the Andes, the lowlands of South America, and to a lesser degree the Mississippi and associated river valleys of what is now the United States.

Closer examination reveals that the effects of European disease were not uniform in terms of timing or across space. In the West, the greatest impacts occurred after the mission systems were built—during the late AD 1700s in California and in the AD 1600s in the Southwest, despite Spanish explorations in both regions in the mid–AD 1500s. The Mississippi River valley and the Columbia Plateau of Washington experienced depopulation in the AD 1500s and 1600s. Some areas in the eastern United States, Canada, and California experienced depopulation, but other places all over the country did not, or remain poorly understood. Although European diseases took a terrible toll, the mosaic of Indigenous languages and cultures of the Americas ensured resilience and persistence. Holocaust it was on a macroscale, but Native American cultures survived and, in many cases, rebounded.

The history of introduced European diseases in the Southwest is relevant to the Great Salt Lake region, especially the populous Wasatch Front. We found the Promontory period left a strong archaeological signature along the Wasatch Front after the decline of farming between AD 1300 and 1600. The Great Salt Lake flooded in the early AD 1600s, about the time Promontory occupation declined, and inundated wetlands and constrained their productivity. Then the lake likely declined for decades because the years between AD 1625 to 1725 saw three successive droughts with only brief wet periods in between. A compilation of hundreds of radiocarbon dates from the eastern Great Basin of Utah and Nevada conveys a proxy measure of human population activity. After the tremendous peak of activity in Fremont times, there was a clear decline in the AD 1300s. This was followed by a rebound between AD 1475 and 1600. Beginning about AD 1625, about the same time as depopulation caused by disease in the Southwest, there was a sharp decline in Utah. This bottomed out by AD 1700 and was followed by a rebound in activity that reached a peak by the time of the Domínguez–Escalante Expedition in AD 1776. Could the decline in the AD 1600s have resulted from European disease vectored Indigene to Indigene to the large populations of the Wasatch Front from either the Pacific coast or the Southwest? Or was the decline in population just due to successive droughts?[8]

Recent research in the Jemez region of the upper Rio Grande Valley near Santa Fe, New Mexico, shows a disease-driven population decline between AD 1620 and 1640. One consequence was reforestation between AD 1650 and 1700 that altered the wildland fire regime. The removal of Native American landscape management practices using fire created a regime of spreading surface fires that persisted into the late 1800s until cattle grazing and active fire suppression disrupted this colonial era pattern. Other areas of the Four Corners have not been as intensively studied as the Jemez, but the evidence suggests an increase in fire after AD 1620 in other areas as well. This is not to say that a single wave of disease in Southwestern Puebloan centers eliminated all the people. Smaller farmsteads and fieldhouses persisted and sustained demographic continuity between the prehispanic and colonial periods.

What the Jemez record shows, however, is there was no disease-driven demographic collapse from the time of Coronado in AD 1542. Rather, disease spread as the Spanish settlements and missions spread in the early 1600s, creating an interaction sphere that included various far-flung Indigenous communities. The cumulative effects were dramatic: the epidemic in AD 1630 eliminated half the population, with the population of the region dropping another 25 percent by 1650. By the time the diseases became endemic around AD 1680, the population of the Jemez region had dropped 87 percent.[9] This tragedy surely changed lives, associations, language, and culture, but Native American populations of the Jemez survive to this day.

Was the decline in Utah's population between AD 1625 and 1700 a result of interaction and disease between the Four Corners region of the Southwest and large populations on the Wasatch Front?[10] Where populations are dense, it only

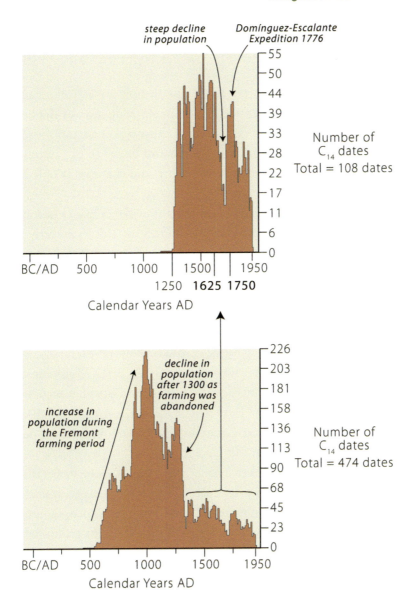

Eastern Great Basin Radiocarbon Dates After AD 500

11.4 Regional radiocarbon dates offer a proxy measure of human activity and population change. The chart on the bottom is a sample of 474 dates. It shows the growth of population during the Fremont farming period, followed by a decline after AD 1300 as farming was abandoned. The upper chart zooms in on the subsample of 108 dates that fall between AD 1250 and 1950. Note the steep decline in dates between AD 1625 and 1725. This anomaly could reflect depopulation from European-introduced diseases and matches a documented period of a 60 to 80 percent decline in Native American populations in the Rio Grande Valley of New Mexico from European diseases. There were also several droughts during this period, exacerbating the misery. Population levels recovered by the time of the Domínguez–Escalante Expedition in AD 1776. Chart by Chelsea McRaven Feeney, redrawn from Lindsay 2005.

takes one infected traveler. Disease vectors among people as they travel, and it is apparent that Indigenous people traveled everywhere across the West. If disease came to the Wasatch Front, it was not sustained as it was in the Jemez region because routine interactions with Europeans had not been established. While the possibility of disease on the Wasatch Front a century before face-to-face contact with the Domínguez–Escalante Expedition is intriguing, we really don't know if that was the case. The sharp decline in activity after the visit of Domínguez and Escalante also raises interest and provokes questions. But then, as usual, science is more about questions than answers.

Images of Indians riding horses and living in tipis are as American as apple pie—witness the endless popular portrayals. The introduction of the horse was a patchwork process that immediately affected those who had and those who did not have horses. Like the shift from the horse and buggy to the automobile, the process would change livelihoods, the economy, and the ways people interacted both cooperatively and through conflict.

The horse was likely introduced earlier than the evidence from historical sources indicates. Horses arrived in the Americas with the Spaniards in the early AD 1500s. The adoption of the horse would be expected to move rapidly in some settings, but more slowly in others. Historical evidence suggests that the Utes of northwestern Colorado had obtained horses by the time of the Pueblo Revolt in New Mexico in AD 1680. The Shoshone of the western Plains of Idaho and Wyoming were thought to have acquired the horse only 10 years later. However, recent archaeological evidence shows the horse was present by the early AD 1600s in several places in North America. At the Blacks Fork River site south of Green River, Wyoming, a foal was ritually cut with metal tools, intentionally buried, and possibly accompanied by three coyote burials by AD 1640. Horse remains from the American Falls Reservoir site on the Snake River Plain near Pocatello, Idaho, date to the same period. The horse spread early into the Great Salt Lake landscape.[11]

The impact of the horse on Native American cultures of the Plains is well documented. For migratory groups, horses enabled larger cargo capacity, leading to the large tipis known in the historic period. Earlier Indigenous peoples used dogs to transport smaller tipis where such transport was feasible. For groups who moved among semipermanent villages, the horse was not necessarily a useful thing given that horses do come with costs. The same is true for dispersed populations in arid regions. Even among groups that adopted the horse, not everyone had one, and many continued to travel by foot. The horse changed the tactics of hunting bison and the cost structure of the economy, as cheap oil did for the modern auto industry. The earlier adoption of the horse in Wyoming and Idaho and its later adoption in the Great Basin could be related to the frequency of bison. The horse expanded mobility, enabled widespread alliances, and expanded trade networks and access to raw materials. Thus power could have become asymmetric between those with and without horses.

A mundane but telling line of archaeological evidence for the impact of the horse is found across the northern rim of the Great Basin. We found previously that the movement of obsidian for tools was extensive among the explorers and pioneers. As the settlers of the Archaic filled the landscape, those distances decreased, but after the introduction of the horse, the distance increased dramatically; obsidian from southeastern Oregon, southern Idaho, and northern Nevada was transported from sources 150 to over 200 miles away. These distances are not necessarily a function of out and back travel for obsidian but may instead reflect the expansion of raw material conveyance mechanisms and the increased cargo capacity the horse provided.

Thirty-four years before Domínguez and Escalante, the explorer Chevalier de la Verendrye observed the equestrian Northern Shoshone traveling from Idaho as far as North Dakota. The horse changed their culture fundamentally, and Verendrye stated, "They are friendly to no tribe. We are told that in AD 1741 they had entirely destroyed 17 villages, and killed all the old men and old women, and made slaves of the young women and had traded them to the seacoast for horses and merchandise."[12]

What then of the Utes of Utah Valley who figured so prominently in the Domínguez–Escalante Expedition? They still did not have horses in AD 1776, suggesting that they did not seek to adopt them. They seem to have been concerned with the horse-mounted Shoshones who lived to the north of them, but Escalante did not make a big deal out of this in the expedition journal. Was there something about their economy, such as the tether to the rich fishery of Utah Lake and the close abundance of other resources, that made the horse less compelling? Their movement among semipermanent villages around Utah Lake may have obviated the use of horses. Perhaps their villages and their numbers at Utah Lake were so great that they could resist incursions by horse-mounted neighbors? Regardless, equestrian societies of the same broad speech community were all around them, causing fundamental changes long before face-to-face contact between European peoples and the "pristine" Natives.

As mentioned earlier, when Domínguez and Escalante reached Toquerville and the Virgin River, they observed Southern Paiutes farming maize. This signaled they were nearing the Southwest, where maize farming had been central to the Indigenous economy for many centuries before the Spaniards arrived in AD 1542.

But the Southern Paiutes are Numic speakers, descendants of Great Basin foragers who ostensibly did not farm. The implication has long been that the Southern Paiutes "began" to farm or "discovered" it from the Hopi or even the Spaniards. Yet we found that pockets of Fremont people across their region hung on to farming into the AD 1500s if not longer. By then the Numic presence in the region was well established; Numic and Fremont peoples' interaction, as evidenced by arrowheads and pottery, had been going on for 500 or more years—at least 25 human generations.

Thus, Numic-speaking peoples had to know about farming, even if they were not Fremont. Rather than reestablishing farming in the St. George Basin, the Southern Paiute's farming is better described as persistence, just as it was for some Fremont peoples. The legacy of farming survived the Little Ice Age, just as it survived all the climate change since maize came north across the Colorado River nearly 2,000 years earlier. What a different story than the stereotype of ancient peoples as timeless, bounded, changeless, and enslaved by their culture.[13]

Denouement

Place is conditioned by landscape and conceptualized in terms of experience and circumstance. We take the notion of place for granted because our attachment to places seems natural and comforting. When people are taken from their familiar places through travel, voluntary or compelled, we recognize a feeling of dislocation. The anthropologist Keith Basso has observed that while social scientists view the concept of place variously—such as a beneficial component of personality or as a means of social integration—he sees it as "a species of involvement with the natural and social environment, a way of appropriating portions of the earth…the familiar province of everyday events."[1]

The fiction writer Annie Proulx also situates sense of place in tangible experience and landscapes. She employs nature as a stage for her gritty stories of everyday life. Her *Wyoming Stories* series, so appropriate to the expansive Great Salt Lake region, convey an almost deterministic power of landscape that can be life-giving, yet stark and even life-threatening.[2]

I am an archaeologist, so deep time has become a source of dislocation of place in my story. The story here transports readers to scales of time that transcend the lives of individuals. We cannot know it through empathy. Place is envisioned through the roles peoples and cultures play at different times and under varying circumstances. We encountered Indigenous peoples engaging place over hundreds of generations. The explorers, the pioneers, and the settlers engaged place differently as the millennia passed. The roles of place changed dramatically with the transition to farming, not just for farmers, but for foragers across the region. Place changed as immigrants arrived, whether they were Basketmakers from the Southwest or Dene from Canada and the Plains of Montana and Wyoming. Place changed as climate altered the way people made their living. Place changed during the centuries when populations grew, and again in the centuries when populations declined. Place changed when Europeans colonized the Atlantic coast, the Southwest, and the California coast centuries prior to face-to-face contact with the Indigenous peoples of the Great Salt Lake region.

The power of landscape is found in my emphasis on natural routes of travel. They exist on geological scales, yet the way they fit into sense of place depends on history and culture. This story is indeed historical, not prehistoric. We encountered the anthropologist Keith Basso learning a lesson from the Western Apache elder Nick Thompson: "White men need paper maps. We have maps in our minds."[3]

The story here resists the tendency toward categorical, binary thinking. There is a subtle ethnocentrism in what I refer to as the Biblical Model where cultures, if only for the sake of classification, become billiard balls rolling around on a table, staying true to their origins lest they risk a loss of authenticity. This amounts to chasing the will-o'-the-wisp of social order in a world of upheaval and change.[4]

Related to this is the challenge of the Pristine Myth. The cultural bias that Indigenous peoples were timeless, changeless children of Nature. The myth that America was sparsely populated. That Native Americans were too primitive and too few to have a role in shaping the places where they lived. Romantic, but inaccurate. In the words of the environmental historian Richard White, such thinking is "an act of immense condensation. For in a modern world defined by change, whites are portrayed as the only beings who make a difference."[5]

Notions of progress seep into writings about the past in popular and social media. Ancient peoples are simultaneously celebrated and minimized as they are presented as remarkable despite their antiquity and primitive technology. Perhaps this tendency arises from our disengagement from Nature. Even the most outdoorsy among us have no touchstone to hunter-gatherers, the ways of their societies, and their ways of making a living—survivalists on YouTube and pseudo-history on television notwithstanding.

These thoughts and positions invite a proposal to employ a lesson found in the passage "The past is a foreign country: they do things differently there."[6] Just as travel in the contemporary world requires us to step outside ourselves, an understanding of the past demands the same, whether this be the casual time traveler, scholars of history, descendants of peoples from deep time, or the scientists who create pasts through their studies.

Genealogy is employed here as a metaphor to engage time. Of course, genealogy on the scales of time considered in the story of the ancients quickly becomes mathematically overwhelming. All humanity has a common ancestor. Our genealogy traced from ancestors to descendants can remind us of our collective heritage and humanity regardless of how the living choose to construct identity.

Sense of place is central to understanding the cultural landscape spanning parts of Idaho, Wyoming, Nevada, and Utah, with Great Salt Lake at the geographic center. I invite you to explore the foreign countries encountered in deep time as you travel the inspiring landscapes north, east, west, and south of Great Salt Lake.

Notes

Preface

1. Annie Proulx is known for her Wyoming short stories that capture sense of place (*Close Range* [1999], *Bad Dirt* [2004], and *Fine Just the Way It Is* [2009]).

Chapter 1: Great Salt Lake Genealogy

1. Details of the Bonneville shoreline are found in Oviatt 2020 and Oviatt, Atwood, Laabs, and others 2021. For field details of associated geological features see Machette 1988. The Stockton Bar is described by Burr and Currey (1988). A recent synthesis of the 368 radiocarbon ages for Lake Bonneville is found in Oviatt 2015. A fascinating story in Oviatt 2020 describes how G. K. Gilbert changed his mind as his observations accumulated. Initially he thought Lake Bonneville had a point of overflow regulating the lake level prior to the Bonneville Flood. By the time of his final report, he no longer promoted overflow to account for the Bonneville level of the lake. In the subsequent 120 years, researchers ignored Gilbert's interpretation; it just seemed natural to them that the lake required an overflow to explain the Bonneville shoreline. Jack Oviatt acknowledges that he too assumed the standard view. But it is now clear that Lake Bonneville did not have an overflow prior to the Bonneville Flood, and the shoreline delineates the boundary between the lake-driven landforms below and the terrestrial, fluvial landforms above.
2. The relationship between levels of Lake Bonneville and glaciers is indirect. The Bonneville Flood resulted from a combination of forces ultimately residing in planetary climate. For an accessible overview see Grayson 2011:209–210. For details and recent dating, see Oviatt, Atwood, Laabs, and others 2021. The indirect relationship between glaciers and Bonneville has long been recognized (Gilbert 1890:310–311). For details about Homestead Cave see Broughton and Smith 2016.
3. For an excellent summary of Bonneville era vegetation and how it is known see Louderback and Rhode 2009.
4. Grayson (2011:173–180) provides an accessible description of Pleistocene mammals in the Great Basin.

Chapter 2: From Bonneville to Great Salt Lake

1. Gilbert 1890. His monograph *Lake Bonneville* is available for free on several websites; a search will provide options. The legislative process describing the founding of the United States Geological Survey is at https://pubs.usgs.gov/circ/c1050/establish.htm.
2. For the naming of Lake Bonneville see Leigh 1958, and for the history of investigation see R. Ives 1948.
3. Stansbury 1852:105.

4. Beckwith 1855:97.
5. Gilbert 1890:171.
6. An interactive website about Lake Bonneville by Paul Inkenbrandt is sponsored by the Utah Geological Survey, Department of Natural Resources. https://storymaps.arcgis.com/stories/f5011189bdc94545b9231d56e4ffc1e4.
7. There is no evidence to support assertions that Lake Bonneville overflowed for 500 to 1,000 years before the flood. The level of the lake oscillated in the millennia prior to the flood, but the chronology is weak, even as the evidence shows that the transgression that caused the flood happened only once (Oviatt 2015:169). The age of the flood is often reported using the radiocarbon age of 14,500 years ago, which calibrates to calendar time as 17,500 years ago.
8. Currey 1983.
9. Gilbert 1890:175.
10. O'Connor 1993 and 2016 are the primary sources of detail about the flood and how the volumes and duration of flow have been calculated. A summary is found in Grayson 2011:102. I took courses from and did fieldwork with Don Currey at the University of Utah and recall his vivid descriptions of a flood that could roll truck-sized boulders like marbles along the Snake River Plain near Twin Falls. Dr. Currey's personalized license plate on his VW station wagon was PLEIST. He defined himself through his work.

Chapter 3: Explorers in an Ecological Moment

1. A proposal by Williams and Madsen (2020) to refer to the American Paleoindian period as the Upper Paleolithic signals this emerging understanding and further reveals the terms "prehistoric" and "prehistory" as inaccurate and ethnocentric.
2. Evolution has a complicated relationship with progress, a notion deep in Occidental/Western culture (Mayr 1982:323–326, 531–534). Social philosophy and the social sciences have a complicated relationship with evolution as well. Unfortunately, and incorrectly, the social sciences retain a strong dose of the writings of Herbert Spencer. The term "social Darwinism" symbolizes a confusion that is more accurately termed "biological Spencerism." This confusion, too, has a complicated intellectual history. For an approachable discussion see Falk's (2020) article in *Smithsonian Magazine*, and for the implications of the confusion for understanding contemporary studies of evolution and adaptation, perhaps Burry 1989 might be helpful. These matters shape how scientists write about ancient peoples and how "they" are presented to a curious public. Cultural baggage matters, even for scientists.
3. For the Tibetan Plateau see Aldenderfer 2011, and for early dates, Xuebin and others 2013. A pioneer of high-altitude archaeology in the United States is James Benedict (1979, 1992, 1996); also see LaBelle and others 2012. A pioneer of the same in Utah is Alice Hunt (1953) and much later Simms (1979). Important high-altitude archaeology in the West has been conducted at Alta Toquima, Nevada (Thomas 1982, 2015, 2020); the White Mountains, California (Bettinger 1991; Morgan et al. 2020); the Wind River Range, Wyoming (Morgan et al. 2012); and the Colorado Rocky Mountains (Brunswig 2020b).
4. Simms 2008a:14–16.
5. A fascinating collection of papers is found in the book *Colonization of Unfamiliar Landscapes: The Archaeology of Adaptation* (Rockman and Steele 2003). Pleistocene colonization of the British Isles was uneven in rate, with standstills, and some areas were colonized on

small scales significantly earlier than the general colonization (Tolan-Smith 2003:116–126). The migration of Neolithic farmers across Europe proceeded at only one kilometer per year, but that was across a landscape already occupied by Mesolithic hunter-gatherers (Fiedel and Anthony 2003:144–146). Given the small number of very early dates across the Western Hemisphere and the nature of radiocarbon dating, it is mathematically unlikely to expect a progression of dates tracing a migration across space (Hazelwood and Steele 2003).

6. The White Sands footprints were reported by Bennett and others (2021). A critique by Madsen and others (2022) challenged the dating of seeds used to age the footprints because that seed plant is known to be a potential source of ancient carbon, making the age appear older than it might be. A rejoinder by Pigati and others (2022) was unable to resolve the problem. Another critique by Oviatt and others (2022) is convincing, leaving the situation one that will be resolved only by new evidence rather than arguments over the limited evidence at hand. Most archaeological dating benefits from more than one line of chronological evidence.

7. The debate over the timing and nature of human colonization of the Americas is voluminous. Claims made by media representatives typically precede the actual scientific reports by a year or years, and the public may be misled by sensationalist reporting that asserts extremely early dates designed to excite and attract clicks. I encourage readers to explore the bigger picture, and I offer some references. The debate over "Clovis first" is often presented as cutting edge, but it is not new, having been challenged directly for five decades. Likewise, coastal migration is not new, having been proposed by Knut Fladmark in the 1970s. Neither coastal nor inland migration routes can be ruled out. Clark and others (2022) have reported evidence that the inland route was not open until 13,800 years ago. For a review of pre-Clovis sites and their legitimacy see Madsen 2015. Investigations claiming earlier dates, especially over 20,000 years ago, remain problematic. Goebel and others (2008) provide an excellent overview in their article "Late Pleistocene Dispersal of Modern Humans in the Americas." Erlandson (2014) is a proponent of coastal migration and the idea of the Kelp Highway. Science is uncertain and deals with varying degrees of probability, not truths or beliefs, and a review of the issues is found in a brief letter to the editor by Potter, Beaudoin, and others (2018). This letter, authored by a "who's who" group of colleagues, offers a restrained, reasoned consideration of a topic overexploited by media and perhaps too polarized by scientists. The peopling of the Americas is an old question. The Spanish Jesuit José de Acosta spent 16 years in the Americas studying ethnography, geography, zoology, and botany. He was known as the most learned man regarding the New World. In AD 1590 he published a tome on his American studies that included an evidence-based, reasoned argument that Native Americans migrated to the Western Hemisphere from northeast Asia via a land route.

8. There is more to this problem than archaeology, and genetic data are vital. Recent reviews of genomic research have been written by Willerslev and Meltzer (2021), Skoglund and Reich (2016), and Raghavan and others (2015). The evidence shows the link with northeast Asia; that there was diversification but common links among all Native Americans; and that the earliest Native Americans were not derived from non–Native American populations. A recent report by Scott and others (2021) titled "Peopling the Americas: 'Not Out of Japan'" helps explain the conditions in northeastern Asia in relationship to the American migration.

9. The ice-free corridor east of the Canadian and American Rockies was open about 500 years before the development of Clovis in the central and eastern United States. For an insightful

overview see Ives and others 2013, and for recent dating see Clark and others 2022. Heaton and Grady (2003) and Ramsey and others (2004) describe Pleistocene coastal faunas, and Erlandson (2014) provides an overview of the coastal migration model.

10. A current review of the Western Stemmed Tradition and a summary of sites, including the Paisley Caves and Cooper's Ferry, is Smith and others 2020 and references therein. For details on Cooper's Ferry see Davis and others 2019.

11. The literature on hunter-gatherer mobility is voluminous, but a recent and interesting take on Great Basin Paleoindian cultural landscapes is found in Newlander 2018. Kelly (2003) considers mobility in unfamiliar landscapes based on hunter-gatherer ethnography. Landscape approaches to archaeology provide useful insights and help break down stereotypes about the anthropological Other. See, for instance, David and Thomas 2008.

12. For a briefing on hunter-gatherer descent see Kelly 1995:278–284. For insight into the anthropology of children and families see Lancy 2022. For a discussion of genetics married with the archaeological evidence see Potter, Baichtal, and others 2018.

Chapter 4: Pioneers and First Settlers

1. A fluted point and a fluted point base were found in the 1949–1953 excavations at Danger Cave. At that time they were described in the field logs as "Misc. points." By the 1980s it was common lore that these were fluted points and similar to Clovis as produced in the Great Basin. Years later a paper by David Rhode and others (2005) reported that Clovis did exist in Danger Cave. A reexamination of the points in the Natural History Museum of Utah collections in 2016 confirmed they are fluted points and could be Clovis or Folsom (Anne Lawlor, NHMU, personal communication 2023). The provenance of the complete point is consistent with the earliest occupation of the cave level DV, but the provenance of the broken base point is level DIV, suggesting it may be out of context. The recently published book *Fluted Points of the Far West* (Rondeau 2023) includes these points.

2. For a magazine-length introduction to Clovis see Mann 2013. For general Clovis perspectives see Goebel and others 2008; Madsen 2015; Potter and others 2017. Clovis as a culture is not as distinctive in the Great Basin as it is on the Plains. An excellent sense of how Clovis fits into the Great Basin is found in a synthesis for the northwestern Great Basin by Smith and Barker (2017).

3. The quote is from Frison and Bradley (1999:22), who describe the cache and how it fit into the Clovis period lifeway. George Frison was a legendary expert on Paleoindian archaeology and taught at the University of Wyoming. Bruce Bradley is a preeminent flintknapper and taught at the University of Exeter in the United Kingdom. Pete Bostrum of the Lithic Casting Lab provided them with high-quality photographs of the Fenn Cache. See Mr. Bostrum's website (www.lithiccastinglab.com) for images of the cache contents. There is some controversy regarding Forrest Fenn, the collector and art dealer from Santa Fe who bought the cache from the daughter-in-law of the finder's son in 1988. Mr. Fenn was a colorful character, but unfortunately, his association with the Fenn Cache has become confused with a scandal over his sponsorship of a treasure hunt in 2010, when he was 80 years old. The questions over the authenticity of the treasure chest he claimed to have hidden and the publicity surrounding the efforts of many to find it, as well as the deaths as recently as 2018 of several who searched

for the treasure, have nothing to do with the Fenn Cache. Mr. Fenn died in 2020. Every lithic tool expert who examined the cache, from Professors Frison and Bradley to the Smithsonian's Dennis Stanford, have expressed confidence in its authenticity. The Fenn Cache is not the only Clovis cache to have been found by avocational archaeologists, construction workers, and landowners. Such caches are often disturbed and scattered, and hence out of context. There are many of these not mentioned here.

4. A paper by Jason Gillespie (2007), "Enculturing an Unknown World: Caches and Clovis Landscape Ideology," is a thoughtful read. The details of the Anzick child genome are in Rasmussen and others 2014.

5. Recent astute reviews of the Western Stemmed Tradition include Smith and others 2020 and Waters and others 2020.

6. A recent integration of the Danger Cave, Bonneville Estates, and Smith Creek Cave Paleoindian chronologies can be found in Goebel and others 2007; see also Bryan 1979; Goebel and others 2021; Jennings 1957; and Rhode and Madsen 1998.

7. An excellent review of ancient Great Basin fiber technology—the selection of raw materials and engineering design—is found in the doctoral dissertation of Anne Lawlor (2020), available online. Lab testing of modern coats and a sleeping bag in comparison to a replica rabbit-skin robe was reported by Yoder and others (2005), "How Warm Were They? Thermal Properties of Rabbit Skin Robes and Blankets."

8. Nineteen obsidian Western Stemmed Tradition points and blanks of the Parman type and thought to be a cache were reported from the McNine collection by Daniel Amick (2004). Evidently, there are other such collections in private hands. Unfortunately, a lot of ink is spilled over whether a cache is utilitarian or ritual, as if these are mutually exclusive. I suspect there was plenty of bundling and storing of tools, but we tend to see only the ones made of stone.

9. G. K. Gilbert 1890:182–183.

10. For an excellent summary of the Old River Bed Delta see Madsen 2016; for the comprehensive monograph see Madsen and others 2015 and references therein.

11. Duke 2015. Note there is some disagreement about the reliability of blood protein residue analysis. It is worth considering the hunting of such large animals with the reminder that everything in so-called primitive society is not just about food. See the paper "Early Paleoindian Big-Game Hunting in North America: Provisioning or Politics?" (Speth et al. 2013).

12. Duke and others 2022. The footprints were found by Daron Duke, who has long worked at Dugway/UTTR, and Thomas Urban, a researcher who imaged the footprints at White Sands, New Mexico, in 2021 (see Chapter 3, note 6). A search will find news articles about the Dugway prints, but formal publication awaits further analysis.

13. For the Melon Gravel as a sacred landscape see Pavesic 2007. For recent methods used to date Idaho rock imagery and results see Andreae and Andreae 2022, noting that rock imagery remains very difficult to date, and estimated ages should be taken only as data to be evaluated against other data.

14. Oviatt 2018.

15. McPhee 1981:45.

16. Middleton and others 2014.

Chapter 5: Transformations of Place

1. Miller 1972. The narrations by Shoshone elder Maude Moon were accompanied by hand gestures. The ending about the rat's tail coming off was a convention Mrs. Moon used for "the end."
2. Small seed use and basketry are discussed in Rhode and others 2006 and Geib and Jolie 2008. The costs of technological investment shaped ancient people's lives just as much as they do for people living today. See Ugan and others 2003; Bettinger and others 2006.

   According to Judson Finley of Utah State University (personal communication), the dating of baskets and the foods they contain shows that some baskets were passed down for generations. The dating was done on two baskets containing food remains in two different houses at Caldwell Village, a Fremont site near Vernal, Utah. Both baskets were centuries older than the food they contained.
3. Exciting starch grain analyses on grinding stones and basket fragments are reported by Herzog and Lawlor (2016). For evidence of mass hunting of jackrabbits see Schmitt and others 2004. For grasshopper collecting at Lakeside Cave see Madsen and Kirkman 1988.
4. Rhode and Louderback 2015; Schmitt and others 2004.
5. See Kay 2002 for the concepts of keystone predator and top-down versus bottom-up ecosystems.
6. Evidence that hunter-gatherer populations shaped game populations and landscapes is rich. For an overview see Alvard 2002, and for a recent examination of tribal territories, social boundaries, and game populations see Bayham and others 2019.
7. For insights on trade and exchange see Hughes 2011.
8. I employed this analogy before (Simms 2008a:132) to help us think about the process of acquiring materials such as toolstone on scales of human lifetimes. This does not challenge models of conveyance of things like toolstone but places it in a temporal framework relevant to human behavior. It also situates our concept of tribal territories in a dynamic conditioned by the life histories of individuals (after Lewis Binford [1983:114–117]).
9. Basso 1996:43. Keith Basso's book *Wisdom Sits in Places: Landscape and Language Among the Western Apache* (1996) is a must read for all students of Native Americans and anthropology.

Chapter 6: A Human Wilderness

1. The best-known treatise on this matter is the book by Charles Mann (2005), *1491: New Revelations of the Americas Before Columbus*. The discussion has a long, torturous history. Two environmental historians were also pioneers; William Cronon (1983, new edition 2011) and Richard White (1980, new edition 1999) faced stiff opposition for situating Indigenous peoples as a part of nature rather than apart from it. White (1995:175) describes "an act of immense condensation. For in a modern world defined by change, whites are portrayed as the only beings who make a difference. [Environmentalists may be]…pious toward Indian peoples, but [they] don't take them seriously [for they] don't credit [Native people] with the capacity to make changes." See Kay and Simmons's (2002) book, *Wilderness and Political Ecology: Aboriginal Influences and the Original State of Nature*. The geographer William Denevan (1992) explicitly critiques "The Pristine Myth: The Landscape of the Americas in 1492." Recent study shows that such things are complex, and there is no single set of landscape influences and management practices that applies monolithically to the continent. Nevertheless, Native Americans were a part of, not apart from, the land.

2. The anthropologist Omer C. Stewart, a native Utahn, was among the first to write seriously about Native American use of fire in a manuscript completed in 1954. It was rejected for decades but finally published in 2002 with an important introduction by the editors, Henry T. Lewis and M. Kat Anderson. The quote of Luther Standing Bear is from Stewart 2002:frontispiece.
3. Great Salt Lake reached a record historic period low of 4,188 feet in November 2022. See Oviatt and others 2021 for the last 12,000 years of Great Salt Lake fluctuations.
4. A classic on collecting roots with Northern Paiute women in southeast Oregon is Couture and others 1986. A long-term study that began in 2003 in the Surprise Valley area, northeastern California, and northwestern Nevada, is a collaboration of James O'Connell, University of Utah; Jenn Rovanpera, United States Bureau of Land Management (BLM); and a host of students. The study employs controlled burns to assess the effects of fire on geophyte productivity. The research also investigates the effects of tillage created when geophytes such as yampa and biscuitroot are harvested. The research employs evaluation of stone artifacts used in geophyte harvesting and processing locations and starch granule analysis on stone tools to identify geophyte species harvested at different times in the past.
5. A book of collected papers, *Engineering Mountain Landscapes: An Anthropology of Social Investment*, edited by Laura L. Scheiber and Maria Nieves Zedeño (2015), situates this topic on a continental scale. One paper in it by David Hurst Thomas (2015) of the American Museum of Natural History in New York provides a readable and rich description of the gravity of "Engineering Alta Toquima." For details of the work at Alta Toquima and nearby Gatecliff Shelter see Thomas 1982, 2020. Thomas (2024) also considers alpine occupation across the Mountain West on a subcontinental scale and in terms of Shoshonean ethnogenesis. I agree with him that there is no synchrony among the use of alpine villages in the West. Alpine villages were built and reoccupied based on local factors, constraints, and opportunities. High-altitude occupation cannot be understood in terms of monolithic socio-historical events such as the Numic Spread or continental-scale climate change. For investigations in the White Mountains see Bettinger 1991 and Morgan and others 2020. For the Wind River Range see Morgan and others 2012 and references therein. For the Rocky Mountains of Colorado see Brunswig 2020b and Kornfeld 2013.
6. Salt Lake City herbalist Merry Lycett Harrison visited the BLM's Moab office and noticed a display in the lobby of a skin bag and contents that she recognized as medicinal herbs organized into proper doses. She obtained permission to study the bundle and published an article in the journal *Utah Archaeology* (Harrison 2003). The age reported in the article can now be recalibrated to AD 1438–1522.
7. Geib and Robins 2008.
8. Intriguing studies in collaboration with Native American elders of sacred landscapes in the Rocky Mountains of Colorado have been reported by Brunswig (2020a) and Chady and others (2020).
9. Simms 2010:83, 2018:19.
10. See the excellent essay by Blackburn and Anderson (1993) on "domesticating the environment."
11. Pyne, *Fire in America* (1982:17).
12. Stewart 2002:70–112.
13. Kelly 1932:82.

14. Darrah, *Powell of the Colorado* (1961:132).
15. Darrah 1961:231.
16. For repeat photography showing vegetation changes around Great Salt Lake over the past century or more see Rogers 1982. For Great Basin fire histories see Kiahtipes 2009; Miller and Wigand 1994; and Ulev 2008. An article by Magargal and others (2017) integrates fire with issues such as resource privatization, intensified plant processing, and forager territories. See Lewis 1973 for an early description of the importance of anthropogenic fire in the Great Basin; Williams (2002), a Forest Service historian, has written a thorough consideration of fire in the West. The quote is from the fire ecologist and environmental historian Stephen Pyne (1982:71).
17. For a recent example of this important understanding see "Native American Fire Management at an Ancient Wildland–Urban Interface in the Southwest United States" (Roos et al. 2021).
18. Experiments with firewood consumption grew out of trips by my family with Reba Rauch and Jim O'Connell. Walter Eiman, a Utah State University student, used an undergraduate research grant to conduct experiments to measure wood consumption using hearth sizes commonly found in archaeological sites. He controlled for fire size, maintenance, fuel feed rate, and duration. He counted dead wood available in various pinyon-juniper forest settings, as well as the total number of trees per unit of land. He conducted the experiments in different places. Walt did this work in 2009, and we recently went back to it to work up the scenarios presented here.
19. Janetski and Smith 2007:58–60. There are site forms and gray literature CRM reports on the recently evaluated sites in the Salt Lake Valley.
20. For Blue Lake see Kiahtipes 2009. For the fire history along the Nevada-Utah border see Kitchen 2015. For the fire history of Newark Valley, Nevada, see Mensing and others 2006. McAdoo and others (2013) describe the aboriginal use of fire in Great Basin sagebrush communities.
21. For the Fort Sage Drift Fence see Pendleton and Thomas 1983; Young and others 2017. The D.C. Corral and Five Mile Draw have only been surveyed, but see Simms 2008b. Howard Egan's experience is described in Steward 1938:34–35. The traps in Park Valley are described by Raymond (1982). For important discussions of communal hunting in the Great Basin see Arkush 2014; Hockett and others 2013; Lubinski 1999; Sprengeler and Morgan 2022. A comprehensive book on the subject is Hockett and Dillingham 2023.
22. Broughton and others 2008; Byers and Broughton 2004.
23. See McGuire and Hildebrandt 2005; and the subsequent debate by Grimstead (2012), Whitaker and Carpenter (2012), and Codding and Jones (2007). The economic, the social, and the ideological are not zero sum.

Chapter 7: Indigenes, Immigrants, and First Farmers

1. Roth and Freeman (2008) provide an accessible synthesis of the transition to agriculture in the American Southwest; more recent literature adds detail. Exciting new evidence that by 3,000 years ago Basketmaker farmers were on the Utah and Arizona border near Kanab is found in Roberts and others 2022. Wilde and Newman (1989) provided evidence of early

maize in the Sevier Valley, Utah, dating maize associated with a burial to between 100 BC and AD 50. An unpublished ^{14}C age by Joan Coltrain on the burial itself dates to AD 100, suggesting that the maize may be sacred, curated, and more ancient than the burial. Maize reached the Uinta Basin by AD 300 (Finley et al. 2020; Talbot and Richens 1996, 2004).

2. The east-west distinction was recognized early in the study of Fremont peoples. By 1956, a symposium of the Society for American Archaeology recommended that horticulturalists in the Great Basin and the northern Colorado Plateau be jointly recognized as Fremont, with the proviso that those in the west be called the Sevier culture (Madsen and Simms 1998:269–270; see also Jennings 1956). The east-west distinction of the preceding Basketmaker II peoples was developed by Matson (1991) and continues to be useful (Matson 2012).

3. "Ancestral Puebloan" is the current and best term. The older moniker, "Anasazi," is a Navajo word that means "enemy ancestors" and does not do justice to the rich and complex Native American histories of the Southwest. Ancestral Puebloan peoples spoke various languages and engaged in a great deal of interaction. Contrary to widespread misinformation, they did not disappear, nor are they lost cultures. They have ethnically and linguistically distinct historical descendants who are very much alive today.

4. Bone chemistry refers to stable isotope analyses, enabling researchers to identify isotopic markers in human bone and teeth indicating general classes of foods. The results are one line of evidence used to reconstruct ancient diets and population movements. The ratios of the stable carbon isotope ^{13}C estimate the relative contributions of domesticated corn and some other grasses to the ancient diet at different times in history. See Coltrain and Janetski 2013 for a thorough review of the bone chemistry. See Coltrain and Janetski 2019 for a review of all the angles of debate over Basketmaker origins. Suffice it to say that framing the debate in binary terms, whether Basketmaker culture developed in situ (an obfuscation) *versus* a migration (migrations are rarely singular), has been done away with. I recommend their review for those who want to get down in the scientific weeds.

5. For a summary see Simms 2008a:197, 201–203. The essence of this growing understanding of migration was synthesized by Matson (1991), although hints of it are found in earlier works. Recent developments of the evidence include McNeil and Shaul 2018, 2020; Ortman and McNeil 2017. For the Steinaker chronology see Talbot and Richens 2004:75; for diet see Coltrain 1996:119–122. Early maize in Cub Creek has been documented by Finley and others (2020).

6. The Prison site in Draper, Salt Lake Valley, has yielded maize phytoliths and nine radiocarbon dates of about 400 BC, but further evaluation of the site to provide more confidence in these ages was not permitted, so the results remain provisional because phytoliths are found in sediments subject to various formation processes. A report by Yentsch and others (2009) is available online.

7. The Grantsville sites were largely destroyed, but an unpublished report by Wayne Shields of preliminary excavations in the 1960s includes a radiocarbon age of AD 500. In contrast, the Dimple Dell site was found in 2015. Dating of numerous burials in the Great Salt Lake Wetlands south of Willard Bay and stable carbon isotope analysis show farming had arrived widely to the Great Salt Lake area by AD 500. See Coltrain and Stafford 1999:62–64; Simms 1999a:31–34.

8. A great deal of political moralizing is made about the story of Ishi. However, there is a responsibility to read the original story by Theodora Kroeber (2004), and a responsibility to experience the mirror image of ethnocentrism. Steve Shackley (2000) describes the study of Ishi's stone tools.
9. The efforts of researcher Deni Seymour (2017) and scholars cited therein go a long way toward bringing the "people without history" in the American Southwest into the pantheon.
10. Noel Morss (2009) was on the early expeditions in Utah in the 1920s ranging from Capitol Reef to Nine Mile Canyon and other lesser-known canyons of the Tavaputs Plateau. Madsen and Simms (1998) trace the history of Fremont studies and the various perspectives and interpretations made over the decades. The book *Crimson Cowboys: The Remarkable Odyssey of the 1931 Claflin Emerson Expedition*, by Jerry Spangler and Jim Aton (2018), focuses on the last year of fieldwork and is a lively, informative read for anyone interested in Utah history.
11. The story of the lost Pillings figurine and how it was authenticated is in Pitblado and others 2013.
12. For responsible, authoritative treatises on Utah rock imagery see Cole 2009 and Schaafsma 1971. For current thinking on the language histories of Eastern and Western Basketmaker peoples see McNeil and Shaul 2018, 2020; Ortman and McNeil 2017.
13. For a synthesis see Simms 2008a:214–217. For the genetic analyses of people living in the Great Salt Lake wetlands see Carlyle and others 2000; O'Rourke and others 1999.
14. The unpublished analysis was done by Douglas Owsley and Shannon Novak of the Smithsonian Institution. Also see Malhi and others 2003.
15. For background on Fremont basketry see Adovasio and others 2002. For an early recognition of Basketmaker basketry at the northern edge of the Southwest see Morris and Burgh 1954, and for the emergence of Basketmaker in the San Juan Basin see especially Coltrain and Janetski 2019, as well as Sesler and Hovezak 2011. A plain-spoken summary relevant to Fremont is in Simms 2008a:199–205.
16. For different perspectives on the adoption of the bow and arrow and its relationship to intergroup relations see Reed and Geib 2013 for the Southwest; Kennett and others 2013 for California; and Smith 2021 for southwest Wyoming.

Chapter 8: The Most Populous Part of Utah
1. The archaeology of the Fallon/Stillwater area is described by Hemphill and Larsen (1999); Kelly (2001); Raven (1990); and Raven and Elston (1989). The article in the *Nevada Magazine* of the *Reno Gazette* is a testimony to the destructive ignorance not only of the collector, but the newspaper reporter of the time. It can be found at https://nevadamagazine.com/issue/march-april-2020/12974/.
2. Quote from the Wheeler Expedition in the 1870s is in Janetski 1990:12.
3. For an excellent summary of the Big Mound at Willard see Stuart 2008:191–193.
4. The move from circular to square housing, in conjunction with other evidence of mobility, is a significant transition worldwide because it correlates with increased tethering to places (Hunter-Anderson 1977; for Fremont see Talbot 2000a).
5. Coltrain and Stafford 1999.
6. The journal *Utah Archaeology* is available online via the Utah Division of State History. The 2018 issue reprints some of the *Utah Archaeology Newsletter* of the Utah Statewide Archae-

ological Society, published by an avocational group since 1955. It includes two reports by Fran Hassell on Willard Bay.

7. For a summary of the archaeology of the Great Salt Lake Wetlands near Willard see Simms and Stuart 2002. For figurines from the Hinkley Mounds see Green 1964. Informative parallels between Utah Valley and Salt Lake Valley are elucidated by Mooney (2014).
8. There is increasing evidence that irrigation was important to Fremont agriculture and, consequently, Fremont settlement decisions. Irrigation is difficult to find and date. Many irrigation ditches are buried. Later use of an irrigation ditch obliterates evidence of prior use except under fortunate circumstances. Archaeologists tend not to search for irrigation, but let it come to them. The following citations show that reports of Fremont irrigation go back many decades. The quotes about Ferron Creek are from Gunnerson 1957:5, 134. The quote from Bull Creek is from Lohse 1980:49. Irrigation in Nine Mile Canyon is described in Reagan 1931a, 1931b:46; and Spangler 2013:154–155. Irrigation on Hill Creek is described in Reagan 1931c:226; and Spangler and Aton 2018:88. Possible irrigation at Median Village, a major site in the Parowan Valley, is mentioned by Marwitt (1970 and original field notes). Metcalfe and Larrabee (1985) reported irrigation near Nawthis Village on Gooseberry Creek above Salina. Irrigation ditches excavated and dated by Talbot and Richens (1996:60–73, 79–82, 188–192) show use early in Fremont times at Steinaker Village. Recent papers suggesting increased awareness and effort to document and study Fremont irrigation include Simms and others 2020 for Pleasant Creek. The work at Cub Creek is recent and is described in a personal communication with Judson Finley, Utah State University. A publication is in preparation.
9. The findings of Boomgarden and others (2019) in Range Creek, central Utah, are that irrigation is mandatory for successful farming, not simply an option. Hart and others (2021) studied ecological indicators in sediments from an ancient Fremont field in Range Creek to evaluate moisture. They found that during the time that field was farmed, summer rainfall was minimal. Such a dry summer environment implies that the maize the field produced must have been watered from the nearby stream fed by snowmelt from high above—irrigation. Baker Village near Great Basin National Park is an obvious candidate for mandatory irrigation given the hydrology and climate of the eastern Great Basin during the Medieval Climatic Anomaly. These and other cases hold implications for all Fremont archaeology.
10. See Johansson and others 2014 for an excellent discussion of architecture at Wolf Village and implications for our understanding of Fremont peoples.
11. Important treatises on Fremont social organization based on the research in Clear Creek Canyon are Janetski and Talbot 2014 and Talbot 2000b.
12. Baker Village is described by Wilde and Soper (1999). Hockett (1998) studied the animal bones and made an argument for feasting. Analysis of a larger sample of bone from Baker Village by Johansson places the activities in the context of communal practice (Richards et al. 2019). David Madsen recently scoured existing collections of ancient ceramics housed in the Nevada State Museum, Carson City. He found a far greater presence of Fremont pottery in central Nevada than previously thought. Much of it was of sufficiently high quality that it implies the presence of skilled potters, not just copies made by local residents. A publication is in preparation.
13. Coltrain 1993; Coltrain and Stafford 1999:Table 4.2; Simms 2008a:214–215. It is helpful to note that some of the maize signal caused by consumption of C_4 photosynthetic pathway

plants could be from wild C_4 plants and from animals consuming C_4 plants. Thus, the percent contribution of maize (a C_4 plant) may be lower, but comparisons with other places remain significant because all Great Salt Lake peoples consumed some wild plants and some bison, who are grass grazers.

14. This project and its results are summarized in a brief nontechnical chapter by Simms and Stuart (2002) in the book *Great Salt Lake: An Overview of Change*, edited by J. Wallace Gwynn and published by the Utah Geological Survey. The references within identify the specialized analyses of biomechanics, bone and dental health, genetic analysis, and stable isotope analysis. The project and its implications for understanding Fremont culture in general are synthesized in Simms 2008a:214–217, and especially Chapter 5 notes 38–40 in that book.

15. I refer to an interesting paper by Deni Seymour (2019) titled "Pliant Communities: Commonalities between Snowbirds and Seasonal Mobile Group Visitation at the Eastern Frontier Pueblos."

16. *The Desert and the Sown* is the title of a book by the early twentieth-century English scholar/diplomat Gertrude Bell (The Desert Queen), who revealed misunderstandings about how traditional Arab tribal societies worked—misunderstandings that led to poor decisions by European policymakers. The lessons of Bell's intimacy with Arab/Bedouin culture hold implications for a less culturally biased understanding of Native Americans. See Simms 2008a:Chapter 5n14.

17. Richards and others 2019; Talbot 2000b.

18. The concept of faceless (not selfless) leadership is discussed by Hegmon (2005).

19. For the notion of a cosmopolitan Indigenous past see Simms 2008a:16. Fremont archaeology has been slow to interpret social organization, and even slower to interpret kinship and descent systems, shying away from the speculations made by early archaeologists. Simms (2008a) has explicitly offered models of Fremont social organization, including kinship and descent; see pages 194–195, 217–219, and 223, and Chapter 5 notes 46–50. After decades of avoiding the topic because we were taught archaeology could not gain purchase on social "things," we owe Pat Barker (1994) for moving us forward into Fremont social organization. Barker's paper was presented at a conference but was widely circulated as a mimeograph and is available on the ResearchGate website. https://www.researchgate.net/search.Search.html?query=Sequential+Hierarchy+and+Political+Evolution+along+the+Western+Fremont+Frontier&type=publication.

Joel Janetski and Richard Talbot (2000; Talbot 2000b) did a great service by interpreting Fremont social organization, with an abbreviated restatement in Janetski and Talbot 2014. A recent synthesis by Richards and others (2019) indicates considerable interest in the topic and welcome progress.

Chapter 9: Upheaval

1. One of the most widely discussed issues in the history of American archaeology is the origins of the Navajo and Apache. Relationships in language between the Southwestern tribes and what was called the "Athabaskan" or "Athapaskan" language family of western Canada were recognized in the nineteenth century. By the 1930s, linguists had determined that there

was a migration from western Canada to the Southwest. Now properly referred to as Dene languages, archaeological research has documented these migrations and their timing. The arrival of Dene speakers to the Southwest was traditionally seen as occurring in the AD 1500s, but there is increasing evidence that the migrations began as early as the late AD 1200s and 1300s. For a recent review of the history of study see Lewandowska 2020, readily available online. For a collection of detailed papers see Seymour 2012. For the mysterious case of the Plains Kiowa and Fremont connections see Ortman and McNeil 2017. For a variety of perspectives on the Numic Spread see the volume edited by Madsen and Rhode (1994), but for other views start with Aikens and Witherspoon 1986; a linguistic analysis by Shaul (2014:Chapter 4); and Simms 1994. For Fremont–Southwestern interaction see McNeil and Shaul 2018, 2020; and Shaul 2014:108–112, 142–143.

2. On the futility of chasing the will-o'-the-wisp of social order in a world of upheaval and change see Simms 1999b. On Native American diasporas and ethnogenesis see Cippola 2017.

3. Sinopolli 1991.

4. Thanks to Scott Ortman and Lynda McNeil (2017:17) for this analogy and the insightful lesson.

5. Fremont presence on the Snake River Plain is reviewed by Mark Plew (2008:130–134). Brooke Arkush (2008) excavated Standing Rock Overhang as well as bison hunting areas in Birch Creek Valley (Arkush and Arkush 2021). Holmer (1990, 1994) argues for Uto-Aztecan/Shoshonean presence in southeastern Idaho beginning about 3,000 years ago. Mark Stuart and Brook Arkush (personal communication) scoured Idaho museum collections and found Great Salt Lake Gray potsherds that appear to have been imported and others that appear to be locally made.

6. A case study along Cub Creek in Dinosaur National Monument shows how Fremont peoples adapted to multiple decades of rainfall variability. From AD 750 to 1050, investment in infrastructure increased, as did maize production, and populations grew. The Uinta Fremont peoples shifted village locations and adjusted their efforts in response to droughts, and this shifting adaptation is a more accurate portrayal than regional abandonment (Finley et al. 2020). A case for return-migration among eastern Fremont peoples is made by McNeil and Shaul (2020).

7. The tree-ring study by Knight and others (2010) used data from the Tavaputs Plateau to show variations in temperature and moisture from 300 BC to the present. Comparisons with tree-ring records in eastern Oregon, central Nevada, and northwestern New Mexico expanded their record to a subcontinental scale. Thomson and MacDonald (2020) employ climate models and paleoclimate data to show how climate shaped choices made by Fremont farmers. Thomson and others (2019) have shown that the decrease in farming was fragmentary and based on local circumstances.

8. Those who noted the affinity between the northern Fremont and Plains peoples include Julian Steward (1937); H. Marie Wormington (1955:160–162, 171, 176–186); Mel Aikens and Erik Reed (Aikens 1967; Aikens and Reed 1966:80); and James Adovasio, David Pedler, and Jeff Illingworth (2002). As stated in note 5 above, Fremont pottery has been found in Idaho. Fremont era pottery in western Wyoming has been evaluated by Finley and Boyle (2014); Middleton and others (2007); and Smith (1992).

9. A paper by James Keyser and George Poetschat (2017), "Uinta Fremont Rock Art in Southwestern Wyoming: Marking the Fremont Northern Periphery," makes a strong case for direct Fremont presence. For the range of shield figures and V-shaped anthropomorphs from the Plains to the Great Basin see Francis and Loendorf 2002:132. For Castle Gardens Style rock imagery see Aikens 1967:201; Francis and Loendorf 2002:136–144; Loendorf and others 2012; Schaafsma 1971:142–145; and Wormington 1955:162. The painted scapulae have been described by Mark Stuart (1988), who examined more than 200 prayerstones in private collections from the same general area where the scapulae were found north of Great Salt Lake (personal communication). On Fremont and Great Basin rock imagery relations and the Great Salt Lake area see Schaafsma 1971:84–85, 91, 109, 138, 143, 146, 148; see also Castleton 1979:15–39. Searcy and Talbot (2015) employ the concept of borderlands to offer insights on Fremont identity.
10. The Texas Creek Overlook site in northwestern Colorado may date as late as AD 1520. See Creaseman and Scott 1987; Simms 2008a:235. Simms and others (2020) offer evidence for Fremont persistence into the fifteenth and sixteenth centuries.
11. The quote about Swedes and Volvos is attributed to Payson Sheets, University of Colorado, Boulder.
12. Julian Steward reported the Promontory Caves excavations in 1937. He later stated that the occupants of the Promontory Caves were "temporary residents...and may even have been Athapascans then on their way south" (Steward 1938:5). Mel Aikens (Aikens 1967; Aikens and Reed 1966) saw relationships between Promontory and Plains peoples. Jesse D. Jennings (1978:173) referred to Promontory pottery as "somehow alien in the Fremont setting," stating that it "superficially resembles pottery from the Plains"; he also noted that "Promontory culture...seems to have existed at the same time as the Levee phase of the local Fremont." Jennings countered Aikens's hypothesis that the Fremont peoples originated on the Plains and moved south because he felt it was clear that the Fremont had Southwestern and Indigenous Utah roots. Jennings did not speak to Steward's earlier proposal that Promontory represents the migration of "Athapascan" peoples to the Southwest, eventually becoming the Navajo and Apache, seemingly missing that Aikens and Steward were proposing different things. I recall that the topic of Promontory as Athapaskan was moot when I was an undergraduate studying under Dr. Jennings in the early 1970s. Madsen and Simms (1998:269–271) review the history of the Promontory problem, which for decades focused only on pottery. Simms (2008a) did not wade into what seemed like an unresolved mystery and avoided the issue. A great error. What had been ignored for decades was that Steward did not base his argument only on the pottery, but on a range of evidence including moccasins, textiles, and basketry. It was not until fresh eyes were brought to the issue and modern fieldwork was conducted at the Promontory Caves between 2011 and 2014 that the error was recognized. We owe a debt to the vision of Jack Ives and Joel Janetski (the latter also a Jennings student) to return to the archaeology itself. They were able to do this because the caves are on a private ranch owned by the Chournos family, who graciously allowed excavation and enthusiastically supported the research. The research benefitted greatly from the participation of Canadian and American tribal members. Subsequent analysis (Ives 2014; Ives et al. 2014; Yanicki and Ives 2017) produced dramatic results. The entire investigation is synthesized in a new book, *Holes in Our Moccasins, Holes in Our*

Stories: Apachean Origins and the Promontory, Franktown, and Dismal River Archaeological Records (Ives and Janetski 2022).
13. Shirazi and others 2022.
14. The timing of the arrival of the Dene to the Southwest continues to be refined with increasing evidence that it was earlier than previously thought. See brief comments by Seymour (2009) for a sense of the argument.
15. For a recent sample of the how and why of Dene migration see Doering and others 2020; Ives 2014; Magne 2012; Malhi 2012; and Yanicki and Ives 2017.
16. Magne and Klassen (2002) describe the setting of Grotto Canyon and the history of interpretation of the site.
17. Metcalfe and others 2021.
18. Yanicki and Ives 2017:160.
19. The connection that the Kiowa of the southern Plains make with their origins in Yellowstone has long been recognized; see, for instance, Mooney 1898. For recent understandings relevant to Promontory and Fremont, see Ives and others 2014; and Ortman and McNeil 2017.
20. Transitions in Promontory Dene lifeways are discussed by Billinger and Ives (2015:77). Lupo and Schmitt (1997) and Grayson (2006) present evidence of declining bison numbers and associate this with a decrease in summer monsoon moisture that altered grassland ecosystems. Mensing and others (2008) have documented the high-altitude Mission Cross Bog in the Jarbidge Mountains of northeastern Nevada, where there appears to have been a wet interval between AD 1300 and 1400, but the seasonality of this moisture is unknown. Bison resurged in the northern Great Basin after AD 1500 in response to cooler temperatures and increased winter moisture. Bowyer and Metcalfe (2022) discuss the complexities of climate, grassland ecosystems, and bison, and show there is much more to be learned to understand the history of the Promontory Dene and bison.

Chapter 10: Descendants
1. Powell 1891. For samples of Great Basin ethnography see the following and references therein: d'Azevedo 1986; C. Fowler 1989, 1992; Garey-Sage and Fowler 2016; Hultkrantz 1986; Kelly 1932, 1964; Liljeblad 1986; Steward 1938.
2. On distributions of Uto-Aztecan and Numic languages, the history of proposed locations of Proto-Uto-Aztecan, and critiques of chronology see Fowler 1972; Merrill 2012; Merrill and others 2009; Shaul 2014:24–98. For the arrival of pinyon pine to the Great Basin see Madsen and Rhode 1990 and Rhode 2000.
3. For an interesting paper by ethnographers and linguists on Proto-Numic kinship, which seems unknown to many who work in the Great Basin, see Hage and others 2004. Some readers may be surprised at the notion of cross-cousin marriages (between children of a parent and those of their opposite-sex siblings), but in several descent systems documented by anthropologists, the relatives known to those of us in Western, industrialized society as cousins are termed brothers and sisters. In those descent systems the kinship terminology reaches broadly across generations and across genetic lineages.
4. Hopi language history, its relationship to the spread of agriculture, and the implications for Western Basketmaker and Fremont peoples are found in McNeil and Shaul 2020; Merrill 2012:231–232, 236; and Shaul 2014:225–229, 253–254, 295–296, 299–301.

5. The concept of borderlands can reduce our reliance on bounded concepts of culture in which lifeway, identity, ethnicity, language, and material culture are seen monolithically. It is heartening to see progress about frontiers and borderlands in works such as Parker 2006, and, with applicability to the Fremont, Searcy and Talbot 2015.
6. Hockett and Morgenstein (2003) describe local and imported Fremont ceramics found near Elko, Nevada. The account for Grass Valley is from a personal communication (2022) with David Madsen, whose search of the Nevada State Museum collections has revealed high-quality Fremont ceramics from central Nevada. Ongoing research suggests that Fremont pottery, and hence Fremont potters, were more common in central and eastern Nevada than previously thought.
7. Tom Connolly (2013) used radiocarbon dating on basketry fragments to show that Shoshonean style coiled basketry had a minor but temporally deep presence in southeastern Oregon for over 2,500 years. This is consistent with Aikens and Witherspoon's (1986:17) argument for a Shoshonean presence in the northwestern Great Basin as early as 2,750 years ago.
8. For Wahmuza and the argument for Uto-Aztecan/Shoshonean presence near Pocatello for the last 3,500 years see Holmer 1990, 1994. For ceramics in southeastern Idaho see Plew 2000:146–151 and Plew and Bennick 1990; and for Shoshonean presence in western Wyoming see Finley, Boyle, and Harvey 2015. For Dinwoody rock imagery in Wyoming see Francis and Loendorf 2002:187. For southwestern Wyoming see Smith 2021. For James Creek Rockshelter see Elston and Budy 1990:274.
9. An excellent introduction to the concept of *puha* is found in Miller 1983. See also the classic accounts of Fowler 1992; Hultkrantz 1986; Jorgensen 1992; Liljeblad 1986; and Park 1938. David Thomas (2019, 2024) has synthesized a wealth of evidence for a temporally deep Shoshonean presence in the Great Basin and Intermountain region.
10. The study of incised stones was pioneered by Trudy Thomas (1983) in a chapter of *The Archaeology of Monitor Valley 2: Gatecliff Shelter*. Over a 20-year period Rich Stoffle and a team that included many Southern Paiute elders (Stoffle et al. 2021) developed the concept of prayerstones. David Thomas (2019) presents a synthesis of prayerstones with the archaeology of a Shoshonean presence in the Great Basin and expands this further in *Shoshonean Ethnogenesis and Numic Origins* (Thomas 2024).
11. The ritual in 1880 described by Richard Ambro in his fieldnotes is cited in Thomas 2024. Southern Paiute elders understand current practice regarding prayerstones (Stoffle et al. 2021).
12. A study of prayerstones from the Great Salt Lake region was done by Diana Call née Azevedo when a private collection was loaned to Utah State University.
13. Fowler 1992:177, Figure 111; Stoffle and others 2004:38; Zedeño 2009.
14. Jack Marwitt (1970:145) cited "incised stones" as being distinctive of Great Salt Lake Fremont. The avocational archaeologist Mark Stuart has seen hundreds of them in private collections in the Great Salt Lake region. He makes the case for prayerstones as an alternative to rock imagery creation in an area where sandstone panels are rare, but it is clear they are part of a regional ideology.
15. For accessible regional syntheses of rock imagery see Schaafsma 2008; and Woody and Quinlan 2008. Sally Cole (2009) reviews rock imagery in Canyon Pintado, Colorado, and

its relationship to Wyoming and Plains cultures. For an argument regarding ancestral Hopi foragers in southeastern Utah see McNeil and Shaul 2018.
16. Janetski and Smith 2007:321–322. For Injun Creek see Aikens and Reed 1966; for Orbit Inn, Simms and Heath 1990; for the Airport site, Cannon and Creer 2010.

Chapter 11: Indigenes Meet Travelers

1. For the most accurate translation of the journal see Chavez and Warner 1995. *Escalante's Dream*, by the popular writer David Roberts (2019), is an interpretive journey as he follows the Domínguez–Escalante Expedition's route through the West. An earlier but less reliable translation is Bolton 1951.
2. Steven Baker (2015) wrote a well-illustrated coffee table tome that corrects popular historical interpretations about the Juan Rivera expedition.
3. The extensive rock imagery at Canyon Pintado has been evaluated by Sally Cole (2009:99, 280, 297). For reviews of evidence of the Femont culture's persistence see Creaseman and Scott 1987; Simms 2008a:235; Simms and others 2020.
4. "Fish-Eaters" is a translation of a term used for a food-named group. Names of food-named groups refer to places where people lived, not necessarily places where people were born, nor names for tribes, bands, and/or ethnic groups. Food-named groups are best known ethnographically for the Northern Paiute in the western Great Basin. The term as applied to the Utah Lake Utes shows the construction of place in relationship to the characteristics of landscapes. See Fowler 1992 and Wheat 1967 for details of Northern Paiute groups and names. Simms (2008a:20–21) explains how food-named groups fit into social organization.
5. Janetski (1991:3–4, 17) and Janetski and Smith (2007:317–326) evaluate the Domínguez-Escalante journal to flesh out Ute lifeways before the horse and address the question of mobility.
6. Recognition of the impact of Old World diseases on Native American populations has been a tough uphill pull spanning nearly five decades. Some key overviews include one by anthropologist Henry Dobyns (1983), who was met with considerable denial of his projections of Indigenous population sizes. The historian Russell Thornton (1987) and the geographer William Denevan (1992) helped to make the case. Charles Mann's (2005) popular volume *1491* is well researched, and the casual reader can find his book condensed in the *Atlantic Monthly* (Mann 2002). Two pioneers of finding depopulation impacts in the archaeology are Ann Ramenovsky (1987) and Sarah Campbell (1990).
7. Koch and others 2019 is a quantitative review of the evidence for population size, land use, carbon levels, and climate history. They argue that the well-documented decline in global atmospheric CO_2 in the late sixteenth and early seventeenth centuries cannot be accounted for until large-scale vegetation regeneration in the Americas is included. The depopulation of Native Americans caused an explosion in vegetation across landscapes on a hemispheric scale.
8. The graphic in Figure 11.4 is from a report by Lindsay (2005) of a large sample of radiocarbon dates from western Utah and eastern Nevada compiled during large-scale archaeological projects for installations such as the Kern River gas pipeline. Because technical reports are often difficult to find, they are referred to as "gray literature."

9. Liebmann and others (2016) found that the Indigenous population of the Jemez region of New Mexico declined by 87 percent following European colonization, but that this reduction occurred during the Mission period in the seventeenth century, nearly a century after initial contact. Depopulation caused regeneration of pine forests, which triggered an increase in the frequency of extensive surface fires between AD 1640 and 1900, after which time fire was suppressed by Euro-Americans. In the Jemez region, fires were suppressed by Indigenes around villages, but the use of small fires was common in remote settings. Depopulation led to the return of forests in this dry environment, increasing fuel loads and fire frequency. The relationships between Indigenous use of fire and range/forest ecology are complex, and there is no one pattern of Native American use of fire, nor uniform consequences for local ecosystems. See, for instance, Hull 2009; Lightfoot and others 2013; and Roos and others 2014.
10. Simms 2008a:n47; Simms and Stuart 2002.
11. Recent research by Taylor and others (2023) presents archaeological, DNA, and stable isotope evidence supporting the suspicion that horse adoption in North America, especially in the Plains and Intermountain regions, was earlier than the Pueblo Revolt in New Mexico in AD 1680. They report the radiocarbon calibrated age range of horse remains from southeastern Idaho as AD 1597–1657 with the most likely portion of that range as the early AD 1600s. The juvenile horse from the Blacks Fork River site south of Green River, Wyoming, is reported in Thornhill 2021. It was radiocarbon dated to a calibrated age range of AD 1521–1667 with a statistical median age of AD 1640. That the foal was butchered with metal tools indicates a range of transitions were occurring earlier than previously demonstrated. The ancient DNA from horses shows that the horse was adopted from European varieties, not from the ancient Pleistocene horses of Beringia.
12. Timing of the introduction of the horse is found, for example, in Haines 1938; Sutton 1986; and Wissler 1914. Bill Hildebrandt (2016:337) has documented the effect of horses on the transport of toolstone. The quote from the explorer Verendrye is from Blegen 1925:118.
13. Merrill 2012:236.

Chapter 12: Denouement

1. The title of this final chapter acknowledges the insight of my colleague Joel Janetski. The ethnographer Keith Basso, who wrote *Wisdom Sits in Places* (1996:106–111, 142), conducted fieldwork at Cibeque, Arizona, from 1979 to 1984. The then-chairman of the White Mountain Apache tribal council, Ronnie Lupe, suggested, "Why don't you make maps over there.... Not whitemen's maps, we've got plenty of them, but Apache maps with Apache places and names" (1996:xv).
2. Proulx 1999, 2004, 2009. The phrase "sense of place" is used so widely in the literature of the last few decades that perhaps it is overused. It is hardly unknown in archaeology but offers a vehicle for archaeologists to tell the story of the past in a dimension other than conventional categories and concepts.
3. Basso 1996:43. Students on field trips often wonder how Indigenous peoples navigated in the outback. I advise them to see Basso's book, where it becomes apparent that one learns the landscape from childhood through the relentless telling of the stories that name literally everything and create a memorized map of their world.

4. Simms 1999b. I was deeply influenced by Eric Wolf, a student of Julian Steward who sought to overcome the dualism and boundedness of Western/Occidental thought in an effort to improve our comprehension of the cross-cultural.
5. White 1995:175. This is from the essay titled "Are You an Environmentalist or Do You Work for a Living? Work and Nature." The title may be off-putting to some, but what White is challenging is the common definition of "nature" as something unaltered by man. That is an impossibility, and such dualism prevents humanity from upholding an environmental ethic. White explores ways to overcome this limitation.
6. The influential novel *The Go-Between* by L. P. Hartley was first published in 1956 and reprinted in 2015.

References

Adovasio, James, David R. Pedler, and Jeff S. Illingworth
2002 Fremont Basketry. *Utah Archaeology* 15:5–26.

Aikens, C. Melvin
1967 Plains Relationships of the Fremont Culture: A Hypothesis. *American Antiquity* 32: 198–209.

Aikens, C. Melvin, and Erik K. Reed
1966 *Fremont-Promontory-Plains Relationships, Including A Report of Investigations at the Injun Creek and Bear River No. 1 Sites, Northern Utah.* Anthropological Papers No. 82. University of Utah Press, Salt Lake City.

Aikens, C. Melvin, and Younger T. Witherspoon
1986 Great Basin Numic Prehistory: Linguistics, Archaeology, and Environment. In *Anthropology of the Desert West: Essays in Honor of Jesse D. Jennings*, edited by Carol J. Condie and Don D. Fowler, pp. 7–21. Anthropological Papers No. 111. University of Utah Press, Salt Lake City.

Aldenderfer, Mark
2011 Peopling the Tibetan Plateau: Insights from Archaeology. *High Altitude Medicine and Biology* 12:141–147.

Alvard, Michael S.
2002 Evolutionary Theory, Conservation, and Human Environmental Impact. In *Wilderness and Political Ecology: Aboriginal Influences and the Original State of Nature*, edited by Charles E. Kay and Randy T. Simmons, pp. 28–43. University of Utah Press, Salt Lake City.

Amick, Daniel S.
2004 A Possible Ritual Cache of Great Basin Stemmed Bifaces from the Terminal Pleistocene–Early Holocene Occupation of NW Nevada, USA. *Lithic Technology* 29:119–145.

Andreae, Meinrat O., and Tracey W. Andreae
2022 Archaeometric Studies on Rock Art at Four Sites in the Northeastern Great Basin of North America. *PLoS ONE* 17:e0263189.

Arkush, Brooke S.
2008 *A Long-Term Record of Bighorn Sheep Hunting and Processing in Southeastern Idaho.* Vol. 3, No. 6, of *The Archaeology of Standing Rock Overhang*. United States Department of Agriculture, Forest Service, Intermountain Region.
2014 Communal Pronghorn Hunting in the Great Basin: What Have We Learned Over the Last Twenty-Five Years? *Pacific Coast Archaeological Society Quarterly* 49:1–19.

Arkush, Brooke S., and Denise Arkush
2021   Aboriginal Plant Use in the Central Rocky Mountains: Macrobotanical Records from Three Prehistoric Sites in Birch Creek Valley, Eastern Idaho. *North American Archaeologist* 42:66–108.

Baker, Steven G.
2015   *Juan Rivera's Colorado, 1765: The First Spaniards Among the Ute and Paiute Indians on the Trails to Teguayo*. Western Reflections, Lake City, Colorado.

Barker, J. Pat
1994   *Sequential Hierarchy and Political Evolution along the Western Fremont Frontier*. Paper presented at the 24th Biennial Great Basin Anthropological Conference, Elko, Nevada. Available on ResearchGate (https://www.researchgate.net).

Basso, Keith H.
1996   *Wisdom Sits in Places: Landscape and Language Among the Western Apache*. University of New Mexico Press, Albuquerque.

Bayham, Jude, Kasey E. Cole, and Frank E. Bayham
2019   Social Boundaries, Resource Depression, and Conflict: A Bioeconomic Model of the Intertribal Buffer Zone. *Quaternary International* 518:69–82.

Beckwith, E. Griffin
2014   [1855] *Report of Explorations for a Route for the Pacific Railroad*. United States War Department.

Benedict, James B.
1979   Getting Away from It All: A Study of Man, Mountains, and the Two-Drought Altithermal. *Southwestern Lore* 45:1–12.
1992   Footprints in the Snow: High-Altitude Cultural Ecology of the Colorado Front Range, U.S.A. *Arctic and Alpine Research* 24:1–16.
1996   *The Game Drives of Rocky Mountain National Park*. Research Report 7. Center for Mountain Archeology, Ward, Colorado.

Bennett, Matthew R., David Bustos, Jeffrey S. Pigati, Kathleen B. Springer, Thomas M. Urban, Vance T. Holliday, Sally C. Reynolds, et al.
2021   Evidence of Humans in North America During the Last Glacial Maximum. *Science* 373:1528–1531.

Bettinger, Robert L.
1991   Aboriginal Occupation at Altitude: Alpine Villages in the White Mountains of Eastern California. *American Anthropologist* 93:656–679.

Bettinger, Robert L., Bruce Winterhalder, and Richard McElreath
2006   A Simple Model of Technological Intensification. *Journal of Archaeological Science* 33:538–545.

Billinger, Michael, and John W. Ives
2015   Inferring Demographic Structure with Moccasin Size Data from the Promontory Caves, Utah. *American Journal of Physical Anthropology* 156:76–89.

Binford, Lewis R.
1983   *In Pursuit of the Past: Decoding the Archaeological Record*. Thames and Hudson, New York.

Blackburn, Thomas, and Kat Anderson
1993   Introduction: Managing the Domesticated Environment. In *Before the Wilderness: Environmental Management by Native Californians*, edited by Thomas C. Blackburn and Kat Anderson, pp. 15–26. Ballena, Menlo Park, California.

Blegen, Anne H.
1925   Journal of the Voyage Made by Chevalier de la Verendrye, with One of His Brothers, in Search of the Western Sea Addressed to the Marquis de Beauharnois. *The Quarterly of the Oregon Historical Society* 26:116–129.

Bolton, Herbert E.
1951   *Pageant in the Wilderness: The Story of the Escalante Expedition to the Interior Basin, 1776.* Utah State Historical Society, Salt Lake City.

Boomgarden, Shannon A., Duncan Metcalfe, and Ellyse T. Simons
2019   An Optimal Irrigation Model: Theory, Experimental Results, and Implications for Future Research. *American Antiquity* 84:252–273.

Bowyer, Vandy E., and Jessica Z. Metcalfe
2022   Bison Ecology, Environmental Conditions, and the Promontory Phase, Northeast Utah. In *Holes in Our Moccasins, Holes in Our Stories: Apachean Origins and the Promontory, Franktown, and Dismal River Archaeological Records*, edited by John W. Ives and Joel C. Janetski, pp. 178–186. University of Utah Press, Salt Lake City.

Broughton, Jack M., David A. Byers, Reid A. Bryson, William Eckerle, and David B. Madsen
2008   Did Climatic Seasonality Control Late Quaternary Artiodactyl Densities in Western North America? *Quaternary Science Reviews* 27:1916–1937.

Broughton, Jack M., and Gerald R. Smith
2016   The Fishes of Lake Bonneville: Implications for Drainage History, Biogeography, and Lake Levels. In *Lake Bonneville: A Scientific Update*, edited by Charles G. Oviatt and John F. Shroder, pp. 292–351. Developments in Earth Surface Processes 20. Elsevier, Amsterdam.

Brunswig, Robert H.
2020a   Ritual Places and Sacred Pathways of Ute Spiritual/Mundane Landscapes in the Southern Colorado Rockies. In *Spirit Lands of the Eagle and Bear: Numic Archaeology and Ethnohistory in the Rocky Mountains and Borderlands*, edited by Robert H. Brunswig, pp. 171–192. University Press of Colorado, Louisville.

Brunswig, Robert H. (editor)
2020b   *Spirit Lands of the Eagle and Bear: Numic Archaeology and Ethnohistory in the Rocky Mountains and Borderlands.* University Press of Colorado, Louisville.

Bryan, Alan L.
1979   Smith Creek Cave. In *The Archaeology of Smith Creek Canyon, Eastern Nevada*, edited by Donald R. Tuohy and Doris L. Rendall, pp. 162–253. Nevada State Museum Anthropological Papers No. 17. Nevada State Museum, Carson City.

Burr, Ted N., and Donald R. Currey
1988   The Stockton Bar. In *In the Footsteps of G. K. Gilbert: Lake Bonneville and Neotectonics of the Eastern Basin and Range Province Guidebook for Field Trip Twelve*, edited by

Michael N. Machette, pp. 66–74. Utah Geological and Mineral Survey Miscellaneous Publication 88, no. 1. Salt Lake City.

Burry, John N.
1989 Social Spencerism Not Social Darwinism. *Medicine and War* 5(3):148–150.

Byers, David A., and Jack M. Broughton
2004 Holocene Environmental Change, Artiodactyl Abundances, and Human Hunting Strategies in the Great Basin. *American Antiquity* 69:235–255.

Campbell, Sarah K.
1990 *PostColumbian Culture History in the Northern Columbia Plateau A.D. 1500–1900*. Garland, New York.

Cannon, Mike, and Sarah Creer (editors)
2010 Data Recovery Excavations at 42Dv2, Davis County, Utah. SWCA Environmental Consultants, Salt Lake City.

Carlyle, Shawn W., Ryan L. Parr, Geoffrey Hayes, and Dennis H. O'Rourke
2000 Context of Maternal Lineages in the Greater Southwest. *American Journal of Physical Anthropology* 113:85–101.

Castleton, Kenneth B.
1979 *Petroglyphs and Pictographs of Utah: The South, Central, West, and Northwest*. Vol. 4. Utah Museum of Natural History, Salt Lake City.

Chady, Christine, David Diggs, and Robert H. Brunswig
2020 Reconstructing a Prehistoric Ute Sacred Landscape in the Southern Rocky Mountains. In *Spirit Lands of the Eagle and Bear: Numic Archaeology and Ethnohistory in the Rocky Mountains and Borderlands*, edited by Robert H. Brunswig, pp. 151–170. University Press of Colorado, Louisville.

Chavez, Fray Angélico, and Ted J. Warner
1995 *The Domínguez-Escalante Journal: Their Expedition Through Colorado, Utah, Arizona and New Mexico in 1776*. University of Utah Press, Salt Lake City.

Cippola, Craig N.
2017 Native American Diaspora and Ethnogenesis. Oxford Handbooks Online. https://doi.org/10.1093/oxfordhb/9780199935413.013.69.

Clark, Jorie, Anders E. Carlson, Alberto V. Reyes, Elizabeth C. B. Carlson, Louise Guillaume, Glenn A. Milne, Lev Tarasov, Marc Caffee, Klaus Wilcken, and Dylan H. Rood
2022 The Age of the Opening of the Ice-Free Corridor and Implications for the Peopling of the Americas. *Proceedings of the National Academy of Sciences* 119(14):1–6.

Codding, Brian F., and Terry L. Jones
2007 Man the Showoff? Or the Ascendance of a Just-So-Story: A Comment on Recent Applications of Costly Signaling Theory in American Archaeology. *American Antiquity* 72:349–357.

Cole, Sally
2009 *Legacy On Stone: Rock Art of the Colorado Plateau and Four Corners Region*. Johnson Books, Boulder, Colorado.

Coltrain, Joan Brenner
1993 Fremont Corn Agriculture: A Pilot Stable Carbon Isotope Study. *Utah Archaeology* 6:49–55.
1996 Stable Carbon and Radioisotope Analysis. In *Steinaker Gap: An Early Fremont Farm-*

stead, by Richard K. Talbot and Lane D. Richens, pp. 115–122. Museum of Peoples and Cultures Occasional Papers No. 2. Brigham Young University, Provo, Utah.

Coltrain, Joan Brenner, and Joel C. Janetski
2013 The Stable and Radio-Isotope Chemistry of Southeastern Utah Basketmaker II Burials: Dietary Analysis Using the Linear Mixing Model SISUS, Age and Sex Patterning, Geolocation and Temporal Patterning. *Journal of Archaeological Science* 40: 4711–4730.
2019 Reevaluation of Basketmaker II Origins. *Journal of Anthropological Archaeology* 56:1–19. https://doi.org/10.1016/j.jaa.2019.10185.

Coltrain, Joan Brenner, and Thomas W. Stafford Jr.
1999 Stable Carbon Isotopes and Great Salt Lake Wetlands Diet: Toward an Understanding of the Great Basin Formative. In *Prehistoric Lifeways in the Great Basin Wetlands: Bioarchaeological Reconstruction and Interpretation*, edited by Brian E. Hemphill and Clark S. Larsen, pp. 55–83. University of Utah Press, Salt Lake City.

Connolly, Thomas J.
2013 Implications of New Radiocarbon Ages on Coiled Basketry from the Northern Great Basin. *American Antiquity* 78:373–384.

Connolly, Thomas J., and Pat Barker
2004 Basketry Chronology of the Early Holocene in the Northern Great Basin. In *Early and Middle Holocene Archaeology of the Northern Great Basin*, edited by Dennis L. Jenkins, Thomas J. Connolly, and C. Melvin Aikens, pp. 241–250. University of Oregon Anthropological Papers No. 62. University of Oregon, Eugene.

Couture, Marilyn, Mary F. Ricks, Lucile Housley
1986 Foraging Behavior of a Contemporary Northern Great Basin Population. *Journal of California and Great Basin Anthropology* 8:150–160.

Creaseman, Steven D., and Linda J. Scott
1987 Texas Creek Overlook: Evidence for Late Fremont (post A.D. 1200) Occupation in Northwest Colorado. *Southwestern Lore* 53:1–16.

Cronon, William
2011 *Changes in the Land: Indians, Colonists, and the Ecology of New England*. Reprinted. Hill and Wang, New York. Originally published 1983.

Currey, Donald R.
1983 *Lake Bonneville: Selected Features of Relevance to Neotectonic Analysis.* United States Geological Survey Open-File Report 82-1070.

Darrah, William Culp
1961 *Powell of the Colorado*. Rev. ed. 2015. Princeton University Press, Princeton, New Jersey.

David, Bruno, and Julian Thomas (editors)
2008 *Handbook of Landscape Archaeology*. Left Coast Press, Walnut Creek California.

Davis, Loren. G., David B. Madsen, Lorena Becerra-Valdivia, Thomas Higham, David A. Sisson, Sarah M. Skinner, et al.
2019 Late Upper Paleolithic Occupation at Cooper's Ferry, Idaho, USA, ~16,000 Years Ago. *Science* 365: 891–897.

d'Azevedo, Warren L. (editor)
1986 *Great Basin*. Handbook of North American Indians, Vol. 11, William C. Sturtevant, general editor, Smithsonian Institution, Washington, D.C.

Denevan, William
1992 The Pristine Myth: The Landscape of the Americas in 1492. In *The Americas Before and After 1492: Current Geographical Research*, edited by Karl W. Butzer, pp. 369–385. Annals of the Association of American Geographers 82(3). Association of American Geographers, Washington, D.C.

Dobyns, Henry F.
1983 *Their Number Become Thinned: Native American Population Dynamics in Eastern North America.* University of Tennessee Press, Knoxville.

Dodd, Walter A., Jr.
1982 *Final Year Excavations at the Evans Mound Site.* Anthropological Papers No. 106. University of Utah Press, Salt Lake City.

Doering, Briana N., Julie A. Esdale, Joshua D. Reuther, and Senna D. Catenacci
2020 A Multiscalar Consideration of the Athabascan Migration. *American Antiquity* 85: 470–491.

Duke, Daron
2015 Haskett Spear Weaponry and Protein-Residue Evidence of Proboscidean Hunting in the Great Salt Lake Desert, Utah. *PaleoAmerica* 1:109–112.

Duke, Daron, Eric Wohlgemuth, Karen R. Adams, Angela Armstrong-Ingram, Sarah K. Rice, and D. Craig Young
2022 Earliest Evidence for Human Use of Tobacco in the Pleistocene Americas." *Nature Human Behaviour* 6:183–192.

Elston, Robert G., and Elizabeth E. Budy (editors)
1990 *The Archaeology of James Creek Shelter.* Anthropological Papers No. 115. University of Utah Press, Salt Lake City.

Erlandson, Jon
2014 After Clovis-First Collapsed: Reimagining the Peopling of the Americas. In *Paleoamerican Odyssey*, edited by Kelly E. Graf, Caroline V. Ketron, and Michael R. Waters, pp. 127–132. Center for the Study of the First Americans, Texas A&M University Press, College Station.

Falk, Dan
2020 The Complicated Legacy of Herbert Spencer, the Man Who Coined "Survival of the Fittest." *Smithsonian Magazine*, April 29.

Fiedel, Stuart J., and David W. Anthony
2003 Deerslayers, Pathfinders, and Icemen: Origins of the European Neolithic as Seen from the Frontier. In *Colonization of Unfamiliar Landscapes: The Archaeology of Adaptation*, edited by Marcy Rockman and James Steele, pp. 144–168. Routledge, Taylor and Francis Group, London and New York.

Finley, Judson Byrd, and Maureen P. Boyle
2014 The Frequency and Typology of Ceramic Sites in Western Wyoming. *Plains Anthropologist* 59:38–57.

Finley, Judson Byrd, Maureen P. Boyle, and David C. Harvey
2015 Obsidian Conveyance in the Mountain World of the Numa. *Plains Anthropologist* 60:375.

Finley, Judson Byrd, Erick Robinson, R. Justin DeRose, and Elizabeth Hora
2020 Multidecadal Climate Variability and the Florescence of Fremont Societies in Eastern Utah. *American Antiquity* 85:93–112.

Fowler, Catherine S.
1972   Some Ecological Clues to Proto-Numic Homelands. In *Great Basin Cultural Ecology: A Symposium*, edited by Don D. Fowler, pp. 105–121. Publication in the Social Sciences. Desert Research Institute, University of Nevada, Reno.
1989   *Willard Z. Park's Ethnographic Notes on the Northern Paiute of Western Nevada, 1933–1940*. Anthropological Papers No. 114. University of Utah Press, Salt Lake City.
1992   *In the Shadow of Fox Peak: An Ethnography of the Cattail-Eater Northern Paiute People of Stillwater Marsh*. Cultural Resource Series 5. United States Department of Interior, Fish and Wildlife Service, Region 1.

Francis, Julie E., and Lawrence L. Loendorf
2002   *Ancient Visions: Petroglyphs and Pictographs of the Wind River and Bighorn Country, Wyoming and Montana*. University of Utah Press, Salt Lake City.

Frison, George, and Bruce Bradley
1999   *The Fenn Cache: Clovis Weapons and Tools*. One Horse Land and Cattle Company, Santa Fe, New Mexico.

Garey-Sage, Darla, and Catherine S. Fowler
2016   *Isabel T. Kelly's Southern Paiute Ethnographic Field Notes, 1932–1934*. Anthropological Papers No. 130. University of Utah Press, Salt Lake City.

Geib, Phil R., and Edward A. Jolie
2008   The Role of Basketry in Early Holocene Small Seed Exploitation: Implications of a ca. 9,000 Year-Old Basket from Cowboy Cave, Utah. *American Antiquity* 73:83–102.

Geib, Phil R., and Michael R. Robins
2008   Analysis and AMS Dating of the Great Gallery Food and Tool Bag. *Kiva* 73:291–320.

Gilbert, Grove Karl
1890   *Lake Bonneville*. United States Geological Survey Monograph 1. Available online at Google Books.

Gillespie, Jason D.
2007   Enculturing an Unknown World: Caches and Clovis Landscape Ideology. *Canadian Journal of Archaeology/Journal Canadien d'Archéologie* 31:171–189.

Goebel, Ted, Kelly Graf, Bryan Hockett, and David Rhode
2007   The Paleoindian Occupations at Bonneville Estates Rockshelter, Danger Cave, and Smith Creek Cave (Eastern Great Basin, U.S.A.): Interpreting Their Radiocarbon Chronologies. In *On Shelter's Ledge: Histories, Theories and Methods of Rockshelter Research*, edited by Marcel Kornfeld, Sergey Vasil'ev, and Laura Miotti, pp. 147–161. BAR International Series. Archaeopress, Oxford.

Goebel, Ted, Bryan Hockett, David Rhode, and Kelly Graf
2021   Prehistoric Human Response to Climate Change in the Bonneville Basin, Western North America: The Bonneville Estates Rockshelter Radiocarbon Chronology. *Quaternary Science Reviews* 260:106930.

Goebel, Ted, Michael R. Waters, Dennis H. O'Rourke
2008   The Late Pleistocene Dispersal of Modern Humans in the Americas. *Science* 319:1497–1502.

Grayson, Donald K.
2006   Holocene Bison in the Great Basin, Western USA. *The Holocene* 16:913–925.
2011   *The Great Basin: A Natural Prehistory*. University of California Press, Berkeley.

Green, Dee C.
1964 The Hinckley Figurines as Indicators of the Position of Utah Valley in the Sevier Culture. *American Antiquity* 30:74–80.

Grimstead, Deanna N.
2012 Prestige and Prejudice: The Role of Long Distance Big Game Hunting as an Optimal Foraging Decision. *American Antiquity* 77:168–178.

Gunnerson, James H.
1957 *An Archeological Survey of the Fremont Area.* Anthropological Papers No. 28. University of Utah Press, Salt Lake City.

Hage, Per, Bojka Milicic, Mauricio Mixco, and Michael J. P. Nichols
2004 The Proto-Numic Kinship System. *Journal of Anthropological Research* 60:359–377.

Haines, Francis
1938 The Northward Spread of Horses Among the Plains Indians. *American Anthropologist* 40:429–437.

Harrison, Merry Lycett
2003 The Patterson Bundle: An Herbalist's Discovery. *Utah Archaeology* 16:53–62.

Hart, Isaac Alfred, Joan Brenner-Coltrain, Shannon Boomgarden, Andrea Brunelle, Larry Coats, Duncan Metcalfe and Michael Lewis
2021 Evidence for a Winter-Snowpack Derived Water Source for the Fremont Maize Farmers of Range Creek Canyon, Utah, USA. *The Holocene* 31:446–456.

Hartley, L. P.
2015 *The Go-Between.* Reprinted. Penguin, U.K. Originally published 1956.

Hazelwood, Lee, and James Steele
2003 Colonizing New Landscapes: Archaeological Detectability of the First Phase. In *Colonization of Unfamiliar Landscapes: The Archaeology of Adaptation*, edited by Marcy Rockman and James Steele, pp. 203–221. Routledge and the Taylor and Francis Group, London and New York.

Heaton, Timothy, and Frederick Grady
2003 The Late Wisconsin Vertebrate History of Prince of Wales Island, Southeast Alaska. In *Ice Age Cave Faunas of North America*, edited by Blaine Schubert, Jim I. Mead, and Russell Wm. Graham, pp. 17–53. Indiana University Press, Bloomington.

Hegmon, Michelle
2005 Beyond the Mold: Questions of Inequality in Southwest Villages. In *North American Archaeology*, edited by Timothy R. Pauketat and Diana DiPaolo Loren, pp. 212–234. Blackwell, Malden, Massachusetts.

Hemphill, Brian E., and Clark S. Larsen (editors)
1999 *Prehistoric Lifeways in the Great Basin Wetlands: Bioarchaeological Reconstruction and Interpretation.* University of Utah Press, Salt Lake City.

Herzog, Nicole, and Anne Lawlor
2016 Reevaluating Diet and Technology in the Archaic Great Basin Using Starch Grain Assemblages from Hogup Cave, Utah. *American Antiquity* 81:664–681.

Hildebrandt, William
2016 Northern Paiute, Western Shoshone, and the Numic Expansion. In *Prehistory of Nevada's Northern Tier: Archaeological Investigations Along the Ruby Pipeline*, by William Hildebrandt, Kelly McGuire, Jerome King, Allika Ruby, and D. Craig Young, pp. 329–339.

Anthropological Papers of the American Museum of Natural History No. 101. American Museum of Natural History, New York.

Hockett, Bryan S.
1998   Sociopolitical Meaning of Faunal Remains from Baker Village. *American Antiquity* 63: 289–302.

Hockett, Bryan, Cliff Creger, Beth Smith, Craig Young, James Carter, Eric Dillingham, Rachel Crews, Evan Pellegrini
2013   Large-Scale Trapping Features from the Great Basin, USA: The Significance of Leadership and Communal Gatherings in Ancient Foraging Societies. *Quaternary International* 297:64–78.

Hockett, Bryan, and Eric Dillingham
2023   *Large-Scale Traps of the Great Basin.* Texas A&M University Press, College Station.

Hockett, Bryan, and Maury Morgenstein
2003   Ceramic Production, Fremont Foragers, and the Late Archaic Prehistory of the North-Central Great Basin. *Utah Archaeology* 16:1–36.

Holmer, Richard N.
1990   Prehistory of the Northern Shoshone. In *Fort Hall and the Shoshone-Bannock*, edited by Ernest S. Lohse and Richard N. Holmer, pp. 41–59. Idaho State University Press, Pocatello.
1994   In Search of Ancestral Northern Shoshone. In *Across the West: Human Population Movement and the Expansion of the Numa*, edited by D. B. Madsen and D. Rhode, pp. 179–187. University of Utah Press, Salt Lake City.

Hughes, Richard E.
2011   *Perspectives on Prehistoric Trade and Exchange in California and the Great Basin.* University of Utah Press, Salt Lake City.

Hull, Kathleen
2009   *Pestilence and Persistence: Yosemite Indian Demography and Culture in Colonial California.* University of California Press, Berkeley.

Hultkrantz, Ake
1986   Mythology and Religious Concepts. In *Great Basin*, edited by W. L. d'Azevedo, pp. 630–640. Handbook of North American Indians, Vol. 11, William C. Sturtevant, general editor. Smithsonian Institution Press, Washington, D.C.

Hunt, Alice
1953   *Archeological Survey of the La Sal Mountain Area, Utah.* Anthropological Papers No. 14. University of Utah Press, Salt Lake City.

Hunter-Anderson, Rosalind L.
1977   A Theoretical Approach to the Study of House Form. *For Theory Building in Archaeology*, pp. 287–315.

Ives, John W.
2014   Resolving the Promontory Culture Enigma. In *Archaeology in the Great Basin and Southwest: Papers in Honor of Don D. Fowler*, edited by Nancy J. Parezo and Joel C. Janetski, pp. 149–162. University of Utah Press, Salt Lake City.

Ives, John W., Duane G. Froese, Joel C. Janetski, Fiona Brock, and Christopher Bronk Ramsey
2014   A High Resolution Chronology for Steward's Promontory Culture Collections, Promontory Point, Utah. *American Antiquity* 79:616–637.

Ives, John W., Duane Froese, Kisha Supernant, and Gabriel Yanicki
2013   Vectors, Vestiges, and Valhallas: Rethinking the Corridor. In *Paleoamerican Odyssey*, edited by Kelly E. Graf, Caroline V. Ketron, and Michael R. Waters, pp. 149–169. Center for the Study of the First Americans, Texas A&M University Press, College Station.

Ives, John W., and Joel C. Janetski (editors)
2022   *Holes in Our Moccasins, Holes in Our Stories: Apachean Origins and the Promontory, Franktown, and Dismal River Archaeological Records.* University of Utah Press, Salt Lake City.

Ives, Ronald L.
1948   The Outlet of Lake Bonneville. *Scientific Monthly* 67:415–426. American Association for the Advancement of Science.

Janetski, Joel C.
1990   Utah Lake: Its Role in the Prehistory of Utah Valley. *Utah Historical Quarterly* 58:5–31.
1991   *The Ute of Utah Lake.* Anthropological Papers No. 116. University of Utah Press, Salt Lake City.
2002   Trade in Fremont Society: Contexts and Contrasts. *Journal of Anthropological Archaeology* 21:344–370.

Janetski, Joel C., and Grant C. Smith
2007   *Hunter-Gatherer Archaeology in Utah Valley.* Museum of Peoples and Cultures Occasional Papers No. 12. Brigham Young University, Provo, Utah.

Janetski, Joel C., and Richard K. Talbot
2000   Social and Community Organization. In *Clear Creek Canyon Archaeological Project: Results and Synthesis*, edited by Joel C. Janetski, Richard K. Talbot, Deborah E. Newman, Lane D. Richens, and James D. Wilde, pp. 247–262. Museum of Peoples and Cultures Occasional Papers No. 7. Brigham Young University, Provo.
2014   Fremont Social Organization: A Southwestern Perspective. In *Archaeology in the Great Basin and Southwest: Papers in Honor of Don D. Fowler*, edited by Nancy J. Parezo and Joel C. Janetski, pp. 118–129. University of Utah Press, Salt Lake City.

Jennings, Jesse D.
1956   The American Southwest: A Problem in Cultural Isolation. In *Seminars in Archaeology, 1955*, edited by Robert Wauchope, pp. 59–127. Memoirs No. 11. Society for American Archaeology, Washington, D.C.
1957   *Danger Cave.* Anthropological Papers No. 27. University of Utah Press, Salt Lake City.
1978   *Prehistory of Utah and the Eastern Great Basin.* Anthropological Papers No. 98. University of Utah Press, Salt Lake City.

Johansson, Lindsay D., Katie K. Richards, and James R. Allison
2014   Wolf Village (42UT273): A Case Study in Fremont Architectural Variability. *Utah Archaeology* 27:33–56.

Jorgensen, Joseph
1992   Foreword. In *Ute Tales*, by Anne M. Smith, pp. xi–xxiv. University of Utah Press, Salt Lake City.

Kay, Charles E.
2002   Are Ecosystems Structured from the Top-Down or Bottom-Up? A New Look at an Old Debate. In *Wilderness and Political Ecology: Aboriginal Influences and the Original State*

of Nature, edited by Charles E. Kay and Randy T. Simmons, pp. 215–237. University of Utah Press, Salt Lake City.

Kay, Charles E., and Randy T. Simmons (editors)
2002 *Wilderness and Political Ecology: Aboriginal Influences and the Original State of Nature.* University of Utah Press, Salt Lake City.

Kelly, Isabel T.
1932 *Ethnography of the Surprise Valley Paiute.* University of California Publications in American Archaeology and Ethnology 31:67–210.
1964 *Southern Paiute Ethnography.* Anthropological Papers No. 69. University of Utah Press, Salt Lake City.

Kelly, Robert L.
1995 *The Foraging Spectrum: Diversity in Hunter-Gatherer Lifeways.* Smithsonian Institution Press, Washington, D.C.
2001 *Prehistory of the Carson Desert and Stillwater Mountains: Environment, Mobility, and Subsistence in a Great Basin Wetland.* Anthropological Papers No. 123. University of Utah Press, Salt Lake City.
2003 Colonization of New Land by Hunter-Gatherers: Expectations and Implications Based on Ethnographic Data. In *Colonization of Unfamiliar Landscapes: The Archaeology of Adaptation*, edited by Marcy Rockman and James Steele, pp. 44–58. Routledge, Taylor and Francis Group, London and New York.

Kennett, Douglas J., Patricia M. Lambert, John R. Johnson, and Brendan J. Culleton
2013 Sociopolitical Effects of Bow and Arrow Technology in Prehistoric Coastal California. *Evolutionary Anthropology: Issues, News, and Reviews* 22:124–132.

Keyser, James D., and George Poetschat
2017 Uinta Fremont Rock Art in Southwestern Wyoming: Marking the Fremont Northern Periphery. *Plains Anthropologist* 62:157–178.

Kiahtipes, Christopher A.
2009 Fire in the Desert: Holocene Paleoenvironments in the Bonneville Basin. Master's thesis, Department of Anthropology, Washington State University, Pullman.

Kitchen, Stanley G.
2015 Climate and Human Influences on Historical Fire Regimes (AD 1400–1900) in the Eastern Great Basin (USA). *The Holocene* 26:397–407.

Knight, Troy A., David M. Meko, and Christopher H. Baisan
2010 A Bimillennial-Length Tree-Ring Reconstruction of Precipitation for the Tavaputs Plateau, Northeastern Utah. *Quaternary Research* 73:107–117.

Koch, Alexander, Chris Brierley, Mark M. Maslin, and Simon L. Lewis
2019 Earth System Impacts of the European Arrival and Great Dying in the Americas After 1492. *Quaternary Science Reviews* 207:13–36.

Kornfeld, Marcel
2013 *The First Rocky Mountaineers: Colorado Before Colorado.* University of Utah Press, Salt Lake City.

Kroeber, Theodora
2004 *Ishi in Two Worlds: A Biography of the Last Wild Indian in North America.* Reprinted. University of California Press, Berkeley. Originally published 1961.

LaBelle, Jason, E. Steve Cassells, and Michael D. Metcalf (editors)
2012   Footprints in the Snow: Papers in Honor of James B. Benedict. *Southwestern Lore* 78(1):3–90.

Lancy, David
2022   *The Anthropology of Childhood: Cherubs, Chattel, Changelings.* 3rd ed. Cambridge University Press, New York.

Lawlor, Anne T.
2020   Plant Fiber and Foraging Tools in the Eastern Great Basin. PhD dissertation, Department of Anthropology, University of Utah, Salt Lake City. ResearchGate publication no. 344674564.

Leigh, Rufus Wood
1958   Lake Bonneville, Its Name. *Utah Historical Quarterly* 26:150–159. Utah State Historical Society, Salt Lake City.

Lewandowska, Magdalena
2020   Athapaskan Migration to the North American Southwest. *Contributions in New World Archaeology* 12:139–163. https://www.researchgate.net/publication/341489440_Athapaskan_Migration_to_the_North_American_Southwest.

Lewis, Henry T.
1973   *Patterns of Indian Burning in California: Ecology and Ethnohistory.* Ballena, Menlo Park, California.

Liebmann, Matthew J., Joshua Farella, Christopher I. Roos, Adam Stack, Sarah Martini, and Thomas W. Swetnam
2016   Native American Depopulation, Reforestation, and Fire Regimes in the Southwest United States, 1492–1900 CE. *Proceedings of the National Academy of Sciences* 113:E696–E704.

Lightfoot, Kent G., Rob Q. Cuthrell, Chuck J. Striplen, and Mark G. Hylkema
2013   Rethinking the Study of Landscape Management Practices Among Hunter-Gatherers in North America. *American Antiquity* 78:285–301.

Liljeblad, Sven
1986   Oral Tradition: Content and Style of Verbal Arts. In *Great Basin*, edited by W. L. d'Azevedo, pp. 660–672. Handbook of North American Indians, Vol. 11, William C. Sturtevant, general editor. Smithsonian Institution Press, Washington, D.C.

Lindsay, Clint
2005   Late Prehistoric/Protohistoric Demography. In *Kern River 2003 Expansion Project*, Vol. 4, edited by Alan D. Reed, Matthew T. Seddon, and Heather K. Stettler, pp. 381–392. Alpine Archaeological Consultants, Montrose, Colorado, and SWCA Environmental Consultants, Salt Lake City.

Loendorf, Lawrence, Laurie L. White, and Greg White
2012   Rock Art Panel Tracing at Castle Gardens, Site 48FR108, Fremont County, Wyoming. Sacred Sites Research, Albuquerque, New Mexico.

Lohse, Ernst S.
1980   Fremont Settlement Pattern and Agricultural Variation. In *Fremont Perspectives,* edited by David B. Madsen, pp. 41–54. Utah State Historical Society, Antiquities Section Selected Papers 7:41–54.

Louderback, Lisbeth A., and David E. Rhode
2009   15,000 Years of Vegetation Change in the Bonneville Basin: The Blue Lake Pollen Record. *Quaternary Science Reviews* 28:308–326.

Lubinski, Patrick
1999   The Communal Pronghorn Hunt: A Review of the Ethnographic and Archaeological Evidence. *Journal of California and Great Basin Anthropology* 21:158–181.

Lupo, Karen D., and Dave N. Schmitt
1997   On Late Holocene Variability in Bison Populations in the Northeastern Great Basin. *Journal of California and Great Basin Anthropology* 19:50–69.

Machette, Michael N. (editor)
1988   *In the Footsteps of G. K. Gilbert: Lake Bonneville and Neotectonics of the Eastern Basin and Range Province Guidebook for Field Trip Twelve.* Utah Geological and Mineral Survey Miscellaneous Publication No. 88-1. Salt Lake City.

Madsen, David B.
2015   A Framework for the Initial Occupation of the Americas. *Paleoamerica* 1(3):217–250.
2016   The Early Human Occupation of the Bonneville Basin. In *Lake Bonneville: A Scientific Update*, edited by Charles G. Oviatt and John F. Shroder, pp. 504–525. Developments in Earth Surface Processes Vol. 20. Elsevier, Amsterdam.

Madsen, David B., Loren G. Davis, David Rhode, and Charles G. Oviatt
2022   Comment on Evidence of Humans in North America During the Last Glacial Maximum. *Science* 375:eabm4678.

Madsen, David B., and James E. Kirkman
1988   Hunting Hoppers. *American Antiquity* 53:593–604.

Madsen, David B., and David Rhode
1990   Early Holocene Pinyon (*Pinus monophylla*) in the Northeastern Great Basin. *Quaternary Research* 33:94–101.

Madsen, David B., and David Rhode (editors)
1994   *Across the West: Human Population Movement and the Expansion of the Numa.* University of Utah Press, Salt Lake City.

Madsen, David B., Dave N. Schmitt, and David Page
2015   *The Paleoarchaic Occupation of the Old River Bed Delta.* Anthropological Papers No. 128. University of Utah Press, Salt Lake City.

Madsen, David B., and Steven R. Simms
1998   The Fremont Complex: A Behavioral Perspective. *Journal of World Prehistory* 12:255–336.

Magargal, Kate E., Ashley K. Parker, Kenneth Blake Vernon, Will Rath, Brian F. Codding
2017   The Ecology of Population Dispersal: Modeling Alternative Basin-Plateau Foraging Strategies to Explain the Numic Expansion. *American Journal of Human Biology* 29(4):e2300.

Magne, Martin P. R.
2012   Modeling Athapaskan Migrations. In *From the Land of Ever Winter to the American Southwest: Athapaskan Migrations, Mobility, and Ethnogenesis*, edited by Deni J. Seymour, pp. 356–379. University of Utah Press, Salt Lake City.

Magne, Martin P. R., and Michael A. Klassen
2002   A Possible Fluteplayer Pictograph Site near Exshaw, Alberta. *Canadian Journal of Archaeology/Journal Canadien d'Archéologie* 25:1–24.

Malhi, Ripan S.
2012   DNA Evidence of a Prehistoric Athapaskan Migration from the Subarctic to the Southwest of North America. In *From the Land of Everwinter to the American Southwest: Athapaskan Migrations, Mobility and Ethnogenesis*, edited by Deni J. Seymour, pp. 241–248. University of Utah Press, Salt Lake City.

Malhi, Ripan S., Holly M. Mortensen, Jason A. Eshleman, Brian M. Kemp, Joseph G. Lorenz, Frederika A. Kaestle, John R. Johnson, Clara Gorodezky, and David Glenn Smith
2003   Native American mtDNA Prehistory in the American Southwest. *American Journal of Physical Anthropology* 120:108–124.

Mann, Charles C.
2002   1491. *Atlantic Monthly* (March):41–53.
2005   *1491: New Revelations of the Americas Before Columbus.* Alfred Knopf, New York.
2013   The Clovis Point and the Discovery of America's First Culture. *Smithsonian Magazine* (November). https://www.smithsonianmag.com/history/the-clovis-point-and-the-discovery=of-americas-first-culture-3825828/.

Marwitt, John P.
1970   *Median Village and Fremont Culture Regional Variation.* Anthropological Papers No. 95. University of Utah Press, Salt Lake City.

Matson, R. G.
1991   *The Origins of Southwest Agriculture.* University of Arizona Press, Tucson.
2012   *Our Changing Understanding of the Basketmaker II Culture: Demography and Ethnicity.* Friends of Cedar Mesa. Available online.

Mayr, Ernst
1982   *The Growth of Biological Thought: Diversity, Evolution, and Inheritance.* Belknap, Harvard University, Cambridge, Massachusetts.

McAdoo, J. Kent, Brad W. Schultz, and Sherman R. Swanson
2013   Aboriginal Precedent for Active Management of Sagebrush–Perennial Grass Communities in the Great Basin. *Rangeland Ecology and Management* 66:241–253.

McGuire, Kelly R., and William R. Hildebrandt
2005   Re-Thinking Great Basin Foragers: Prestige Hunting and Costly Signaling During the Middle Archaic Period. *American Antiquity* 70:695–712.

McNeil, Lynda D., and David L. Shaul
2018   Western Basketmakers: Social Networking among Uto-Aztecan Foragers and Migrant Farmers on the Colorado Plateau. *Kiva* 84:203–236.
2020   Itamu umumi yooya'ökiwn i ("We Will Arrive as Rain to You"): Evidence of Historical Relationships among Western Basketmaker, Fremont, and Hopi Peoples. *Kiva* 86:245–273.

McPhee, John A.
1981   *Basin and Range.* Farrar, Straus, and Giroux, New York.

Mensing, Scott, Stephanie Livingston, and Pat Barker
2006   Long-Term Fire History in Great Basin Sagebrush Reconstructed from Macroscopic Charcoal in Spring Sediments, Newark Valley, Nevada. *Western North American Naturalist* 66:64–77.

Mensing, Scott, Jeremy Smith, Kelly Burkle Norman, Marie Allan
2008 Extended Drought in the Great Basin of Western North America in the Last Two Millennia Reconstructed from Pollen Records. *Quaternary International* 188:79–89.

Merrill, William L.
2012 The Historical Linguistics of Uto-Aztecan Agriculture. *Anthropological Linguistics* 54:203–260.

Merrill, William L., Robert J. Hard, Jonathan B. Mabry, Gayle J. Fritz, Karen R. Adams, John R. Roney, and Art C. MacWilliams
2009 The Diffusion of Maize to the Southwestern United States and Its Impact. *Proceedings of the National Academy of Sciences* 106(50):21019–21026.

Metcalfe, Duncan, and Lisa V. Larrabee
1985 Fremont Irrigation: Evidence from Gooseberry Valley. *Journal of California and Great Basin Anthropology* 7:244–254.

Metcalfe, Jessica Z., John W. Ives, Sabrina Shirazi, Kevin P. Gilmore, Jennifer Hallson, Fiona Brock, Bonnie J. Clark, and Beth Shapiro
2021 Isotopic Evidence for Long-Distance Connections of the AD Thirteenth-Century Promontory Caves Occupants. *American Antiquity* 86:526–548.

Middleton, Emily S., Geoffrey M. Smith, William J. Cannon, and Mary F. Ricks
2014 Paleoindian Rock Art: Establishing the Antiquity of Great Basin Carved Abstract Petroglyphs in the Northern Great Basin. *Journal of Archaeological Science* 43:21–30.

Middleton, Jessica L., Patrick M. Lubinski, and Michael D. Metcalf
2007 Ceramics from the Firehole Basin Site and Firehole Phase in the Wyoming Basin. *Plains Anthropologist* 52:29–41.

Miller, Jay
1983 Basin Religion and Theology: A Comparative Study of Power (Puha). *Journal of California and Great Basin Anthropology* 5:66–86.

Miller, Richard F., and Peter E. Wigand
1994 Holocene Changes in Semiarid Pinyon-Juniper Woodlands. *Bioscience* 44:465–474

Miller, Wick R.
1972 *Newe Natekwinappeh: Shoshoni Stories and Dictionary.* Anthropological Papers No. 94. University of Utah Press, Salt Lake City.

Mooney, Adrien
2014 An Analysis of the Archaeological Work of the Provo River Delta, Utah. Master's thesis, Department of Anthropology, Brigham Young University, Provo. https://scholarsarchive.byu.edu/cgi/viewcontent.cgi?article=4973&context=etd.

Mooney, James
1898 *Calendar History of the Kiowa Indians.* 17th Annual Report of the Bureau of American Ethnology. United States Government Printing Office, Washington, D.C.

Morgan, Christopher, Marielle Black, Amanda R. Richey, Kristina Crawford, and Mark Giambastiani
2020 The Ecology of the Alpine Villages of Eastern California. In *Cowboy Ecologist: Essays in Honor of Robert L. Bettinger*, edited by Roshanne S. Bakhtiary, Terry L. Jones, and Michael G. Delacorte, pp. 135–155. Center for Archaeological Research, Davis, California.

Morgan, Christopher, Ashley Losey, and Richard Adams
2012   High-Altitude Hunter-Gatherer Residential Occupations in Wyoming's Wind River Range. *North American Archaeologist* 33:35–79.

Morris, Earl H., and Robert F. Burgh
1954   *Basket Maker II Sites Near Durango, Colorado.* Carnegie Institution of Washington Publication No. 604. Washington, D.C.

Morss, Noel
2009   *The Ancient Culture of the Fremont River in Utah.* Peabody Museum Papers, Vol. 12, No. 3. Harvard University. Reprinted, University of Utah Press, Salt Lake City. Originally published 1931.

Newlander, Khori
2018   Imagining the Cultural Landscapes of Paleoindians. *Journal of Archaeological Science: Reports* 19:836–845.

O'Connor, Jim E.
1993   *Hydrology, Hydraulics, and Geomorphology of the Bonneville Flood.* Geological Society of America Special Paper No. 274. Geological Society of America, Boulder.
2016   The Bonneville Flood—A Veritable Débâcle. In *Lake Bonneville: A Scientific Update*, edited by Charles G. Oviatt and John F. Shroder Jr., pp. 105–126. Developments in Earth Surface Processes No. 20. Elsevier, Amsterdam.

O'Rourke, Dennis H., Ryan L. Parr, and Shawn Carlyle
1999   Molecular Genetic Variation in Prehistoric Inhabitants of the Eastern Great Basin. In *Prehistoric Lifeways in the Great Basin Wetlands: Bioarchaeological Reconstruction and Interpretation*, edited by Brian E. Hemphill and Clark S. Larsen, pp. 84–102. University of Utah Press, Salt Lake City.

Ortman, Scott G., and Lynda D. McNeil
2017   The Kiowa Odyssey: Evidence of Historical Relationships among Pueblo, Fremont, and Northwest Plains Peoples. *Plains Anthropologist* 63:152–174.

Oviatt, Charles G.
2015   Chronology of Lake Bonneville, 30,000 to 10,000 yr BP. *Quaternary Science Reviews* 110:166–171.
2018   *The Gilbert Episode in the Great Salt Lake Basin, Utah.* Utah Geological Survey Miscellaneous Publication No. 14-3. Utah Department of Natural Resources, Salt Lake City.
2020   G. K. Gilbert and the Bonneville Shoreline. *Geology of the Intermountain West* 7:300–320. An open access journal of the Utah Geological Association. https://doi.org/10.31711/giw.v7.

Oviatt, Charles G., Genevieve Atwood, Benjamin J. C. Laabs, Paul W. Jewell, and Harry M. Joi
2021   A Field Trip to Observe Features of Lake Bonneville, Mountain Glaciation, and Great Salt Lake near Salt Lake City, Utah, USA. In *GSA in the Field in 2020* 60:71–94.

Oviatt, Charles G., Genevieve Atwood, and Robert S. Thompson
2021   History of Great Salt Lake, Utah, USA: Since the Termination of Lake Bonneville. *Limnogeology: Progress, Challenges and Opportunities, Syntheses in Limnogeology*, pp. 233–271. Springer, Cham. https://doi.org/10.1007/978-3-030-66576-0_8.

Oviatt, Charles G., David B. Madsen, David Rhode, and Loren G. Davis
2022   A Critical Assessment of Claims that Human Footprints in the Lake Otero Basin, New

Mexico Date to the Last Glacial Maximum. *Quaternary Research* 2022:1–10. https://doi:10.1017/qua.2022.38.

Page, David, and Daron G. Duke
2015 Toolstone Sourcing, Lithic Resource Use, and Paleoarchaic Mobility in the Western Bonneville Basin. In *The Paleoarchaic Occupation of the Old River Bed Delta*, edited by David B. Madsen, Dave N. Schmitt, and David Page. Anthropological Papers No. 128. University of Utah Press, Salt Lake City.

Park, Willard Z.
1938 *Shamanism in Western North America: A Study in Cultural Relationships.* Cooper Square Publishers, New York.

Parker, Bradley J.
2006 Toward an Understanding of Borderland Processes. *American Antiquity* 71:77–100.

Pavesic, Max G.
2007 The Bonneville Flood Debris Field as Sacred Landscape. *Journal of California and Great Basin Anthropology* 27:15–28.

Pendleton, Lorann S., and David Hurst Thomas
1983 *The Fort Sage Drift Fence, Washoe County, Nevada.* Anthropological Papers of the American Museum of Natural History Vol. 58, Pt. 2. American Museum of Natural History, New York.

Pigati, Jeffery S., Kathleen B. Springer, Matthew R. Bennett, David Bustos, Thomas M. Urban, Vance T. Holliday, Sally C. Reynolds, Daniel Odess
2022 Response to Comment on "Evidence of Humans in North America During the Last Glacial Maximum." *Science* 375(6577), eabm6987.

Pitblado, Bonnie L., Molly Boeka Cannon, Megan Bloxham, Joel Janetski, J. M. Adovasio, Kathleen R. Anderson, and Stephen T. Nelson
2013 Archaeological Fingerprinting and Fremont Figurines: Reuniting the Iconic Pilling Collection. *Advances in Archaeological Practice: A Journal of the Society for American Archaeology* 1:3–12.

Plew, Mark G.
2000 The Archaeology of the Snake River Plain. Faculty and Staff Authored Books 72. Department of Anthropology, Boise State University, Idaho. https://scholarworks.boisestate.edu/fac_books/72.

Plew, Mark G., and Molly K. Bennick
1990 Prehistoric Ceramics in Southwestern Idaho: A Report on the Southwest Idaho Ceramic Project. In *Hunter-Gatherer Ceramics in the Great Basin*, edited by Joanne Mack, pp. 107–122. Nevada State Museum Anthropological Papers No. 23. Nevada State Museum, Carson City.

Potter, Ben A., James F. Baichtal, Alwynne B. Beaudoin, Lars Fehren-Schmitz, C. Vance Haynes, Vance T. Holliday, et al.
2018 Current Evidence Allows Multiple Models for the Peopling of the Americas. *Science Advances* 4:eaat5473.

Potter, Ben A., Alwynne B. Beaudoin, C. Vance Haynes, Vance T. Holliday, Charles E. Holmes, John W. Ives, Robert Kelly, et al.
2018 Letter to the Editor: Arrival Routes of First Americans Uncertain. *Science* 359:1224–1225.

Potter, Ben A., Joshua D. Reuther, Vance T. Holliday, Charles E. Holmes, Shane Miller, and Nicholas Schmuck

2017   Early Colonization of Beringia and Northern North America: Chronology, Routes, and Adaptive Strategies. *Quaternary International* 444B:36–55.

Powell, John Wesley

1891   *North of Mexico. Indian Linguistic Families of America* No. 7. United States Government Printing Office, Washington, D.C.

Proulx, Annie

1999   *Close Range: Wyoming Stories.* Simon and Schuster, New York.

2004   *Bad Dirt: Wyoming Stories 2.* Simon and Schuster, New York.

2009   *Fine Just the Way It Is: Wyoming Stories 3.* Simon and Schuster, New York.

Pyne, Stephen

1982   *Fire in America: A Cultural History of Wildland and Rural Fire.* Princeton University Press, Princeton, New Jersey. Rev. ed., University of Washington Press, Seattle, 2017.

Raghavan, Maanasa, Matthias Steinrücken, Kelley Harris, Stephan Schiffels, Simon Rasmussen, Michael DeGiorgio, et al.

2015   Genomic Evidence for the Pleistocene and Recent Population History of Native Americans. *Science* 349 (6250).

Ramenovsky, Ann F.

1987   *Vectors of Death: The Archaeology of European Contact.* University of New Mexico Press, Albuquerque.

Ramsey, Carolyn, Paul A. Griffiths, Darly W. Fedje, Rebecca J. Wigen, and Quentin Mackie

2004   Preliminary Investigation of a Late Wisconsinan Fauna from K1 cave, Queen Charlotte Islands (Haida Gwaii), Canada. *Quaternary Research* 62:105–109.

Rasmussen, Morten, Sarah L. Anzick, Michael R. Waters, Pontus Skoglund, Michael DeGiorgio, Thomas W. Stafford Jr., Simon Rasmussen, et al.

2014   The Genome of a Late Pleistocene Human from a Clovis Burial Site in Western Montana. *Nature* 506(7487):225–229.

Raven, Christopher

1990   *Archaeological Field Tests of Model Predictions.* Pt. 2 of *Prehistoric Human Geography in the Carson Desert.* Cultural Resource Series No. 4. United States Fish and Wildlife Service, Portland, Oregon.

Raven, Christopher and Robert G. Elston

1989   *A Predictive Model of Land-Use in the Stillwater Wildlife Management Area.* Cultural Resource Series No. 3. United States Fish and Wildlife Service, Portland, Oregon.

Raymond, Anan

1982   Two Historic Aboriginal Game-Drive Enclosures in the Eastern Great Basin. *Journal of California and Great Basin Anthropology* 4:23–33.

Reagan, Albert B.

1931a Some Archaeological Notes on Nine Mile Canyon, Utah. *El Palacio* 31:45–71.

1931b Notes from the Field. *Discoveries* 2:8.

1931c Some Archaeological Notes on Hill Canyon in Northeastern Utah. *El Palacio* 31: 223–244.

Reed, Paul F., and Phil R. Geib
2013 Sedentism, Social Change, Warfare, and the Bow in the Ancient Pueblo Southwest. *Evolutionary Anthropology: Issues, News, and Reviews* 22:103–110.

Rhode, David
2000 Holocene Vegetation History in the Bonneville Basin. In *Late Quaternary Paleoecology in the Bonneville Basin*, by David B. Madsen, pp. 149–163. Utah Geological Survey No. 130. Utah Geological Survey, Salt Lake City.

Rhode, David, Ted Goebel, Kelly E. Graf, Bryan S. Hockett, Kevin T. Jones, David B. Madsen, Charles G. Oviatt, and Dave N. Schmitt
2005 Latest Pleistocene–Early Holocene Human Occupation and Paleoenvironmental Change in the Bonneville Basin, Utah–Nevada. In *Interior Western United States*, edited by J. Pederson and C. M. Dehler, 10–29. Geological Society of America Field Guide 6. Geological Society of America, Boulder.

Rhode, David, and Lisbeth A. Louderback
2015 Bonneville Basin Environments During the Pleistocene–Holocene Transition. In *The Paleoarchaic Occupation of the Old River Bed Delta*, edited by David B. Madsen, Dave N. Schmitt, and David Page, pp. 22–29. Anthropological Papers No. 128. University of Utah Press, Salt Lake City.

Rhode, David, and David B. Madsen
1998 Pine Nut Use in the Early Holocene and Beyond: The Danger Cave Archaeological Record. *Journal of Archaeological Science* 25:1199–1210.

Rhode, David, David B. Madsen, and Kevin T. Jones
2006 Antiquity of Early Holocene Small-Seed Consumption and Processing at Danger Cave. *Antiquity* 80:328–339.

Richards, Katie K., James R. Allison, Lindsay D. Johansson, Richard K. Talbot, and Scott M. Ure
2019 Houses, Public Architecture, and the Organization of Fremont Communities. In *Communities and Households in the Greater American Southwest: New Perspectives and Case Studies*, edited by Robert J. Stokes, pp. 201–228. University Press of Colorado, Denver.

Roberts, David
2019 *Escalante's Dream: On the Trail of the Spanish Discovery of the Southwest*. W. W. Norton, New York.

Roberts, Heidi, Richard V. N. Ahlstrom, and Jerry D. Spangler (editors)
2022 *Far Western Basketmaker Beginnings: The Jackson Flat Reservoir Project*. University of Utah Press, Salt Lake City.

Rockman, Marcy, and James Steele
2003 *Colonization of Unfamiliar Landscapes: The Archaeology of Adaptation*. Routledge, Taylor and Francis Group, London and New York.

Rogers, Garry F.
1982 *Then and Now: A Photographic History of Vegetation Change in the Central Great Basin Desert*. University of Utah Press, Salt Lake City.

Rondeau, Michael F.
2023 *Fluted Points of the Far West*. University of Utah Press, Salt Lake City.

Roos, Christopher I., David M. J. S. Bowman, Jennifer K. Balch, Paulo Artaxo, William J. Bond, Mark Cochrane, Carla M. D'Antonio, et al.
2014 Pyrogeography, Historical Ecology, and the Human Dimensions of Fire Regimes. *Journal of Biogeography* 41:833–836.

Roos, Christopher I., Thomas W. Swetnam, Thomas J. Ferguson, Matthew J. Liebmann, Rachel A. Loehman, John R. Welch, Ellis Q. Margolis, et al.
2021 Native American Fire Management at an Ancient Wildland-Urban Interface in the Southwest United States. *Proceedings of the National Academy of Sciences* 118:e2018733118.

Roth, Barbara J., and Andrea Freeman
2008 The Middle Archaic Period and the Transition to Agriculture in the Sonoran Desert of Southern Arizona. *Kiva* 73:321–353.

Schaafsma, Polly
1971 *The Rock Art of Utah*. University of Utah Press, Salt Lake City.
2008 Shamans, Shields, and Stories on Stone. In *The Great Basin: People and Place in Ancient Times*, edited by Catherine S. Fowler and Don D. Fowler, pp. 145–152. School for Advanced Research Press, Santa Fe, New Mexico.

Scheiber, Laura L. and Maria Nieves Zedeño (editors)
2015 *Engineering Mountain Landscapes: An Anthropology of Social Investment*. University of Utah Press, Salt Lake City.

Schmitt, Dave N., David B. Madsen, and Karen D. Lupo
2004 The Worst of Times, the Best of Times: Jackrabbit Hunting by Middle Holocene Human Foragers in the Bonneville Basin of Western North America. In *Colonisation, Migration, and Marginal Areas: A Zooarchaeological Approach*, edited by Mariana Mondini, Sebastian Munoz, and Stephen Wickler, pp. 86–95. Oxbow Books, Oxford, U.K.

Scott, Richard, Dennis H. O'Rourke, Jennifer A. Raff, Justin C. Tackney, Leslea J. Hlusko, Scott A. Elias, Lauriane Bourgeon, et al.
2021 Peopling the Americas: Not "Out of Japan." *PaleoAmerica*. https://doi:10.1080/20555 563.2021.1940440. Available at https://www.researchgate.net/publication/355254236 _Peopling_the_Americas_Not_Out_of_Japan.

Searcy, Michael T., Richard K. Talbot
2015 Late Fremont Cultural Identities and Borderland Processes. In *Late Holocene Research on Foragers and Early Farmers in the Desert West*, edited by Barbara J. Roth and Maxine E. McBrinn, pp. 234–264. University of Utah Press, Salt Lake City.

Sesler, Leslie M., and Timothy D. Hovezak
2011 Farming at the Edge of Paradise: Basketmaker II Emergence in New Mexico's San Juan Basin. *Southwestern Lore* 77:9–19.

Seymour, Deni J.
2009 Comments on Genetic Data Relating to Athapaskan Migrations: Implications of the Malhi et al. Study for the Southwestern Apache and Navajo. *American Journal of Physical Anthropology* 139:281–283.
2019 Pliant Communities. In *Communities and Households in the Greater American Southwest: New Perspectives and Case Studies*, edited by Robert J. Stokes, pp. 131–151. University Press of Colorado, Denver.

Seymour, Deni J. (editor)
2012 *From the Land of Ever Winter to the American Southwest: Athapaskan Migrations, Mobility, and Ethnogenesis.* University of Utah Press, Salt Lake City.
2017 *Fierce and Indomitable: The Protohistoric Non-Pueblo World in the American Southwest.* University of Utah Press, Salt Lake City.

Shackley, M. Steven
2000 The Stone Tool Technology of Ishi and the Yana of North Central California: Inferences for Hunter-Gatherer Cultural Identity in Historic California. *American Anthropologist* 102:693–712.

Shaul, David Leedom
2014 *A Prehistory of Western North America: The Impact of Uto-Aztecan Languages.* University of New Mexico Press, Albuquerque.

Shirazi, Sabrina, Nasreen Broomandkhoshbacht, Jonas Oppenheimer, Jessica Z. Metcalfe, Rob Found, John W. Ives, and Beth Shapiro
2022 Ancient DNA-Based Sex Determination of Bison Hide Moccasins Indicates Promontory Cave Occupants Selected Female Hides for Footwear. *Journal of Archaeological Science* 137:105533.

Simms, Steven R.
1979 High Altitude Archaeology in Utah: A Cultural Resource Inventory of 11 Projects and a Test Excavation (42SV1357) in the Fishlake National Forest. Reports of Investigations 79–36. Archaeological Center, Department of Anthropology, University of Utah, Salt Lake City. Available on ResearchGate (https://www.researchgate.net).
1989 The Structure of the Bustos Wickiup Site, Eastern Nevada. *Journal of California and Great Basin Anthropology* 11:2–34.
1990 Fremont Transitions. *Utah Archaeology* 3:1–18.
1994 Unpacking the Numic Spread. In *Across the West: Human Population Movement and the Expansion of the Numa*, edited by David B. Madsen and David Rhode, pp. 76–83. University of Utah Press, Salt Lake City.
1999a Farmers, Foragers, and Adaptive Diversity: The Great Salt Lake Wetlands Project. In *Prehistoric Lifeways in the Great Basin Wetlands: Bioarchaeological Reconstruction and Interpretation*, edited by Brian E. Hemphill and Clark S. Larsen, pp. 21–54. University of Utah Press, Salt Lake City.
1999b Chasing the Will-o'-the-Wisp of Social Order. In *Models for the Millenium: The Current Status of Great Basin Anthropological Research*, edited by Charlotte Beck, pp. 105–110. University of Utah Press, Salt Lake City.
2008a *Ancient Peoples of the Great Basin and Colorado Plateau.* Routledge, Taylor and Francis Group, London and New York.
2008b Making a Living in the Desert West. In *The Great Basin: People and Place in Ancient Times*, edited by Catherine S. Fowler and Don D. Fowler, pp. 95–104. School for Advanced Research Press, Santa Fe.
2010 *Traces of Fremont: Society and Rock Art in Ancient Utah.* University of Utah Press, Salt Lake City.
2018 Rock Art as Social Geography. *Archaeology Southwest* 32:19.

Simms, Steven R., and Kathleen M. Heath
1990   Site Structure of the Orbit Inn: An Application of Ethnoarchaeology. *American Antiquity* 55:797–812.

Simms, Steven R., Carol J. Loveland, and Mark E. Stuart
1991   *Prehistoric Human Skeletal Remains and the Prehistory of the Great Salt Lake Wetlands.* Contributions to Anthropology No. 6. Utah State University, Logan.

Simms, Steven R., Tammy M. Rittenour, Chimalis Kuehn, and Molly Boeka Cannon
2020   Prehistoric Irrigation in Central Utah: Chronology, Agricultural Economics, and Implications. *American Antiquity* 85:452–469.

Simms, Steven R., and Mark E. Stuart
2002   Ancient American Indian Life in the Great Salt Lake Wetlands: Archaeological and Biological Evidence. In *Great Salt Lake: An Overview of Change*, edited by J. Wallace Gwynn, pp. 71–83. Utah Department of Natural Resources Special Publication. Utah Geological Survey, Salt Lake City.

Sinopolli, Carla M.
1991   Style in Arrows: A Study of an Ethnographic Collection from the Western United States. In *Foragers in Context: Long-Term Regional and Historical Perspectives in Hunter-Gatherer Studies*, edited by Preston T. Miracle, Lynn E. Fisher, and Jody Brown, pp. 63–87. Michigan Discussions in Anthropology Vol. 10. University of Michigan, Ann Arbor.

Skoglund, Pontus, and David Reich
2016   A Genomic View of the Peopling of the Americas. *Current Opinion in Genetics and Development* 41:27–35.

Smith, Craig
1992   The Fremont: A View from Southwest Wyoming. *Utah Archaeology* 5:55–75.
2021   The Bow and Arrow, Population, Environment, and Seeds: Intensification in Southwest Wyoming. *Journal of Anthropological Archaeology* 62:101300.

Smith, Geoffrey M., and Pat Barker
2017   The Terminal Pleistocene/Early Holocene Record in the Northwestern Great Basin: What We Know, What We Don't Know, and How We May Be Wrong. *Paleoamerica* 3:13–47.

Smith, Geoffrey M., Daron Duke, Dennis L. Jenkins, Ted Goebel, Loren G. Davis, Patrick O'Grady, Dan Stueber, Jordan E. Pratt, and Heather L. Smith
2020   The Western Stemmed Tradition: Problems and Prospects in Paleoindian Archaeology in the Intermountain West. *PaleoAmerica* 6:1–20.

Spangler, Jerry D.
2013   *Nine Mile Canyon: The Archaeological History of an American Treasure.* University of Utah Press, Salt Lake City.

Spangler, Jerry D., and James M. Aton
2018   *The Crimson Cowboys: The Remarkable Odyssey of the 1931 Claflin Emerson Expedition.* University of Utah Press, Salt Lake City.

Speth, John D., Khori Newlander, Andrew A. White, Ashley K. Lemke, and Lars E. Anderson
2013   Early Paleoindian Big-Game Hunting in North America: Provisioning or Politics? *Quaternary International* 285:111–139.

Sprengeler, Kari, and Christopher Morgan
2022 An Evaluation of Demographic and Sociocultural Factors Affiliated with Cooperative Artiodactyl Hunting in the Prehistoric Great Basin, USA. *Hunter Gatherer Research* 4:467–493.

Stansbury, Howard
1852 *Exploration of the Valley of the Great Salt Lake.* Smithsonian Institution Press, Washington, D.C. Reprinted 1988.

Steward, Julian H.
1938 *Basin Plateau Aboriginal Sociopolitical Groups.* United States Bureau of American Ethnology Bulletin 120. Washington, D.C.
2009 *Ancient Caves of the Great Salt Lake Region.* Reprinted. University of Utah Press, Salt Lake City. Originally published 1937.

Stewart, Omer C.
2002 *Forgotten Fires: Native Americans and the Transient Wilderness.* University of Oklahoma Press, Norman.

Stoffle, Richard W., Fletcher Chmara-Huff, Kathleen Van Vlack, and Rebecca Toupal
2004 *Puha Flows from It: The Cultural Landscape Study of the Spring Mountains.* Bureau of Applied Research in Anthropology, University of Arizona, Tucson. Submitted to USDA Forest Service. Available as a PDF from University of Arizona via Google Scholar.

Stoffle, Richard, Kathleen Van Vlack, Sean O'Meara, Richard Arnold, and Betty Cornelius
2021 Incised Stones and Southern Paiute Cultural Continuity. *Journal of California and Great Basin Anthropology* 41:19–36.

Stuart, Mark E.
1988 An Unusual Cache of Painted Bison Bone from Eastern Box Elder County, Utah. *Utah Archaeology* 1:46–51.
2008 The Big Village at Willard. In *Ancient Peoples of the Great Basin and Colorado Plateau*, by Steven Simms, pp. 191–193. Routledge, Taylor and Francis Group, London and New York.
2015 A Painted Fremont Pit House. *Utah Archaeology* 28:77–80.

Sutton, Mark Q.
1986 Warfare and Expansion: An Ethnohistoric Perspective on the Numic Spread. *Journal of California and Great Basin Anthropology* 8:65–82.

Talbot, Richard K.
2000a Fremont Architecture. In *Clear Creek Canyon Archaeological Project: Results and Synthesis*, edited by Joel C. Janetski, Richard K. Talbot, Deborah E. Newman, Lane D. Richens, and James D. Wilde, pp. 131–184. Museum of Peoples and Cultures Occasional Papers No. 7. Brigham Young University, Provo.
2000b Fremont Settlement Patterns and Demography. In *Clear Creek Canyon Archaeological Project: Results and Synthesis*, edited Joel C. Janetski, Richard K. Talbot, Deborah E. Newman, Lane D. Richens, and James D. Wilde, pp. 201–230. Museum of Peoples and Cultures Occasional Papers No. 7. Brigham Young University, Provo.

Talbot, Richard K., and Lane D. Richens
1996   *Steinaker Gap: An Early Fremont Farmstead.* Museum of Peoples and Cultures Occasional Papers No. 2. Brigham Young University, Provo, Utah.
2004   *Fremont Farming and Mobility on the Far Northern Colorado Plateau.* Museum of Peoples and Cultures Occasional Papers No. 10. Brigham Young University, Provo, Utah.

Taylor, William Timothy Treal, Pablo Librado, Mila Hunska Tasunke Icu (Chief Joseph American Horse), Carlton Shield Chief Gover, Jimmy Arterberry, Anpetu Luta Win (Antonia Lorettta Afraid of Bear-Cook), Akil Nujipi (Harold Left Heron), et al.
2023   Early Dispersal of Domestic Horses into the Great Plains and Northern Rockies. *Science* 379:1316–1323.

Thomas, David H.
1982   *The 1981 Alta Toquima Village Project: A Preliminary Report.* Social Sciences Technical Report Series 27. Desert Research Institute, Reno.
1983   *The Archaeology of Monitor Valley 2: Gatecliff Shelter.* Anthropological Papers of the American Museum of Natural History Vol. 59, Pt. 1. American Museum of Natural History, New York.
2015   Engineering Alta Toquima: Social Investments and Dividends at 11,000 Feet. In *Engineering Mountain Landscapes: An Anthropology of Social Investment*, edited by Laura L. Scheiber and Maria Nieves Zedeño, pp. 49–74. University of Utah Press, Salt Lake City.
2019   Shoshonean Prayerstone Hypothesis: Ritual Cartographies of Great Basin Incised Stones. *American Antiquity* 84:1–25.
2020   *Alpine Archaeology of Alta Toquima and the Mt. Jefferson Tablelands (Nevada).* The Archaeology of Monitor Valley Contribution No. 4. Anthropological Papers of the American Museum of Natural History No. 104. American Museum of Natural History, New York.
2024   *Shoshonean Ethnogenesis and Numic Origins.* The Archaeology of Monitor Valley Contribution No. 6. Anthropological Papers of the American Museum of Natural History, in press. American Museum of Natural History, New York.

Thomas, Trudy
1983   Material Culture of Gatecliff Shelter: Incised Stones. In *The Archaeology of Monitor Valley 2: Gatecliff Shelter*, by David H. Thomas, pp. 246–278. Anthropological Papers of the American Museum of Natural History Vol. 59, Pt. 1. American Museum of Natural History, New York.

Thomson, Marcus J., Juraj Balkovič, Tamás Krisztin, and Glen M. MacDonald
2019   Simulated Impact of Paleoclimate Change on Fremont Native American Maize Farming in Utah, 850–1449 CE, Using Crop and Climate Models. *Quaternary International* 507:95–107.

Thomson, Marcus J., and Glen M. MacDonald
2020   Climate and Growing Season Variability Impacted the Intensity and Distribution of Fremont Maize Farmers During and After the Medieval Climate Anomaly Based on a Statistically Downscaled Climate Model. *Environmental Research Letters* 15:105002.

Thornhill, Cassidee A.
2021   Reanalysis of Equid Faunal Remains from the Blacks Fork River Site (48Sw8319):

A Unique Look at a Protohistoric Horse in Wyoming. *Plains Anthropologist* 66(257): 58–73.

Thornton, Russell B.
1987 *American Indian Holocaust and Survival: A Population History Since 1492*. University of Oklahoma Press, Norman.

Tolan-Smith, Christopher
2003 The Social Context of Landscape Learning and the Lateglacial-Early Postglacial Recolonization of the British Isles. In *Colonization of Unfamiliar Landscapes: The Archaeology of Adaptation*, edited by Marcy Rockman and James Steele, pp. 116–126. Routledge, Taylor and Francis Group, London and New York.

Ugan, Andrew, Jason Bright, and Alan Rogers
2003 Is Technology Worth the Trouble? *Journal of Archaeological Science* 30:1315–1329.

Ulev, Elena (compiler)
2008 Effects of Fall and Spring Prescribed Burning in Sagebrush Steppe in East-Central Oregon. In Fire Effects Information System. United States Department of Agriculture, Forest Service, Rocky Mountain Research Station, Fire Sciences Laboratory. Available at http://www.fs.fed.us/database/feis/, accessed February 28, 2009.

Waters, Michael R., Ted Goebel, and Kelly E. Graf
2020 The Stemmed Point Tradition of Western North America. *PaleoAmerica* 6(1):1–3.

Wheat, Margaret M.
1967 *Survival Arts of the Primitive Paiute*. University of Nevada Press, Reno.

Whitaker, Adrian R., and Kimberley L. Carpenter
2012 Economic Foraging at a Distance Is Not a Question of If but When: A Response to Grimstead. *American Antiquity* 77:160–167.

White, Richard
1995 Are You an Environmentalist or Do You Work for a Living?–Work and Nature. In *Uncommon Ground: Toward Reinventing Nature*, edited by William Cronon, pp. 171–185. W. W. Norton, New York.
1999 *Land Use, Environment, and Social Change: The Shaping of Island County, Washington*. Rev. ed. University of Washington Press, Seattle. Originally published 1980.

Wilde, James D., and Deborah E. Newman
1989 Late Archaic Corn in the Eastern Great Basin. *American Anthropologist* 91:712–720.

Wilde, James D., and Reed A. Soper
1999 *Baker Village: Report of Excavations, 1990–1994*. Museum of Peoples and Cultures Technical Series No. 99-12. Brigham Young University, Provo.

Willerslev, Eske, and David J. Meltzer
2021 Peopling of the Americas as Inferred from Ancient Genomics. *Nature* 594:356–364.

Williams, Gerald W.
2002 Aboriginal Use of Fire: Are There Any "Natural" Plant Communities? In *Wilderness and Political Ecology: Aboriginal Influences and the Original State of Nature*, edited by Charles E. Kay and Randy T. Simmons, pp. 179–214. University of Utah Press, Salt Lake City.

Williams, Thomas J., and David B. Madsen
2020 The Upper Paleolithic of the Americas. *PaleoAmerica* 6:4–22.

Wissler, Clark
1914 *The Influence of the Horse in the Development of Plains Indian Cultures.* Memoir 16. American Anthropological Society, Washington, D.C.

Woody, Alana, and Angus Quinlan
2008 Rock Art in the Western Great Basin. In *The Great Basin: People and Place in Ancient Times*, edited by Catherine S. Fowler and Don D. Fowler, pp. 137–144. School for Advanced Research Press, Santa Fe, New Mexico.

Wormington, H. Marie
1955 *A Reappraisal of the Fremont Culture.* Proceedings No. 1. Denver Museum of Natural History.

Xuebin Qi, Chaoying Cui, Yi Peng, Xiaoming Zhang, Zhaohui Yang, Hua Zhong, Hui Zhang, et al.
2013 Genetic Evidence of Paleolithic Colonization and Neolithic Expansion of Modern Humans on the Tibetan Plateau. *Molecular Biology and Evolution* 30(8):1761–1778.

Yanicki, Gabriel M., and John W. Ives
2017 Mobility, Exchange, and the Fluency of Games: Promontory in a Broader Sociodemographic Setting. In *Prehistoric Games of North American Indians: Subarctic to Mesoamerica*, edited by Barbara Voorhies, pp. 139–162. University of Utah Press, Salt Lake City.

Yentsch, Andrew T., Ronald L. Rood, Kevin T. Jones, Lindsay A. Fenner
2009 *The Prison Site: An Archaic Campsite along the Jordan River, Salt Lake County, Utah.* Antiquities Section, Utah Division of State History, Salt Lake City.

Yoder, David, Jon Blood, and Reid Mason
2005 How Warm Were They? Thermal Properties of Rabbit Skin Robes and Blankets. *Journal of California and Great Basin Anthropology* 25:55–68.

Young, D. Craig, William R. Hildebrandt, and Far Western Anthropological Research Group
2017 *Tufa Village (Nevada): Placing the Fort Sage Drift Fence in a Larger Archaeological Context.* Anthropological Papers of the American Museum of Natural History No. 102. American Museum of Natural History, New York.

Zedeño, Maria Nieves
2009 Animating by Association: Index Objects and Relational Taxonomies. *Cambridge Archaeological Journal* 19:411–421.

Index

Please note that italicized page numbers in this index indicate illustrative material.

Acoma people, 109
Adobe Rock, 139
agriculture: farming lifeway contrasted with foraging lifeway, 83–85; Fremont and Numic peoples, 142; irrigation, 97-98, 100, 113, 120, 175nn8–9; maize farming, 77, 81–82, 151, 154, 159; Numic speakers in Great Basin, 159–60; Three Sisters, 77; transition to/spread of, 76–77, 172–73n1
Airport archaeological site, 42, 70, 143
alpine landscape settlement, 16, 60–61
Alta Toquima, 60, 171n5
American Falls Reservoir site (Idaho), 158
American Fork Cave, 70
American Fork River, 92
Anasazi culture, 80. *See also* Ancestral Puebloan culture
Ancestral Puebloan culture, 80–81, 83–85, 88, 101, 105, 120, 122, 173n3
Antelope Valley (Nevada), 74–75
Anzick Cache, 31–32
Apache people, 108, 111. *See also* Navajo/Apache Dene peoples
archaeological methodology, x, 109
Archaic period/Settlers, 58–59, 132
arrowheads: Bull Creek points, 90; Desert Side-notched points, 133-34, 143–44; Fremont styles contrasted with Ancestral Puebloans, 89–90; Kayenta points, 90; modern collecting of, 91–92; Rosegate points, 133, 136. *See also* Clovis culture; Western Stemmed Tradition
artifacts, 109–10; perishable, 33–35. *See also* prayerstones
Athabaskan people. *See* Dene peoples
Athapaskan people. *See* Dene peoples
ATK Thiokol Corporation land, 115–16
atlatl darts, 22, 89–90
Aztec people, 132

Backhoe Village, 101
Baker Village, 98, 100, 106, 120
Barrier Canyon rock imagery style, 86
basalt boulders, 39–42. *See also* Melon Gravel
Basin and Range Tradition of rock imagery in prayerstones, 137
Basketmakers: basketmaking traditions, 88; Eastern Basketmakers, 78–80, 81, 133; migration, 85, 136; rock imagery style, 86; Western Basketmakers, 80, 120, 133
basketry, 49, 55; coiled, *48*, 134; Fremont traditions, 87–88
Basso, Keith, 57, 161, 162
Bear River, 10–11, 120, 123; Clovis caches, 29, *31*
Bear River Migratory Bird Refuge, 59, 97, *102*
Bear River Range, 70
Beckwith, E. Griffen, 9
Biblical Model of humanity, x, 109, 133, 144, 162
Bighorn Mountains (Wyoming), 29; Bighorn Basin, 117
Big Village (Willard, Utah), 94–95, 96–97
biscuitroot, 21, 50, 59

211

Black Forks River site (Wyoming), 158
Blackwater Draw (New Mexico), 27
Blue Hills, 116
Blue Lake, 6, 70
Bonneville, Benjamin, 8
Bonneville Basin: Clovis culture, 26–32; evidence of earliest human habitation, 24–25; social organization and lineage lines, 38; Western Stemmed Tradition, 32–38. *See also* Lake Bonneville
Bonneville Estates Rockshelter, 33, 52
Bonneville Flood, 11–13, 41, 141
Bonneville Salt Flats, 70
Bonneville Shoreline Trail, 1–3, *2*
borderlands and human interactions, 116, 120, 133, 134–35, 178n9, 180n5
bow and arrow technology, 71, 89–90. *See also* arrowheads
Bull Creek, 97
Bull Creek points, 90
Buzz Cut Dune, 106

Cache Valley, 70, 104, 111
caching of equipment, 59–60, *63*
Cahokia (Mississippian culture city), 122
Caldwell Village, 98, 101
Camels Back Cave, *9*, 50, 52, 137
campfires, firewood for, 68–69
Canyon Pintado (Colorado), 148
Capitol Reef National Park, 80, 98, 120
Carr Creek (Colorado), 148
cartography. *See* maps
Castle Gardens (Wyoming), *115*, *116*, 141; Castle Gardens Style rock imagery, 114–15
cattails: cattail rafts, 143; cattail roots, 38–39
caves: as archaeological sites, 46–47, 50–52, 91, 116, 120–21; cave occupation and planning depth, 23; cave occupation of pioneers and first settlers, 27, 33, 121–22, 125; Great Salt Lake region, 24, 51–52, 54
Chacoan society, 109, 122, 142
Chaco Canyon, 83, 122

Chemehuevi language, 131
chi-tho tool, *142*, 143
Christian symbolism, 110
Clear Creek Canyon, 98, 99–100, 120
climate change: cave site evidence in Great Salt Lake region, 51–52, 59; drought periods, 136, 156; and Fremont settlement, 113–14; Little Ice Age, 129; 13th and 14th centuries, 108
climate modeling, 113
Clovis culture, 26–32, 168n1; caches of Clovis points, 27–32, *28*, *30*, 168–169n3; contrasted with Western Stemmed Tradition, 36–37; trade and networks, 29–31, 35–36
Cochiti people, 109
colonization, 110, 155–56, 162, 167n7
Colorado Plateau, 141–42
Colorado River, 80, 154
Columbia River, 10
Comanche language, 131
Connor Springs, 116, 120
Connor Springs-Blue Creek, 139
Connor Springs rock imagery, 141
Continental Divide, 117
Cooper, James Fenimore, 58
Cooper's Ferry (Idaho), 19
Crossing of the Fathers, 154
Cub Creek, 81, 97, 113, 177n6
cultural assumptions and stereotypes, 21, 32–33, 100–101, 106–7
Curlew National Grasslands, 111

Danger Cave (Wendover, Utah), 33, 137
D.C. Corral (Nevada), 70–72, *72*
Debra L. Friedkin site (Texas), 17
Deep Creek, 6
Deep Creek Mountain Range, 46, 68, 69–70, 106
deer hunting, 65
Dene peoples, 108, 121, 127, 176–77n1; *chi-tho* tool, 143; migrants, 110–11; Promontory Caves, 121–25

Desert Side-notched points, 133, 143–44
Desolation Canyon, 66
dialect chains, 133, 137, 150, 154
Dimple Dell archaeological site, 70, 82
Dinosaur National Monument, 81, 97, 113
Dinwoody rock imagery, *135*
Dirty Shame Rockshelter (Oregon), 134
disease: disease-driven population decline, 156–58; epidemic, 155, 156
DNA evidence: for early human migration, 19; Fremont burial remains, 86–87, 105
Domínguez, Francisco Atanasio, 145–54
Domínguez-Escalante Expedition (1776), 86, 143, 145–54, *146*
Douglas Creek (Colorado), 77, 148
Drake Cache, 31
drought periods, 136, 156. *See also* climate change
Duchesne River, 78, 147, 149, 150
Dutch Mountain, 68, 76

Earth as living being, 136
earthworks, 76
Eastern Agricultural Complex, 76
Eastern Basketmakers, 78–80, 81, 133; migration routes, *79*
Egan, Howard, 74–75
Ely, Nevada, 100
epidemic disease, 155, 156
equestrian-based lifeways, 150–51, 158–59, 182n11
Escalante, Silvestre Vélez de, 145–54
Escalante River/canyon country, 80, 81, 90, 120
ethnogenesis, 109, 111, 136, 144, 154; Fremont, 114, 120, 125; Kiowa, 108
Evans Mound (Parowan Valley, Utah), 95–96, *96*, 101

farming. *See* agriculture
Fenn Cache, 27–30, *31*, 61, 168–69n3
Fiftymile Bench, 80
firearms, 151

fire as environmental management tool, *60*, 64–67, 70, 156
firewood, 68–69
fishhooks, *34*
Fish Springs National Wildlife Refuge, 69, 76, *77*
Five Finger Ridge, 98, 99–100, 106, 120
Five Mile Draw (Montello, Nevada), 72–74
food processing and storage, 48–51, *50*
footwear, 89; moccasins, *88*, 88–89, *89*, 121, *122*, 123, *123*, 125; sandal styles, *35*, 55
foraging peoples: cultural groups and lifeways, 83; kinship systems, 132–33; in Late Archaic period, 134; mobility within landscape, *56*; motifs on prayerstones, 141; territories and geography, 54–57, 147, 149–50
Fort Hall Bottoms (Idaho), 134
Fort Sage Drift Fence (Nevada), 70–72, *71*
Four Corners region, 88, 101
Fox site, 143–44
Franktown Cave (Colorado), 125
Fremont, John, 9
Fremont Indian State Park, 100
Fremont peoples/culture, 85–86, *125*, 133; agriculture, 101, 103–4; along Wasatch Front, 92–107; basketry, 87–88; burial practices, 86, 89, 103–4, *105*; climate change and settlement, 113–14; decline of farming, 142; diet, 100–101, 103–4; DNA evidence, 86–87, 105; drought periods and upheaval, 111–13; dwellings and settlements, 98–101, 105–6; footwear, 89; founding of, 106; Fremont style pottery, 134; gendered roles, 104; in Great Salt Lake, 135; Indigenous roots, 142; irrigation, 97–98, 100, 111; language history, 121, 125, 127, 134; maize, 111; mounds, 93–97; natural travel routes, 117–20; pithouses, *84*, *94*; prayerstones, 141; projectile points, 133; remains exposed in flooding incident, 101–3; residential sites in Piceance Basin, 148–49; rock imagery,

86, 114–15, *148*; settlement practices, 80, 93, 106–7, 113–14; shield figures, 114–15; upheaval in 13th and 15th centuries, 108–9
Fremont River, 80
Fremont State Park, 98
Fremont Wasatch Front, 107

Gatecliff Shelter (Nevada), 141
genetic evidence. *See* DNA evidence
Gentile Valley, 6
geophytes, 38, 171n4
Gilbert, Grove Karl, *3*, 8–13, 37
Gilbert Episode, 42–43
G. K. Gilbert Geologic View Park, 5
glacial events, 5, 13, 165n2; and coastal ecosystems, 19
Glen Canyon, 81
Gooseberry Creek, 101
Goshen Island South site, 143
Goshute language, 131. *See also* Numic languages
Goshute people, 87, 130
Grantsville archaeological site, 82
graptolite fossils, 139
Graptolite Summit, 139, 141
grasshopper collection/consumption, 50–51, 65
Grass Valley (Nevada), 137
Grassy Mountain, 139
Great Basin Carved Abstract Style, 41, 44
Great Basin curvilinear rock imagery style, 86, 115
Great Basin mountain ranges, 44
Great Basin National Park, 98, 100
Great Basin Scratched Style of prayerstones, 137
Great Gallery rock imagery site, 62
Great Salt Lake: "benches," 1, 8; first humans, 13; 17th century flood, 156; formation and prehistoric conditions, 1, 3–4, 7; history and levels, *11*; Late Archaic settlers, 76–90; 20th century flooding, 101
Great Salt Lake basin/region: archaeology and material culture, 91–92; Basketmaker migration, 78–82; cave sites and evidence of cultural transformation, 51–52; Fremont settlement, 111; housing sites, 69–70; hunting, 52–54; map, *xvi*; overview, x; Promontory period, 155–56; settler phase and cultural transformation, 46–57; transition of wetlands to desert, 52
grinding stones, 48–50, 54, 101
Grotto Canyon (Alberta), 123
Grouse Creek Mountains, 69–70
Gunnison River, 147

Harrison, Holly "Cargo," 16
Hassell, Fran, 96
hearths, 39, 85, 92
Hebior site (Wisconsin), 17
Heron Springs site, 143
Hill Creek, 97
Hinkley Mounds, 97
Hinkley village, 106
Hogup Cave, 50, 90, 137
Hogup Mountain, 139
Hole-in-the-Rock Trail, 80
Homestead Cave, 3, 52
Hopi language community, 109, 131, 133
Hopi peoples, 78, 142, 154
horses, impact on Indigenous groups, 150–51, 158–59, 182n11
Hot Springs archaeological site, 70
human migration: Basketmaker migration, 78–82; climate change as cause, 114; DNA evidence, 86–87; explorer phase and mobility, 21–25, *23*, 46–47; Great Salt Lake natural routes, 117–20; interaction between ethnic/linguistic groups, 82–83; pioneer phase, 26–37, 46–47; return migrations, 113; settler phase, 37–45, 47; settler phase and built environment, 59–75; settler phase and continuing mobility, 54–56; settler phase

and cultural transformations, 51–52; settler phase and game populations, 54; social networks, 22–25. *See also* Indigenous peoples; Paleoindians

Human Wilderness, 154, 170n1; fire as environmental management tool, 64–67, 70, 171n2; Fremont culture at most populous, 91–107; Salt Lake Basin as, 58–75

hunter-gatherer societies: kinship systems, 23–24; mobility tempo and mode, 21-23; sense of "home," 24; social networks, 23, 35–36

hunting: big game drives, 70–75; big game hunting, 33, 53–54; bison, 125; caribou, 123; deer, 65; fire used in hunting drives, *65*, 65–66; and food processing, 21–25; and food storage, 50; humans as keystone predator, ix, 54; mammoth hunting, 38; pronghorn, 70, 72–75, *73*; rabbit drives, 65; shamans, 73; small game hunting, 52–53

Hurricane, Utah, 154

Indigenous peoples: diversity among, 150–51; first explorers of the Americas, *17*; myth of "first contact," 154; Native American depopulation from disease, 155, 156, 182n9; stories linked to geography, 136. *See also* human migration; Paleoindians

Injun Creek site, 143

irrigation, 97-98, 100, 113, 120, 175nn8–9

Ishi (Yana individual), 82–83

James Creek Shelter (Nevada), 135–36
Jemez region (New Mexico), 156–58, 182n9
Joaquin (Laguna Ute guide), 147, 151
Jordan River (Utah), 39, 92, 143
José Maria (Laguna guide), 151
juniper forests, 66–67, 68–69

Kaibab Plateau, 110
Kawaiisu language, 131

Kayenta points (arrowheads), 90
Kay's Creek, 92
Kelly, Isabel, 65
Kelp Highway, 19
Keresan language community, 109
kinship systems: in forager societies, 23–24; terminology, 132–33, 179n3
Kiowa-Tanoan languages, 78, 86, 105, 108–9, 114, 127, 133
Kiowa-Tanoan people, 108, 125, 142

Lake Bonneville, *6*; Bonneville Flood, 11–13, *12*, 42; ecosystem surrounding, 5–6; evidence of earliest human habitation, 24–25; formation and prehistoric conditions, 1, 3–4, 5, 7, 10–13; glacial events, 5, 11, 13; Gunnison arm, 37; history of and levels of, *11*; inflow, sources of, 10; initial human exploration, 16–21; map, *4*; Old River Bed Delta, 37–39; and Pleistocene Lakes, *20*; Pleistocene megafauna, 7; recession of/transition to Great Salt Lake, 26; shoreline "benches," 1, 10; wetlands surrounding, 6

Lake Bonneville (Gilbert, 1890), *3*, 8
"lake effect", 11
Lakeside Cave, 50–51
Lakeside Mountains, 139
landscape management, ix, 156; fire as management tool, *60*, 64–67, 70, 156, 171n2
landscape: cultural knowledge of, 57; foraging cultures contrasted with farming cultures, 83–85; human investment in, 75; and migration routes, *112*. *See also* place, sense of; sacred landscapes; territory
language: anthropological linguistics, 10–11, 109, 121
language history, x–xi, 121; contrasted with ethnicity, 110; dialect chains, 133, 137, 150, 154; Native American, nineteenth century, 130; shaped by geography and lifeways, 132; Shoshone and Ute, 130; story, significance of, 110–11

languages: map of language families, *131*
Little Cottonwood Canyon, 5
Little Dry site, 143
Little Ice Age, 129
Logan Canyon, 5
Long Lake (Oregon), 44
Lovelock Cave (Nevada), 61
Luther Standing Bear, 58

maize: and Basketmaker migrations, 136; consumed by Fremont peoples, 100–101; maize farming, 77, 81–82, 151, 154, 159
mammoth hunting, 38
maps: cartography, 162; Domínguez-Escalante Expedition route, *146*; Eastern Basketmaker migration routes, *79*; first explorers of the Americas, *17*; Great Salt Lake Basin, *xvi*; Lake Bonneville, *4*; Lake Bonneville and Pleistocene Lakes, *20*; landscapes and migration routes, *112*; language families, *131*; Miera's map of Domínguez-Escalante Expedition, 145, *146*; prayerstone styles, *140*; pronghorn hunting drives, *73*, *74*; toolstone sources, *40*
material culture, 109–10. *See also* artifacts
mats and bags, 33–34
Mazama Ash, 44
McConkie Ranch rock imagery, 141
McGuire, Don, 94
McPhee, John, 44
Meadowcroft Rockshelter (Pennsylvania), 17
Median Village, 97–98
medicine bundles, 61–62
Meegan, George, 16
megafauna species, 7, 38
Melon Gravel, 39–42, *41*, *42*, *43*, 141
Miera y Pacheco, Bernardo, 145
Miller, Wick, 46
Mississippian culture, 122
moccasins, *88*, 88–89, *89*, 121, *122*, 123, *123*, 125
Monitor Range, 141
Mono language, 131

Monte Verde (Chile), 17
Moon, Maude, 46, 47–48, 49
"Moqui" people, 154
Mormon immigrants, 80
Morss, Noel, 85, 98
Mount Jefferson Tablelands, 60
Muddy River, 81

Nahuatl language, 132
Native Americans: population fluctuations, 76–77, *157*; present day in Great Salt Lake region, 130–44
Navajo/Apache Dene peoples, 108, 111, 154, 176–77n1
Nawthis Village, 97, 101
nets, 34–35, *36*
Newark Valley (Nevada), 70
Nine Mile Canyon, 81, 85, 89, 97
Noble Savage, myth of, 58
Numic languages, 120, 129, 131–33, 179n3; contrasted with Fremont languages, 134; dialect chains, 133; divergence of, 136; linked to prayerstones, 137; Numic Spread, 109
Nunamiut Eskimo lifetime foraging ranges, 57

obsidian, 39, 69, 114, 159; obsidian tools, 72
Ogden River, 92;, Ogden Valley, 104
Old Pony Express Route, 37
Old River Bed Delta, 37–39, 69, 139; decline of, 45; early wetland sites, 39; evidence of climate change, 52
Oneida Narrows, 10–11
oolitic sand, 50–51
Orbit Inn site, 143

Page-Ladson site (Florida), 17–19
Pahvant Butte, 151
Paisley Caves (Oregon), 19
Paiute languages, Northern and Southern, 131
Paiute peoples, 59, 87, 150, 154; arrows, 110;

deer hunting drives, 65; maize farming, 151, 154, 159
Paleoindians: and built environment in Great Salt Lake region, 59–75; cultural sophistication of, 14–16, 107; early arrival in the Americas, 16–21; initial migrations to new landscapes, 15. *See also* human migration; Indigenous peoples
Panamint language, 131
Paria River, 80
Parowan Valley, 93, 97–98, 100, 101
Patterson Bundle, 61–62, *62*
Pence-Duerig Cave (Idaho), 111
Piceance Basin (Colorado), 77, 120, 148
pickleweed seeds: harvesting and processing, 46–50
Pickleweed Winter, 46–47
Pillings figurines, 86, *87*
Pineview Reservoir, 44
Pinyon Flat, 68
pinyon forests, 66–67, 68–69, 132; pine nut harvest, *49*, 52, *53*, *55*, 60
pithouses, *84*, 85, *94*
place, sense of, ix–x, 161–64, 182n2. *See also* landscapes
Pleasant Creek, 98
Pleistocene epoch: glaciation, 5, 11; megafauna, 7, 47
Pliant communities, 105, 176n15
Pony Express National Historic Trail, 76
Portneuf River, 10
Pottery: Fremont peoples, 85–86, 100, 111, 114, 117, 121, 142, 143, 177n8, 180n6; Promontory peoples, 121, 143, 144, 178n12; Fremont pottery among foragers, 114, 134, 180n6
Poverty Point (Louisiana), 76
Powder Mountain ski resort, 104
Powell, John Wesley, 8, 66, 94, 110, 130
power: and sacred landscapes, 64, 136-137, 141, 162; and shamans in hunting context, 73; and technology, 151, 158
"power" in Indigenous languages, 136

prayerstones, 115–16, 136–42, *138–39*; design and motifs, 137; distribution of styles, *140*; ritual emplacement, 137, 139
"primitive people" as inappropriate label, 14–16, 107
Prison archaeological site, 70, 82
Pristine Myth, ix, 58, 64, 76, 109, 114, 144, 162
private/public property distinctions in foraging societies, 69–70
projectile points, 133–34. *See also* arrowheads
Promontory Caves, 121–27, 139, 143
Promontory Dene culture, *124*, 134, 142–43, 178–79n12, 179n20
Promontory Mountains, 120–21
Promontory period in Great Salt Lake basin, 155–56
pronghorn hunting, 70, 72–75
Proto-Uto-Aztecan language, 132
Proulx, Annie, ix, 161, 182n2
Provo bench, 13
Provo River, 92, 93, 149
public/private property distinctions, 69–70
Pueblo Revolt, 158
pueblos, 150
Pyne, Stephen, 64, 67
Pyramid Lake (Nevada), 150

rabbits: rabbit fur robes, 34–35; rabbit hunting drives, 65
rafts, cattail, 143
Range Creek Canyon, 98
Red Bear "Silvestre" (Ute guide), 147–49, 151
Red Man of Timpie, 115, *117*
red ochre, 29
Richey Cache, 31
Rio Grande Valley, 156
Rivera, Juan María de, 145, 147
Roan Cliffs (Colorado), 77
Roan Creek, 148
rock art, portable. *See* prayerstones
rock imagery, *43*, 110, *118*, *119*, *126–29*, 135; Basketmaker style, 86; Castle Gardens

Style, 114–15; Classic Vernal Style, 86; Dinwoody tradition, *135*; Fremont culture, 86, 114–15; sites, 39–42, 44, 64; social geography of, 64; Western Stemmed Tradition, 36-37, 44
Rock Springs (Idaho), 111
roots, 49-50, 53, 59, 66, 171n4; roots and hydration, 38
Rosegate arrow points, 133, 136
Rousseau, Jean Jacques, 58

sacred landscapes: and prayerstones, 136–37, 141, 162; rock imagery sites, 39–42, 44, 64
sand, oolitic, 50–51
sandal types, *35*, 55
Sandy Beach site, 143
San Juan River, 80
San Rafael River, 81
San Rafael Swell, 81
Schaefer site (Wisconsin), 17
Seamons Mound, 97
Sevier culture, 80
Sevier Desert, 37, 151
Sevier Lake, 4
Sevier River Valley, 6, 80, 81
sewing materials, 33–34
Shaman Bundle, 61
shaman's sucking tube, 61, *62*
shield figures/motifs, 114–15, *116*, *117*
Shoshone Knives, *144*
Shoshone language history, 120, 131. See also Numic languages; Uto-Aztecan language family
Shoshone peoples, 86, 87, 101–2, 108, 109, 110, 111, 130, 150; foragers, 135; Late Archaic settlement, 134
Silvestre "Red Bear" (Ute guide), 147–49, 151
Simon Cache, 31
Simpson Park Mountains, 141
Simpson Springs Pony Express Station, 37
Six Mile Creek, 29, 31
Smith Creek Cave (Nevada), 33

Smith Family Archaeological Preserve, 116
Snake Range, 52, 100
Snake River, 10, 13, 134; basalt beds, *12*
Snake River Canyon rock imagery sites, 39–42, 44
Snake River Plain, 86, 114, 117, 158
social geography of rock imagery, 64
social networks and hunting, 22–25
Spanish explorers, 143
Spanish Fork, 143
Spanish Fork River, 92, 149
Spanish Spit site, 143
Standing Rock Overhang (Idaho), 111
Stansbury, Howard, 8–9
Stansbury Mountains, 82
Steinaker Gap site, 81, 97, 113
stemmed points, 22. See also Western Stemmed Tradition
stereotypes, cultural, 21, 32–33, 100–101, 106-7
Stillwater Marsh (Nevada), 91
Stockton Bar, 3
stones, incised. See prayerstones
stone tools, 22, 39, 144
Strawberry Reservoir, 149
Strawberry River, 78, 147, 149, 150
Surprise Valley (California), 65

Takic language subfamily, 131
Tavaputs Plateau, 77, 81, 85, 97, 113, 114, 120
territory: concept of, 70; and human investment in land, 75; mobility of foraging peoples, *56*; as way of living, 57. See also landscapes; sacred landscapes
Thompson, Nick, 57, 162
Thoreau, Henry David, 58
Timbisha language, 131
time, measurement of, 1–3
Timpanogos Cave, 70
Timpanogots Ute people, 78, 148, 149–50, *152–53*
tobacco, 39
tools: caching of equipment, 59–60; fish-

hooks, *34*; Shoshone Knives, 144; stone tools, 22, 39, 144. *See also* artifacts
toolstone, *40*, 135
Toquima Range (Nevada), 141
Tosawihi quarry (Nevada), 106
tree-ring records, 113, 177n7
Tubatulabal language, 131

Uinta Basin, 77, 78, 86, 97, 101, 114
United States Geological Survey, 8
urbanization, 155
Utah Lake, 4, 149–50; villages, 150
Utah Test and Training Range, 52
Utah Valley, 116
Ute language, 31, 120; Ute-Numic language, 110. *See also* Numic languages
Ute peoples, 87, 108–11, 130; adoption of horse, 159; Late Archaic settlement, 134; in Utah Valley 18th century, 148–51
Uto-Aztecan language family, 80, 105, 109, 111, 120, 131–132. *See also* Numic languages

Verendrye, Chevalier de la, 159
Vermilion Cliffs, 80, 154
Vernon, Utah, 139
Virgin River, 80, 154

Wahmuza site (Idaho), 134, 144
Walker Lake, Nevada, 150
Warren village, 106
Wasatch Front, 5; and Basketmaker farmland, 81; decline of farming, 143; Fremont settlers, 98; geology, 141; oak brush, 44; peak populations, 92; Promontory period artifacts, 155–56; submersion as part of Lake Bonneville, 19, 21
water, symbolism and imagery, 41–42
Waterpocket Fold, 80

Weber River, 92
Western Basketmakers, 80, 120, 133
Western Stemmed Tradition, *18*, 26, 32–35; contrasted with Clovis culture, 36–37; Haskett type, 33, 38, 44; shift to smaller, triangular points, 52; use of landscape, 36–37; rock imagery 36-37, 44
wetlands: Great Basin and migration, 92; Great Salt Lake and food resources, 37–39, 43, 82; and human burials, 103–4; Lake Bonneville wetlands, 6–7; shrinking of, 52–54
Wheeler Expedition, 93
White, Richard, 162
White Mountains (California), 60
White River ash eruption, 123
White Sands (New Mexico), 19, 167n6
Willard Bay State Park, 96
Willow Creeks, 93
Wilson Butte Cave (Idaho), 111
Wind River basin (Wyoming), 114–15, *115*, 141
Wind River Range, 60, 117
Winnemucca Lake (Nevada), 44
Wishbone site (Old River Bed Delta), 39
Wolf Village, 98–99, *99*, 106
women's economies and food provision, 21, 33
Woodard Mound/village, 97, 106
Wyoming Basin, 134
Wyoming Stories (Proulx), 161

yampa harvest, 21, 50, 59–60, *60*
Yana tribelets, 82–83
Yellowstone Plateau, 134–35
Younger Dryas, 42–43
Yuta language, 150

Zia peoples, 109

About the Author

STEVEN R. SIMMS is Professor Emeritus of Anthropology at Utah State University, Logan, Utah, where he taught since 1988. He also taught at Weber State College and the University of Utah. He conducted archaeological field work across the United States and in the Middle East for 50 years, participating in hundreds of field trips. Simms authored over 100 scientific publications. His books include *Ancient Peoples of the Great Basin and Colorado Plateau* (2008), and *Traces of Fremont: Society and Rock Art in Ancient Utah* (2010) awarded the Society for American Archaeology Book award in the public audience category and the Utah Book Award for non-fiction. He directed over 60 archaeological projects, including the Great Salt Lake Wetlands Project 1990–93, funded by the state of Utah, U.S. Bureau of Reclamation, and the National Science Foundation. He served on the scientific advisory board of Friends of Great Salt Lake since the organization was founded in 1994. Since childhood he has hiked the mountains and deserts of the American West and slept on the ground nearly a thousand nights. In retirement he lives with his partner Judy Nelson, a ceramicist and artist on "Piney Island" at the foot of the Bighorn Mountains in Story, Wyoming.